THE CRIME WITHOUT A NAME

THE CRIME
WITHOUT
A NAME

ETHNOCIDE AND THE ERASURE OF CULTURE
IN AMERICA

Barrett Holmes Pitner

COUNTERPOINT
Berkeley, California

The Crime Without a Name

Library of Congress Cataloging-in-Publication Data
Names: Pitner, Barrett Holmes, author.
Title: The crime without a name : Ethnocide and the erasure of culture in
    America / Barrett Holmes Pitner.
Description: First hardcover edition. | Berkeley, California : Counterpoint,
    2021. | Includes bibliographical references.
Identifiers: LCCN 2020057707 | ISBN 9781640094840 (hardcover) |
    ISBN 9781640094857 (ebook)
Subjects: LCSH: African Americans—Race identity. | African
    Americans—Social conditions. | Racism in language—United States. |
    Language and culture—United States. | Racism—United States. |
    United States—Race relations.
Classification: LCC E185.625 .P55 2021 | DDC 305.896/073—dc23
LC record available at https://lccn.loc.gov/2020057707

Jacket design by Na Kim
Book design by Jordan Koluch

COUNTERPOINT
2560 Ninth Street, Suite 318
Berkeley, CA 94710
www.counterpointpress.com

Printed in the United States of America

10 9 8 7 6 5 4 3 2 1

To Andrea and our son

CONTENTS

THE CRIME WITHOUT A NAME

PROLOGUE

Thus the task is not so much to see what no one yet has seen, but to think what nobody yet has thought about that which everybody sees.

ARTHUR SCHOPENHAUER

American society lacks the language to describe itself, and as a result it is incapable of diagnosing and rectifying its own destruction. The severity of America's linguistic void became unmistakable during the presidency of Donald Trump as his vulgar existence crippled the nation, and we struggled to precisely articulate the severity of the problem. Our discourse that focused on morality, emotion, religion, bipartisanship, economics, and race repeatedly proved inadequate for describing the monster before us. And while Trump highlighted the problem, he was not its source. America lacks this language because our problem derives from our culture. Our destructive culture created an inadequate language, and so America empowers dangerously flawed people like Trump. To change this dynamic, we need new language.

Much of my work that led to the creation of The Sustainable Culture Lab seeks to address this need, to bring language—new and lesser-known—into common parlance so we may define ourselves and create a more equitable society. America is built upon ethnocide—the destruction of a people's culture while keeping the people—but this word is both new and uncommon. *Ethnocide*, along with its more famous sibling, *genocide*, was coined in 1944 by Raphael Lemkin, a Polish Jewish refugee to the United States. Its original purpose was to describe the atrocities committed against the Jewish people by the Nazis during the Holocaust. The creation of the words *ethnocide* and *genocide* filled a linguistic vacuum by describing a form of violence that was previously unimaginable. To persuade Europeans to stop destroying themselves and to ensure that humanity could learn and improve, the continent's greatest thinkers developed new philosophies and words to describe their horrible actions. However, since 1944 the term *ethnocide* has lived in relative obscurity, and only now is it being used to describe the transatlantic slave trade.

The absence of language is a beguiling problem, especially since English, being a merging of Romance and Germanic languages, has an abundance of words. American English suffers from an absence of *meaningful*—and yet a profusion of *meaningless*—language due to our systemic ethnocidal divisions.

The inadequacy of our language even extends to how we describe ourselves as a society. Linguistically, we are encouraged to casually interchange *America* and *United States* as our collective identifier. However, the latter speaks to the name of a government and the former to a European-based concept of existence that is built upon the linguistic erasure of Indigenous culture. It is also the namesake of a man who never set foot on the land that became the United States of America. These words do not have the same meaning, but we are encouraged to act as if they do. In a language built upon domination and destruction, the meanings of words—and life— become afterthoughts because dominance precedes everything else. Most Americans probably understand *America* to be a de facto cultural identifier, but a seed of doubt still exists because we are unsure of what exactly constitutes American culture. Since this book is an exploration of language and culture, I use *America* to express our culture, which has existed since before the creation of the United States.

Also, the confusion that occurs from the word *we* in American English speaks to this absence or inadequacy. As a Black man, when I use *we* most people infer that I am speaking about the Black community, my common people, and not about a *we* that refers to a collective American people. This is because our society has never aspired to have a common people; if you share commonality you are less likely to create an other whose culture you can destroy and exploit. The centuries-long ethnocide of the transatlantic slave trade consisted of European colonizers forcefully bringing Africans to the Americas so that they could destroy African culture, exploit African bodies, and build a society upon perpetual division and the absence of a collective *we*. The United States' racial divisions of Black and white were created to sustain and normalize ethnocidal division. When Americans say *we* we struggle to understand the denotation of the word, and we are unaccustomed to non-white Americans having the agency to represent and define our collective society. America is a muted society with a plethora of words.

Scarcity within linguistic abundance seems contradictory, but this is our reality. We have an excess of words for nearly everything except our own identity and culture. We can define ourselves as a democracy and a nation that celebrates freedom and liberty, yet this language and narrative lose their legitimacy in the face of American legacies like slavery and Jim Crow. Democracies are imperfect by design, with systems of exclusion and marginalization baked into even the best of them, but the *faith* in democracy resides in the system's philosophical commitment and capacity to rectify these inequalities. American democracy does not work this way. Our reliance on ethnocidal division has created a society dependent on sustaining inequality, which we mask with the façade of democracy.

Freedom has Germanic roots and *liberty* has French roots, and these are two English words that mean the same thing and yet mean nothing when applied to the American experience. When the American ideals of democracy, freedom, and liberty are juxtaposed against the American practices of chattel slavery or Indigenous genocide, we confront a hypocrisy and an absence of words because we do not have the language for our unique American hypocrisy. The concept of ethnocide provides the beginning of the necessary language.

Rarely do we confront the insufficiency of our own language. Instead, we prefer to imagine a society devoid of our systemic tyranny, and in so doing we can attach ourselves to inaccurate, yet clearly preferable identifiers such as democracy, freedom, and liberty. As a Black man I have never been able to accept this status quo because my culture stems from America's systemic tyranny. American hegemony relies on the deliberate and strategic silencing of voices—including mine—and there are many methods for making one mute in America. One's voice can be forcefully silenced, or one can be bribed into embracing one's oppression. Yet once one can express their voice, their words must do more than describe the oppression and hypocrisy that befalls their community, because America's corrupted, oppressive, and hypocritical language will work to silence their liberating discourse or turn it into meaningless gibberish. For our liberating words to have meaning in America, they must speak to the collective "we" that America has never wanted to exist.

This book is equal parts memoir and philosophical journey because recognizing the absence of language encompasses both the journey to find one's own voice and the process of finding the language for one's voice to convey its intended meaning and create sustainable change. Despite how outspoken I was growing up, I struggled to find the language to describe my environment in the American South.

I grew up in the suburbs of Atlanta, Georgia, and I had a bunch of white friends growing up. It was normal for one of my friends to casually describe me as "white like us." Every time I heard this I would recoil. Sometimes I'd brush it off, other times I would remind them that I'm not white, and they'd respond by insisting, "You know what I mean." But now the question is *What do they mean?* What is the intended meaning of their words? Did they even know what they meant or said? I knew there was a chasm between what they said and what they meant, but did they?

I have never wanted to be white. Being called white felt like the worst insult in the world, not because I thought being white was inherently bad, but because that accusation existed to erase my Blackness. Why should I ever want to be white like them? The statement was, of course, intended as a compliment. They were not trying to harm me; they were trying to explain why and how much they liked me. They aspired to no longer see me as Black, and they would become defensive when I reminded them that I was. Eventually, it became clear to me that I did not have the language to describe these friends. What is the word for a well-meaning person whose language, whose very ideas are not intentionally, but inherently, racist? Whose idea of a compliment is a grave insult built upon cultural erasure. Despite this dynamic being normal throughout most of America, I knew of no words to describe this common occurrence. The onus was not on me to find my voice, but to excavate the concealed meaning of their words.

America is a society that focuses on action ahead of philosophy and language, and people love to ask *What's next?* Americans want to know the actions they can take more than the words they can say or the thoughts they should cultivate. When talking about my book, I have encountered countless people who find the ideas and concepts fascinating, but what they really want to know is *What's next?* What action can I tell them to take?

My point is not to dismiss the necessity of action, but action without language or philosophy is chaotic. Language and philosophy precede action; comprehension should precede action. The last two chapters of this book are devoted to action and change, but first we need to be able to identify the problems of our society and speak the revolutionary language necessary to make the changes and guide the actions.

1

DISCOVERING
ETHNOCIDE

We are in the presence of a crime without a name.

WINSTON CHURCHILL, August 1941

When a new word enters our vernacular, it is hard to imagine how we ever functioned without it. When provided with a better way to describe any facet of existence, it is almost impossible to continue articulating and imagining your environment without incorporating that new concept. It is used to depict the past, present, and future. People project an awareness of the word, and its impact, upon previous generations who lived without it, and it becomes difficult to imagine the calamitous impact of this absence.

In the United States, we have a propensity to coin or reinvent words related to business, which is a problem since businesses will always value profit over people. If our language becomes the language of business, it ceases to be the language of the people.

During journalism school, I was told of the necessity of branding our-selves to be more attractive to businesses. I understood the practicality of this idea but was taken aback by the redefining of a word to articulate this need, and I recoiled at the idea of reshaping myself to fit into a brand that businesses would want to buy. Our branding consisted not of red-hot irons seared into our flesh, but the creation of a disposition yearning to become consumed by a corporation. I wanted an education to grow into a better person, not a more desirable commodity. Journalism as a craft requires you to write well, listen to others, ask good questions, and forge authentic rela-tionships; all of which can make you a better person. It vexed me that the American way to thrive in this profession encouraged me to simplify, limit, and reduce myself into something marketable. I was asked to create and apply my own shackles.

Americans often shape our lives around this business-centric language. We refer to each other as *consumers*, and we value disruption so long as corporations or start-ups lead the way. Despite America's cultural reliance on the language of business and the desire for it to shape our lives, we have remained unaware of its obsolescence. When a business runs out of money everything attached to it dies, including its language. The language has a short shelf life partially because it is rare for a business to have a life span as long as that of a human being, and it is highly unlikely for a business to exist for generations. The language of a culture and a people is obviously more sustainable than that of a business, but America tragically attempts to create a sustainable language from the unsustainable language of business.

A simple example of this dynamic would be the 108-story Willis Tower in Chicago. Until 2009 it was known as the Sears Tower because the Amer-ican department store chain Sears, Roebuck and Co. wanted their name emblazoned upon the tallest building in the world. Upon completion in 1974, the then Sears Tower became the tallest building in the world, surpassing the World Trade Center in New York City. (In 2013, the new One World Trade Center building, which replaced the old World Trade Center building following 9/11, reclaimed the title of tallest building in the United States.) However, by the early 2000s, Sears fell into financial decline and the meaning, value, and relevance of their name had become nearly obsolete. Another company took over their building and the language of Sears essentially died out. Yet Chicagoans still loath calling this building the Willis Tower. They insist on calling it the Sears Tower, and in print the building is often written as "Willis (Sears) Tower." Chicagoans are attempting to revive a dying language because they believe that the language of a dying business is a vital part of their culture. Eventually, the Willis Group will fade away and Chicago will again confront the specter of their skyline being defined by a nameless building.

The constant threat of extinction due to the potential absence of money also inclines businesses to produce hollow, shortsighted, self-interested, and manipulative language in order to stay afloat. The language of business exists to extract the money and resources it needs to live, therefore truth and honesty become afterthoughts. If the truth might result in a loss in revenue, then lies will now become a necessity for survival. As America works to merge humanity and business—corporations are also people according the the U.S. Supreme Court—we cultivate and encourage a hollow, meaningless, and dishonest discourse. Unsurprisingly, America's pro-business politicians are frequently our most dishonest and two-faced, yet their lies rarely harm them because their claimed monopolization of America's business culture positions them as the saviors and protectors of America's unsustainable business-centric culture.

In 1607, America's first permanent British settlement in Jamestown, Virginia, was established by the Virginia Company of London, or London Company. John Smith was a leader of the Virginia Company of London's expedition to America and their prioritization of profit ahead of human life shaped their interactions with Indigenous people. Despite depending on the knowledge and food of Indigenous people to survive in the New World, Smith and the English colonists never aspired to become one with Indigenous people. Their thirst for gold and profit shaped their relationship with the Powhatan tribe and the land. The land became a commodity, and human beings became either impediments or accomplices in their quest for wealth. The lifesaving aid that the Indigenous people provided to the colonizers mattered for not because they refused to allow colonizers to consume their resources. Smith and the colonizers always wanted more resources and more land, and only a couple years after their arrival in the New World, war erupted. The First Anglo-Powhatan War began in 1609, and Smith had already returned to England by its start, but the seed of destruction had already been planted.

When America talks about Smith, we often speak of Smith and Pocahontas as a symbol of peace between colonizers and Indigenous people, but this is a false narrative that presents a more appealing brand that America prefers to sell to ourselves and the world.

The language of business has shaped America from the beginning. It should surprise none of us that our language has always supported the dehumanization, oppression, and enslavement of non-European people for the profit of the companies, and their societal derivatives who colonized America.

As a Black American, I have never felt much comfort in my mother tongue in part because of its tacit encouragement of human commodification. This corresponds to a dearth of common, everyday language required to succinctly describe the complex joys and sorrows of life that exist outside the parameters of *branding*.

Years ago, a friend introduced me to the French phrase *l'appel du vide*, or the "call of the void." For years I felt alone in my fear of heights—not of slipping and falling, but of going momentarily insane and jumping off a ledge. This perceived psychological solitude made me wonder if I was actually insane. When I learned of *l'appel du vide* I felt relieved and more equipped to handle an aspect of life that was so common that the French named it. *L'appel du vide* is the sensation that you get when you peer over a cliff and a little voice in your head says, "I wonder what it would feel like to jump off." People also feel the call of the void when driving their car and they suddenly wonder what it would feel like to cause an accident. The fear caused by *l'appel du vide* is not a fear of heights or driving, but the recognition that sometimes the last voice you should listen to is your own. By knowing this phrase, I was no longer trapped within my own emotions, knowing that countless others knew the gripping fear of doubting your ability to trust yourself. This phrase and others like it have everything to do with life, and nothing to do with business, and are far more prevalent outside of American English.

—

In 2015 I wrote an article titled "OK, This Trump Thing Isn't Funny Anymore." At that point Donald Trump was a presidential candidate in the Republican primaries, and most commentators treated Trump's campaign as a joke and a harmless extension of his *brand*. I found his rhetoric decidedly unfunny and dehumanizing. Trump launched his campaign with a speech in which he called Mexicans "rapists," and his dangerous vitriol grew with each passing day. He called for the deportation of all twelve million undocumented immigrants in the country. Chants of "white power" would sporadically erupt at his rallies. In mid-August two white men in Boston assaulted a homeless Latino man. Upon their arrest they told the police, "Donald Trump was right, all these illegals need to be deported."

Following this attack, I reached out to my editors and asked to write a column calling Donald Trump a fascist. They rejected this story idea. Trump's language might have been dangerous or "racially charged," but they determined that proclaiming him a fascist was a step too far.

Trump had only been in the race for a couple of months, so the comparisons to Benito Mussolini or Adolf Hitler seemed premature to my editors. Trump had only advocated for mass deportations but had not forcibly removed anyone himself. And considering that most people did not think he even had the slightest chance of winning the Republican nomination, let alone the presidency, what would be the benefit of this proclamation? I remember being told, "You can't call Donald Trump a fascist!"

Eventually my editors relented, but with the caveat that I could not directly call Trump a fascist. I could only compare him to one. I wrote the article. In it, I wondered why Americans were not more actively combatting Trump's rhetoric. I mentioned, for instance, how quickly people had dismissed Trump's promise to deport all undocumented immigrants. Many argued that it was a logistical impossibility, and others argued that America's inherent morality would prevent the rampant forced removal of millions of people. I saw the opposite. The demonization of non-white people has long been the American norm, and the growing influence of communities of color made the toxicity of the normalized American discourse that Trump spewed more visible. Despite being able to see it, we still lacked the language to describe our cultural vitriol, and many Americans pushed back at using the destructive European language of the early twentieth century to describe America today.

When Trump demonized Latinos, I thought of my family, who had been free persons of color (FPCs) in Charleston, South Carolina, since the late 1700s. FPCs were legally required to carry papers proving that they were not enslaved, and in the years leading up to the Civil War white

Charlestonians began demanding that all FPCs show their papers. Those who could not were rounded up and forced into a life of slavery. Most of my ancestors fled the city to avoid a life of enslavement. At this time South Carolina also made it illegal for Black people to leave the state, so my family had to smuggle themselves out. The increased demand and illegality of transporting Black people resulted in extortionist prices, and Black people needed to sell most of their belongings to afford safe passage out of South Carolina. During the Civil War, two of my ancestors fled Charleston for Haiti, and after staying for a little over a year they set sail for New York City and enlisted in the Union Army to fight for our freedom.

Based on my own family's history, I knew that rounding up people without documentation was not a far-fetched idea for the United States. However, one has to be willing to take a broad, honest look at our history to recognize this truth. Only a myopic view of American life could characterize Trump's rhetoric as a cultural impossibility with no historical precedent. Otherwise, it was obvious that he had tapped into our disgusting, unspoken zeitgeist, which most Americans wanted to believe had been confined to our distant past. Our inability to recognize Trump and America for what they are made American society ill-equipped to stop him.

At the time, *fascist* happened to be the best word to describe the rise of Trump, but it still led people astray. The word *fascist* was coined to describe the rise of twentieth-century authoritarianism in Italy, so it failed to adequately describe the uniquely American danger Trump posed. Trump was a feature, not a bug, of American culture. Calling Trump, various members of his campaign, his supporters, and members of the media who supported him racist also felt inadequate to me. In American society, calling someone a racist requires proving explicitly racist intent, such as an official affiliation with a racist organization like the Ku Klux Klan. Yet this standard only emboldens and empowers racist and ignorant people. Outside the individuals with obvious racist intent who mask their motives, there remains a large mass of individuals whose ignorance and racist upbringing allow them to fiercely deny their racism while perpetuating it. I grew up around these people, but I felt American English lacked the words to capture this nuance. For decades, I struggled with how to articulate this feeling pertaining to what I saw in the world, but as a journalist I now had the obligation to find the words.

American society emphasizes individualism, and we prefer to see our successes or failures as the result of an individual's actions. Concepts like systemic racism are met with such hostility in part because racism is a concept many Americans prefer to interpret in the most individualistic sense, and we are attempting to attach it to a systemic problem. Then come the debates about whether each individual connected to systemic racism is in fact a racist, and the primary purpose of the phrase is corrupted. Language that speaks to a collective problem becomes corrupted and effectively meaningless because it does not adhere to America's individualistic narrative, and our fixation on individualism prevents us from articulating and comprehending collective problems. We are a people bereft of the language to diagnose what ails us.

To address our linguistic void, I searched through Greek and Latin prefixes and suffixes trying to construct a word that conveyed what I intended, and I eventually settled on *ethnocide* to denote the "killing of culture." I had no idea, initially, that the word had first been coined by Raphael Lemkin in 1944 as a response to the Holocaust. *Ethnocide* explained with stunning exactitude the more invisible destruction wreaked by the transatlantic slave trade. How Europeans kept enslaved Africans from practicing their religions or speaking their languages. How Europeans cut the hair of African people to remove their cultural identifiers and separated members of the same tribe or family to break cultural bonds. Prevented enslaved people from identifying as Igbo or Yoruba or Malian, and lumped them all together as African or Black or nigger.

For decades, many people have described the transatlantic slave trade as a genocide, African Holocaust, Holocaust of Enslavement, or Black Holocaust. But these terms never resonated with me. The events Lemkin witnessed that prompted him to coin both *genocide* and *ethnocide* consisted of mass atrocities with the intent to exterminate a particular type of people from a specific place through mass killings and/or forced removals. Europeans didn't want to exterminate African *people*, but rather African *culture*. Ethnocide's endgame is perpetual oppression, exploitation, and inequality. Once European colonizers engaged in the slave trade, ethnocide became the bedrock of the societies they built in the New World.

Trump's rhetoric during his campaign and throughout his presidency has represented a manifestation of ethnocide. It demands that white Americans know and reclaim their place at the top of American society. Barack Obama's presidency was purported to herald an era of racial equality, and his ideology threatened to dismantle America's unequal ethnocidal norm. Like America, Trump rose to the top by successfully marketing the Trump *brand* and convincing people of the authenticity of an image that, in fact, has always been a fragile façade. Trump's campaign and presidency sought to return ethnocide to the fore, yet we could not adequately combat his agenda without the awareness of the concept. To combat ethnocide, we must also examine the arduous journey of Raphael Lemkin, the man who committed his life to creating the language and laws to respond to a nameless crime that killed and terrorized millions of people.

—

Raphael Lemkin was born to a Polish Jewish family on June 24, 1900, in a small town along the Poland-Belarus border within the Russian Empire.

Anti-Semitism spread across Europe as Lemkin was growing up. When he was five, the Russian Empire killed nearly a hundred Jews and wounded a similar amount during the Białystok pogrom, just a few dozen miles from Lemkin's hometown. In his autobiography *Totally Unofficial*, Lemkin describes how Russian mobs cut open the bellies of victims and stuffed them with feathers from pillows and comforters. "A line, red from blood, led from the Roman arena through the gallows of France to the pogrom of Białystok," wrote Lemkin.

Lemkin demonstrated a compassion for oppressed peoples from an early age. During his teenage years, Lemkin was drawn to the plight of the Armenian people, who during World War I were rounded up and systematically exterminated by the Ottoman Empire. An estimated one and a half million Armenians were murdered. (The Turkish government disputes these claims.) Lemkin was horrified by these crimes, and even more horrified when the perpetrators were never convicted.

In 1926, having studied linguistics and philosophy at university, Lemkin attended the Jan Kazimierz University of Lwów, Poland (now Lviv, Ukraine), to study law with the lofty goal of creating a legal framework for outlawing these mass atrocities. At Lwów, his professors explained to him that the acquittals of the Ottoman officials who oversaw the killing of over a million Armenians was a matter of Turkish sovereignty. They claimed that, with regard to international law, the Armenian people were the equivalent of "chickens on a farm," and that a farmer (in this case, the Turkish government) has the right to do as he chooses with his chickens. Lemkin refused to accept this justification and argued that sovereignty consisted of "all types of activity directed toward the welfare of people," but "cannot be conceived as the right to kill millions of innocent people."

After finishing law school, and during the years between World Wars I and II, Lemkin worked as a public prosecutor in Warsaw. Following the 1933 Simele massacre, in which armed forces of the Kingdom of Iraq systematically targeted and killed nearly three thousand Assyrians in Iraqi Kurdistan, Lemkin made his first attempt at outlawing this crime. That year, Lemkin published a report for an international law conference in Madrid that formulated two crimes: the crime of barbarity and the crime of vandalism. "The first consisted of destroying a national or religious collectivity; the second consisted of destroying the works of culture, which represented the specific genius of these national and religious groups. I wanted to preserve both the physical existence and the spiritual life of these collectives." The report made little headway, and the only noticeable outcome was to outrage the Polish foreign minister, who eventually forced Lemkin to resign from the prosecutor's office in 1934. Until the start of World War II, Lemkin worked in private practice in Warsaw.

On September 1, 1939, Germany invaded Poland, and less than a week later, on September 6, Lemkin fled Warsaw after the Polish government ordered all able-bodied men to leave the city immediately. Lemkin took the first train he could out of the city, but during his journey the train was bombed by the Germans. Lemkin escaped and ran to safety into the Polish forest. He and other survivors assembled and began marching to freedom through the forests and small rural villages outside the clutches of the pursuing German army. Many of these Poles hoped to escape to America, but first they would have to successfully escape Poland and find refuge in another European nation that the Germans had not consumed. During their journey they sought shelter in the homes and barns of Poles who had not yet attempted to leave.

Lemkin eventually made it out of Poland and headed east into Russia to see his family for what would be the final time. After two years of chronic migration—from Lithuania to Latvia to Sweden to Russia to Ja-

pan to Canada—Lemkin entered the United States in 1941 and secured a
faculty position at Duke. By train it took Lemkin one and a half days of
continuous travel to reach Chicago from Seattle, and he was astonished
that he was only halfway to Durham, North Carolina. "It was then I realized that America is more than a country, it is a continent. In Europe,
in the same amount of time, I would already have passed through several
countries," Lemkin wrote in *Totally Unofficial*. Lemkin's observation about
the immense size of America is important, because as a Polish Jew living at
the intersection of German, Polish, and Russian culture, he was always exposed to new languages and philosophies. Lemkin soaked in these cultures.
He became fluent in nine languages and could read fourteen. America, in
contrast, was a continent of sterilized sameness so vast that it took days to
traverse. Additionally, the wide expanses allow people to imagine a society devoid of racial division by physically distancing themselves from our
systemic oppression. The dystopian status quo of Jim Crow can be hard for
anyone to image if they never venture to the South.

In North Carolina, Lemkin witnessed the Jim Crow South for the first
time in his life. He was baffled by segregated restrooms "For Whites" and
"For Colored," and struggled to comprehend the scope of America's systemic racism. Upon seeing segregated restrooms, he asked a Black man if
this was real. The man looked confused and angered by the question and
refused to answer. Lemkin soon realized the embarrassment that his ignorance caused.

Despite the security of academia, Lemkin could not ignore the horrors
occurring in Europe, and especially the mass extermination of millions of
Jews by the Nazis. Soon after arriving in America, Lemkin began lecturing,
consulting, and lobbying the U.S. military to address what he would in a
matter of years define as genocide. He wrote papers and published books,
but his pleading fell on deaf ears. Americans were too focused on what

Lemkin called the "war on the armies," and unwilling to see the "war on the peoples" driving the Nazis. In the face of constant opposition, Lemkin eventually got in touch with President Franklin Delano Roosevelt, but FDR responded to Lemkin by urging "patience." The absurdity of requesting patience as you are being confronted by a Nazi death squad was not lost on Lemkin, and he spent a long time contemplating how America and other powerful societies could allow genocide to occur even after being confronted with evidence of the mass killings. "I thought: genocide is so easy to commit because people don't want to believe it until after it happens," Lemkin recalled in *Totally Unofficial*.

Rumors ran through Washington about a mass annihilation of Jews by the Nazis, but the government failed to act. Lemkin began having nightmares of the terror inflicted upon his people, and his family. His health deteriorated rapidly, but he continued to write and in 1944 he published his magnum opus, *Axis Rule in Occupied Europe*, where the definition of *genocide* appeared in print for the first time.

> New conceptions require new terms. By "genocide" we mean the destruction of a nation or of an ethnic group. This new word, coined by the author to denote an old practice in its modern development, is made from the ancient Greek word *genos* (race, tribe) and the Latin *cide* (killing), thus corresponding in its formation to such words as tyrannicide, homicide, infanticide, etc.

Following the war, the Nuremberg trials convicted Nazis of war crimes, but never mentioned genocide. The convictions from Nuremberg sent a strong message to the world, but the convictions alone did not develop an international framework for preventing future genocides. Lemkin had little interest in litigating the past. He wanted to use the law to create a safer future. For the rest of his life, Lemkin remained a one-man lobbyist for codifying the crime of genocide at the international and national level. One could always find him at the United Nations talking to diplomats, but his life was anything but glamorous. Lemkin essentially self-funded his lobbying work, and frequently had to beg friends for money to pay rent and buy food. His clothes were tattered, and many onlookers at the UN felt sorry for him. None of these obstacles stopped him, and on December 9, 1948, the Convention on the Prevention and Punishment of the Crime of Genocide was formally presented and adopted by the UN General Assembly. On January 12, 1951, it came into force after the twentieth nation ratified the treaty. In December 1951, American civil rights leaders, including W. E. B. Du Bois and Paul Robeson, introduced a petition to the UN accusing the United States of genocide against Black people. No charges were levied against the United States, and America did not ratify the Genocide Convention until nearly forty years later, in 1988.

Lemkin was eventually nominated for the Nobel Peace Prize multiple times, but he never won. In 1959, he died of a heart attack while walking down the street in New York City. He was either on his way to or leaving his agent's office to present the latest draft of his autobiography, *Totally Unofficial*. The book saw the light of day in 2013, only after his unfinished manuscripts were discovered and compiled. Lemkin's death did not make much headway in the news, and few passersby had any idea of the life-altering importance of the disheveled fifty-nine-year-old man who had suddenly collapsed on the sidewalk.

Lemkin, despite becoming a respected lawyer, worked outside of our social norms, and was considered totally unofficial by many in his profession. I believe we must pay particular importance to what made him no longer official. Lemkin's career did not adhere to social or bureaucratic norms once he began to defend the oppressed. Challenging a government's right to terrorize and exterminate its own people made Lemkin a persona non grata, and this remained the case for the rest of his life. And while Lemkin has been largely forgotten, *genocide* has not, and many people are amazed to learn that the word was invented less than eighty years ago. The mass killing of Armenians by the Ottoman Empire that first launched Lemkin on this linguistic crusade is now known as the Armenian Genocide, which clearly demonstrates the altering perceptions that new words can create.

But Lemkin also invented another word, which, until now, has been largely obscured and forgotten: *ethnocide*. In a footnote for *genocide* in *Axis Rule in Occupied Europe*, Lemkin wrote, "Another term could be used for the same idea, namely *ethnocide*, consisting of the Greek word 'ethnos'—nation—and the Latin word 'cide.'"

Since these mass atrocities were inflicted upon a particular nation or culture of people, Lemkin felt that *ethnocide* and *genocide* could be interchangeable. However, the few scholars who decided to examine ethnocide determined that this word was essentially dependent on genocide to have any cultural relevance. With genocide, the killing of a people would also result in the killing of their nation or culture, so ethnocide essentially lived within genocide. For ethnocide to have any independent legitimacy, one would need to provide an example of a culture that was destroyed, yet the people remained. In 1970, French ethnologist Robert Jaulin published *La Paix blanche: Introduction à l'ethnocide* (White Peace: Introduction to Ethnocide), which detailed the ethnocide being inflicted upon the Indigenous Bari people living between Venezuela and Colombia. Jaulin understood ethnocide as destroying the spirit or soul of a people while keeping their bodies. Spanish historian and jurist Bartolomé Clavero has expanded upon Jaulin's definition, but his concentration is on the law, and his exploration of genocide and ethnocide does not focus on the transatlantic slave trade.

When I first struggled to define and name the world I experienced, I was not able to apply Lemkin's *ethnocide* to help make sense of things. I went on my own linguistic journey and formulated a word that, unbeknownst to me, already existed. Despite this, my application represents an extension of Lemkin's ideas into an environment in which he lived, but inadequately explored. In the South, at the segregated restrooms, he looked ethnocide in the face but could not see it. I do not begrudge him for his lack of vision. He spent the rest of his life—withstanding social ridicule and poverty—to codify genocide within international law. In the footnotes of his work, he left a clue for explaining an America he never sufficiently understood—that never embraced his brilliance—via a word that can empower oppressed people in America today and see through America's façade.

The idea of ethnocide redefined my work as a journalist discussing race, culture, and politics in America. As a Black man in America who was taught Western ideas, my task for understanding my environment will always consist of incorporating European ideas, factoring in their ignorance of the lives of Black people, and modifying these ideas so that they can become applicable to my existence. Lemkin is one of many great European men whose ideas require this type of recalibration.

2

POLDEREN AND CULTIVATING CULTURE

Beyond myself

somewhere

I wait for my arrival

OCTAVIO PAZ, "The Balcony"

What exactly is culture? There are various forms of culture—popular culture and folk culture and even work culture. The various applications of the word *culture* can obscure its meaning, and thus will limit our understanding of exactly what ethnocide kills.

I define a culture as a collection of people in a specific place who work together to survive in perpetuity. A collection of people hunt and harvest food unique to their environment. They build houses and clothes conducive to the weather. They develop a language, customs, art, practices, and beliefs

specific to their community. At its core, sustainable culture has an attachment to place.

A quick exploration of various untranslatable words and a consideration
for the cultures that created them will show how the environment in which
those people live greatly influenced the creation of that word. My favorite
of these words, which I believe also succinctly articulates the importance
of equality and an attachment to place when forging culture, is the Dutch
word *polderen*.

About one-third of the Netherlands is below sea level, and since about
the twelfth century the Dutch have waged a sustained land reclamation
battle against the North Sea. The Dutch people developed dikes, canals,
and windmills to pump out water and create new land, called polders. *Polder* basically means "reclaimed land," but there is a spirit to the word that
makes it hard to translate into another language. Every inch of a polder has
purpose, and none of the land can go to waste. The creation of polders has
become increasingly ambitious as the Dutch population has grown in the
twentieth century. The combined population of the three massive polders
built from the 1920s to the 1960s is nearly four hundred thousand people.
Many residents can still remember when their land was just water. They can
recall, and all residents learn, the effort required to make their land, and,
intriguingly, this creates the inverse of the relationship most people and
cultures have with their land.

In most cases, the land precedes the people. Land can seem a fixed,
ever-present resource. But the Dutch, in many ways, have preceded their
land and can easily envision a future where their land could disappear. A
faulty dam, a massive storm, and the threat of climate change could legit-
imately result in the North Sea swallowing up huge swaths of the country.
On January 31, 1953, a combination of high tides and a large windstorm on
the North Sea resulted in sea levels rising nearly nineteen feet and flood-

ing 150,000 hectares (roughly 370,000 acres) of the Netherlands. Nearly two thousand people died and over seventy thousand were evacuated. This constant environmental threat has made the Dutch keenly aware of the danger of cultural extinction, and to counter this threat they have created the philosophy of *polderen*.

Polderen loosely translates as putting aside one's political, class, religious, and other differences in order to come together for the benefit of the community. Originally, Dutch people needed to employ *polderen* to save the polder from a heavy storm. The people faced an existential crisis, and they could easily envision a tomorrow where their polder (and most likely themselves, too) would no longer exist. They came together so frequently, as they stared death in the face, that they needed to give this action a name, yet the application of *polderen* extends to aspects of everyday Dutch life with little concern for the dangers of the North Sea. Starting in the 1500s, as Europe was consumed with religious conflicts between Catholics and Protestants, the Dutch became Europe's beacon of religious tolerance. The practice of putting religious and other differences aside for the betterment of humanity created a culture of tolerance and togetherness that still influences the Dutch today. The Dutch parliament, for example, has never had a one-party governing majority, but instead has always relied on forming coalitions. The Dutch believe that the political parties will put differences aside for the betterment of the people, and thus far they always have, even if it takes a while to form a coalition government. Following the 2017 parliamentary elections, it took a record 225 days to form the new cabinet because Dutch politicians had to form a new government coalition made up from four different political parties. On average it takes the Dutch about 90 days to form a coalition government, and the previous record was 208 days in 1977. Clearly, there will be some political parties whose ideologies provide almost no opportunity to find common ground, but in a nation with over eighty registered political parties, Dutch culture encourages these groups to find a way to work together. The Dutch govern via *polderen* too.

As a soccer (football) fanatic, I first encountered *polderen* as I watched Ajax Amsterdam and the Dutch national team play soccer. At the global level, soccer becomes a fascinating exploration of cultural expression. Prior to the Dutch soccer revolution, soccer had a very industrialized, specialized philosophy. The attackers were only good at scoring goals. Defenders were only good at defending. Midfielders were good at both, but not good enough to specialize in either. The Dutch considered this approach to be too inefficient, so they devised Total Football with the goal of ensuring that all of the players had roughly equal technical abilities and could switch positions. This flexibility allowed them to maximize every inch of the soccer field and the potential of each player. The collective philosophy of Total Football has revolutionized soccer around the globe, and now all top teams employ some iteration of this philosophy. We might call Dutch soccer Total Football, but it is an obvious application of *polderen*.

Polderen also shapes Dutch agricultural development and the Dutch response to the threat of rising sea levels from climate change. The Dutch are the second-largest agricultural exporter in the world, only behind the United States, yet they have vastly fewer resources. In 2019, Dutch agricultural exports increased by 4.6 percent and surpassed $114 billion (94.5 billion euros), and U.S. exports were $137 billion (113 billion euros), a 2.1 percent decrease from 2018. To maximize space, the Dutch have built gigantic greenhouses so that they can control the development and growth of their crops. This expedites production and makes it possible to grow crops for a global market in a densely populated region. Despite being half the size of the U.S. state of Maine, the Netherlands has more than ten times the population at over seventeen million. The density of the Netherlands means its global agricultural production mixes with urbanized communities, so the

Dutch heavily regulate the use of pesticides and industrial waste to prevent them from harming the greater community. Their experience with dikes, dams, and manipulating water has made them the preeminent source for information and infrastructure development to address rising sea levels from climate change. New Jersey enlisted the help of the Dutch following Hurricane Sandy in 2012, and New Orleans has been collaborating with Dutch engineers since 2006 to confront coastal erosion, rising sea levels, and increasingly dangerous and frequent hurricanes brought on by climate change.

Whenever I have been to the Netherlands, I notice that the people keep their curtains open. The monotony of daily life largely remains a communal activity even when you are within your own home. Not all Dutch people live on a polder, but as I pass by and see people inside their homes and they look at me, I meditate on how communal existence seems to come first, and how private space, such as your home, appears to exist as part of a larger communal space. One's home does not create a private sanctuary apart from the world, but instead creates personal space within a community.

An important difference between the United States and the Netherlands is how efficiently and sustainably each country uses their resources and the philosophy that guides their practices. *Polderen* manifests not only in the physical creation of culture via polders and the people, animals, and plants that live on them, but also in the metaphysical due to the ideas, philosophies, practices, and art that *polderen* creates. In comparison to *polderen*, American ethnocide represents an inversion of culture so severe that one must question if American society even has culture.

—

What we might define as American culture starts with the colonization of North America, which was predicated on the genocide of Indigenous people through taking their land and forcefully removing and exterminating their people. Soon thereafter chattel slavery also became a pillar of American life, and the transatlantic victims of ethnocide were forced to grow European crops on the stolen land. European colonizers have no relationship to the land apart from taking it away from Indigenous people. Europeans cultivated the land in order to grow crops from the Old World, rather than those native to the land. The connection to the land existed only as a way to generate revenue. American culture was never a collective culture focused on existence, but a divided culture that valued money more than human life.

The ethnocidal culture of exploitation and appropriation does not have the longevity of *polderen*, which the Dutch have applied for nearly a thousand years. The culture forged in what became the United States divided the community between Europeans, who could profit from the land, and exploited people, who were forced to work the land and receive nothing in return. Barbarism would be a more apt descriptor of the culture of colonization, yet we still call it culture, and this poses a profound problem. Two opposing ways of life—one values existence and the other does not—are defined with the same word: culture. America does not have the language to define our culture, and this linguistic absence makes it alarmingly difficult to combat our destructive culture. For example: if America's destructive practices are called culture and the Dutch's sustainable practices are also called culture, then we no longer have language for differentiating between good and bad practices. Instead, we use the language of sustainability and cultivation to describe our unsustainable destruction. Bad actions are now good. Lies become the truth. The world has become inverted, and existence has become a secondary concern that we are encouraged to neglect.

The inversion of culture that Americans call culture is both acultural and decultural. European colonizers both negated and acted without culture as they engaged in genocidal and ethnocidal practices in the New

World, but what makes America and other colonized societies unique and distinct from cultures such as Germany's, Cambodia's, or Rwanda's, which regressed into genocide, is that the negation and lack of culture became the foundation of the country that we know today. Any society can regress into cultural destruction, but few are built upon it. In ethnocide, the exploiters (the ethnociders) survive off the culture of the oppressed (the ethnocidees). Ethnocide is foundationally parasitic, so the final solution is not extermination, but perpetual oppression.

In America the distinction between ethnocider and ethnocidee is denoted by race. White Americans have created a culture, or race, and have defined themselves based on their capacity to exploit their surroundings and distinguish themselves from the other. The name that white people have given themselves is not attached to a place. Their eponym has no connection to a physical place nor an understanding of a collective people. Here again the Dutch provide the perfect juxtaposition. The name of their country, The Netherlands, literally means the "low-lying region," and the word *Dutch* derives from *diutisc*, which means "people" in Old High German. The cultural identity of the Dutch articulates that they are a collective people from a specific place. America, with its foundation of ethnocide and genocide, defines itself by the division of people and the denial of place.

Not only does America's name signify no attachment to place, but the name *America* comes from Amerigo Vespucci, an Italian sailor who never landed in what is today called the United States of America. Vespucci eventually distinguished himself from the pack of lost European explorers who thought they were in India during his 1501 voyage to the tip of South America. He was able to see the other side of the continent and realized, for the first time, their error. America is named after a man who, in many ways, has zero attachment to this place, and this disconnect still influences our society.

The ethnocidal culture of European colonizers and the racial distinctions that white people made in order to perpetuate it are atrocities unlike anything the world has ever seen, but as Americans we are pressured, cajoled, and inclined to view our society as anything other than atrocious. We can stare an ethnocidal atrocity in the face and think nothing of it because it is all we have ever known. As with the perversion of the word *culture* when applied to ethnocide, those who live within an ethnocidal environment can see something that is bad, but still call it good, because the word for good is the only one that exists. Ethnocide creates this inversion of the truth, and it all starts with the division of people.

—

An ethnocidal society divides the people of its society by relegating truth to a negative influence; the source of truth resides exclusively with the ethnociders because the culture depends on sustaining ethnocidal division. They need to keep their power to divide society and possess the truth regardless of whether it is true or false. Truth is irrelevant within ethnocide. America has countless examples of the meaningless truths that ethnocide creates, but race is the most obvious one.

The narratives that America professes regarding the white and Black races have no legitimacy, but within American ethnocide we all yearn to make them at least partially legitimate because these identifiers of perpetual, systemic, ethnocidal division are the only identifiers and identities most Americans know. This is why, when Americans talk about being post-racial, we never talk about what a post-racial people would look like. Instead, we imagine America remaining essentially the same, but without racial strife. America wants to either move beyond or deconstruct race, but I believe we need to move to *before* race and focus on culture instead. We need to talk

about being *pre*-racial, so that we can properly see our ethnocidal divisions
and how they corrupt all of us. If Americans are not these toxic identities,
we do not know who we are and what we should call ourselves.

Many recent immigrants to America have the option of identifying
with their non-American identity to counter the contagion of American
ethnocide, but the longer they stay in America the harder it is to continue.
Eventually, they too are divided within the white and non-white ethnocidal
paradigm of America.

Within ethnocide, the ethnocider lives off the exploitation and the denial of the culture of the ethnocidee. In many cases, the ethnocider is fully
aware that their livelihood depends on exploitation. They must either disregard the impact of their actions because exploitation generates relative
stability or use the irrelevance of truth within ethnocide to convince themselves that their exploitation is instead something more palatable.

In recent years, factions of the white nationalist and white supremacist
movements in America have even employed the terminology of ethnocide
to describe what they perceive to be the threat of non-white immigration
to the United States. American white nationalist Richard Spencer has cited
the work of French writer and New Right movement leader Alain de Benoist's interpretation of ethnocide as having helped inspire his desire to create
an ethnostate in America. Ethnocide for de Benoist is merely the idea that
combining cultures equates to a killing of culture. As a result, Spencer and
others claim that the presence of non-white people poses a threat to white
culture. The ethnocide white nationalists claim is happening bears no resemblance to the prolonged, systemic, ethnocidal campaign of the transatlantic slave trade, which had an explicit objective of murdering the culture
of African people. The alleged ethnocide of white nationalists merely acknowledges that these white people are aware that their complexion-based
culture will not survive if it interacts with people of a darker complexion.

Their identity relies on the creation of an other, and the potential of the other to become an equal threatens the continuation of their unsustainable culture-less identity. The other will always strive for liberation, so these white people will live in a state of perpetual conflict as they wage an unwinnable war against culture and existence.

Ethnociders may actively denounce their capacity to exploit while still benefiting from a system built to generate profit from exploitation. Within the perverse discourse of American English, the individualistic manifestation of a system of exploitation that ethnocidal white Americans constructed for themselves is commonly referred to as white privilege, and even that terminology represents an inversion of the truth. Their privilege is wealth in the guise of culture, so it would be more apt to describe this celebrated cultural absence as a hindrance.

White supremacy is another example. A white person erroneously believes they are supreme or superior, so America calls them a white supremacist. That is what they believe, but not what they are. This is a deference to whiteness even as whiteness is criticized, and this steadily erodes the truth in America's ethnocidal society. Ethnociders are given the linguistic upper hand despite it undermining our actions and the truth of our society. American society is conditioned to defer to the exploiter and to see them as the inverse of what they are. Ethnociders survive off this imbalance.

However, unlike ethnociders, ethnocidees cannot live off exploitation and must instead live off the culture they create, all while an oppressive force steadily undermines and extracts it. American ethnociders depend on extracting and profiting off vibrant Black culture because it both sustains the division of ethnocide and masks ethnocidal oppression.

Years ago, I asked my mother what she considered Black culture to be, and she listed famous Black Americans, referencing music, art, and food; and all of this made sense. Next, I asked about when she actively gets to do culturally Black things, and she mentioned the church, the hair salon, and, of course, when she's at home with my dad and sister; and this made sense too. Nothing out of the ordinary about these answers, but they all suggested that Blackness was allowed to exist primarily in an absence of whiteness. Without explicitly saying so, she articulated that Black culture could flourish in spaces without white people, and thus she could only exist within her own culture for a fraction of the day.

My mother was initially quite upset with me from these questions because she believed that I was minimizing or delegitimizing Black culture. We live in a society that spends much of its time denigrating Black culture, so as a Black man I am expected to celebrate and champion Black culture to the hilt. We remain primed and ready to defend our culture since we expect the attacks. Expressing the limitations of Black culture as a Black man does not fit within this script. The foundation of this tension and confusion derives from the unquestioned acceptance of white culture as legitimate. If Black people can only express their culture for a fraction of the day, the assumption is that white people can express their culture more than we can, and therefore we have lost the unspoken cultural battle. This logic only makes sense if we erroneously decide to perceive white ethnocidal culture as the same as, and not as the opposite of, culture. In that conversation, my mother needlessly gave white ethnocidal culture a legitimacy that it did not warrant, and my examination of Black culture appeared to be an attack. However, when compared to the absence of culture that is white ethnocidal culture, the Black community's confined and oppressed culture represents arguably the strongest cultural force in American society today.

Black culture in America must find enclaves beyond the reach or concern of ethnocidal white America to forge our culture, yet we also know that our culture within these spaces will still be attacked by white Americans once it grows to a point where it could threaten America's ethnocidal status quo.

Black churches are bombed and attacked once the ideas cultivated within this Black cultural space grow beyond the walls of the church and influence the actions of Black people as they exist within spaces that white Americans feel they must dominate. Black neighborhoods are attacked once their businesses pose any sort of competitive threat to white-owned businesses and the Black residents behave as if they are equal to their white neighbors.

The 1921 Tulsa massacre is one of the clearest manifestations of white American ethnocidal terror. In the late 1880s, free Black Americans started moving into Oklahoma, which did not become a state until 1907. To the recently freed Black Americans, the territory of Oklahoma offered an opportunity to live outside of the oppression of the South and the erasure of recently claimed rights following the collapse of Reconstruction in 1877. In the city of Tulsa, the Black community congregated in the Greenwood district, and by the early twentieth century it had become one of the most prosperous Black communities in America, even earning the name "Black Wall Street." However, on May 30, 1921, Black Greenwood resident Dick Rowland entered an elevator with Sarah Page, a white woman, and soon Black Wall Street would be no more. Page either yelled "Rape!" or said that Rowland sexually assaulted her. Soon, white vigilante lynch mobs had formed, and a newspaper headline even read "To Lynch Negro Tonight." With the support of the local law enforcement, white Tulsans attacked Greenwood and burnt down thirty-five city blocks. A police directive urged white Tulsans to "get a gun, and get busy and try to get a nigger." As white Tulsans destroyed Greenwood, thirty to forty trucks carrying Black bodies "stacked up like cordwood" could be seen leaving the district. Thirty-six deaths were officially recorded, but estimates range from one hundred to three hundred. Nearly a thousand people were admitted to the hospital, and ten thousand Black Americans were left homeless as their homes and businesses were burnt to the ground. In 2020, nearly a century after the massacre, a mass grave was discovered in Tulsa's Oaklawn Cemetery suspected to be the final resting place of nearly twenty Black victims of the massacre.

Though the Tulsa massacre only lasted for two days, generations of Black prosperity were destroyed, as was much of the documentation of this prosperity, allowing white ethnociders to dismiss the severity of their terror and craft a new narrative that ignores Black prosperity. White Tulsans ranging from poor whites to influential government and political officials participated in the terror, and as white Tulsans controlled the city and the cultural narrative after the massacre, they worked to conceal their atrocity. Many of the Black survivors of the massacre also refrained from retelling the horrors inflicted upon them because they did not want to relive the trauma or suffer further abuse from white Tulsans who wanted their terrorism erased from history. Remembering the terror of the past can create terror and trauma in the present, and because of this dystopian reality, many Black Tulsans never learned about the massacre of their own people. Remembering Tulsa and the many other similar massacres will never become the white American norm so long as ethnocide dominates our society. Black Americans must continually pick up the ashes of our culture and start anew, despite our knowledge of the inevitability of another conflagration and the disregard of our trauma.

Seventeen years after Tulsa, on November 9–10, 1938, the Nazis destroyed Jewish businesses throughout Germany, killed nearly a hundred people, and sent thirty thousand Jews to the concentration camps. To this day, Germany annually remembers *Kristallnacht*, the "Night of Broken Glass." German culture does not aspire to conceal and condone Nazi terrorism. America's terror emerges from our foundational ethnocidal culture. Without the language to define our culture, we are prone to ignore and perpetuate the terror ethnocide requires.

—

When I was younger, I felt the cultural void created by ethnocide, and I was fascinated that so many transformative Black Americans, including Malcolm X and Dr. Martin Luther King Jr., used philosophies and cultures from outside of America to form the foundations of their work and our liberation movements.

The philosophy of Dr. Martin Luther King Jr. played a significant role in my maturation. Neither of my parents are academics, so I was not inundated with King's written work as a child, but as a Black man from metro Atlanta, I saw Dr. King's presence everywhere. Many of the murals and depictions of Dr. King also feature another transformative figure for the Black community: Mahatma Gandhi. I remember, at first, being confused why he was there alongside celebrated figures in Black history, but my elders told me how Gandhi's philosophy of nonviolence inspired Dr. King's work. They did not spend much time on Gandhi's philosophy of Satyagraha, which helped India defeat the British and end colonial rule, but instead emphasized how he inspired Dr. King. This was a transformative moment for me as a child. Even in elementary school, I was introduced to the need to look beyond America for answers to America's problems. This belief only grew as I got older.

Gandhi was not the only, or even the most significant, philosopher to shape the ideas and work of Dr. King. In 1934, only five years after his birth, his father, Martin Luther King Sr., who was the minister at Ebenezer Baptist Church in Atlanta, traveled to Berlin, Germany, for the Baptist World Alliance conference. King Sr. left for the conference days in advance and traveled to Rome, Tunisia, Egypt, Jerusalem, and Bethlehem before arriving in Germany. While in Germany he witnessed the rise of the Nazi Party and condemned their treatment of the Jewish people and other minority groups. He also traveled throughout the country and learned about the revolutionary religious and social ideas of the sixteenth-century German monk Martin Luther, who started the Protestant Reformation, a protest against the Catholic Church's abuse of power and corruption. The ideas and actions of Luther radically transformed King Sr.'s worldview, and when he returned to America, he changed his and his son's name from Michael King to Martin Luther King. (Martin Luther King Jr.'s birth certificate listed Michael King as his name until Dr. King legally changed his name when he was twenty-eight years old.) The ideas of people and cultures beyond America shaped how Dr. King saw the world and defined himself starting at the age of five, and his global knowledge helped him fight against American ethnocidal injustices.

As a student at Harvard University, Dr. King studied the work of German philosopher Georg Wilhelm Friedrich Hegel (just as Raphael Lemkin did decades earlier as a student at Heidelberg University), and he used Hegel's concept of the dialectic as the foundation for incorporating the philosophy of Gandhi into his civil rights activism. In Hegel's theory, history evolves through a dialectic that consists of a thesis, antithesis, and finally a synthesis. The thesis and antithesis clash, and suffering is inevitable, but the outcome will ideally be a synthesis that elevates their best parts. The violent oppression of Black people had long been the American thesis regarding race, and instead of countering the thesis of violence with more violence, King believed that Gandhi's nonviolent philosophy of Satyagraha would be the proper antithesis to American violence. The synthesis would arguably be the Civil Rights Act of 1964, the Voting Rights Act of 1965, and Lyndon Johnson's Great Society. Dr. King also studied Immanuel Kant and Friedrich Nietzsche and had an academic understanding of foreign philosophy and ideas. Malcolm X, on the other hand, had a more visceral and emotive relationship to the non-American world.

When I was ten years old, Spike Lee's *Malcolm X* hit the theaters. Malcolm was strong, intelligent, commanded respect, and stood up to white America, and my Black friends loved seeing this Black man on the big screen. I loved that, too, but what captivated me the most was Malcolm's pilgrimage to Mecca after he had left the Nation of Islam.

Malcolm X said in his "Letter from Mecca,"

> I have eaten from the same plate, drank from the same glass and slept on the same bed or rug . . . with fellow Muslims whose skin was the whitest of white, whose eyes were the bluest of blue, and whose hair was the blondest of blond—but I could look into their blue eyes and see that they regarded all of us as the same (Brothers), because their belief in One God (Allah) had actually removed the "white" from their mind, which automatically changed their attitude and their behavior towards people of other colors. Their belief in the Oneness of God has made them so different from American whites, that their color played no part in my mind in all of my dealings with them . . . If white Americans could accept the religion of Islam, if they could accept the Oneness of God (Allah), they too could then sincerely accept the Oneness of Man, and cease to measure others always in terms of their "difference in color." And with racism now plaguing America like an incurable cancer, all thinking-Americans should be more receptive to Islam as an already-proven solution to the race problem.

I liked how leaving America helped him see America more clearly. His pilgrimage allowed him for the first time to differentiate white Americans from all white people, and his new ideas exacerbated his break from the Nation of Islam. After returning from Mecca, Malcolm X continued to voice opinions that did not align with Elijah Muhammad, the leader of the Nation of Islam. Prior to his trip to Mecca, Malcolm X was already unwelcome in the religious community he had helped lead, but the division and tension continued to grow. Malcolm X left for Mecca on April 13, 1964, and on February 21, 1965, he was assassinated in the Audubon Ballroom in New York City. In 2020, the documentary miniseries *Who Killed Malcolm X?* speculates that his assassins came from a Nation of Islam mosque in Newark, New Jersey, and that law enforcement did very little to protect him.

Malcolm X could speak to an American toxicity that was neither the norm of the world nor inescapable. He left America, came back, and found a way to articulate his new philosophy in a way that resonated with an American people who were accustomed to being trapped within ethnocide. Yet the tragedy of his enlightenment is that his awareness of America's toxicity resulted in increased tensions and threats to his life in America. This tension can occur with all Americans regardless of race, and the violent silencing of non-white voices who challenge ethnocide has always been an acceptable act within American ethnocide. Malcolm X's non-American ideas contributed to his assassination, and the same thing can be said of Dr. King.

The revolutionary thinkers within the Black community foster the cultural philosophies that can influence Black Americans for generations, and as they search for culture, they must often look beyond America for answers. The strength of the emerging cultural philosophies within the Black community is the disdain of America's ethnocidal society, and, like Tulsa and the countless other massacres against Black communities across America, ethnocidal white Americans aspire to exterminate the metaphysical—along with the physical—manifestations of Black culture in America. For most of my life I have gravitated toward the liberation of non-American worlds, but never as an escape from America. Foreign lands have always served the purpose of generating ideas and language to better understand the tragedy of my ethnocidal society and cultivating revolutionary solutions to our systemic problems.

—

Lemkin was one of the fortunate European Jews who was able to immigrate to the United States. By the 1920s, America had implemented new immigration quotas designed to protect America's racial stock by limiting "undesirable" immigrants, including Africans, Asians, and Jews. By the start of World War II, the United States had hardly adjusted its immigration policies to accommodate European Jews fleeing Nazi terror. The tragedy of American immigration is that the image of America projected to the world derives from ethnociders and therefore has no obligation to be grounded in the truth.

Lemkin came to America to escape oppression and almost certain death, but once here, American ethnocide pressured him to live as the oppressor. Upon arriving in America, Lemkin may have been an "undesirable" Jew, but he still did not have to use colored restrooms and suffer the brunt of segregation. He obtained a position at Duke University that no Black person would obtain for at least another twenty years. Duke did not start the process of desegregation until 1961; Duke was one of the last major universities to desegregate, and in 1961, it agreed to admit Black students into its graduate program. In 1963, it admitted five Black undergraduate students. Lemkin also had access to influential people in the United States government and United Nations that would have been impossible for a Black American to obtain at the time. Lemkin could pass as white, yet his life's work focused on protecting all people from murder and the oppression of their own government. His work represented the

POLDEREN AND CULTIVATING CULTURE

cultural and moral antithesis of white American ethnocidal society and, unsurprisingly, was largely dismissed in America and primarily embraced by non-Americans.

Lemkin did not know that he was immigrating to an ethnocidal society as he fled genocide. As a voice that worked to outlaw ethnocidal and genocidal violence, his privileged position gave him access to people who had a vested interest in ignoring his work. He had the opportunity to talk to the culturally deaf. Combatting genocide opened America to criticism of its oppression of non-white Americans, and the forced removal and murder of Indigenous people.

The Black community felt empowered by the creation of the word *genocide*, and his lesser-known word can empower us even more. Since the coining of *genocide*, we have consistently used it to describe our treatment in America, and *ethnocide* can only enhance our discussion about American culture and the systemic oppression we endure. Within an understanding of ethnocide are tools for articulating our systemic oppression and dismantling ethnocide. To understand America, you must leave America so that you can acquire the language, perspective, and philosophy to articulate America's destructive culture.

As I explore the nature of American ethnocide, I grow empowered by the cultural wisdom of non-American words. I feel more equipped to describe my society, yet I must use foreign words and ideas to do so. However, Americans cannot rely solely on foreign words to define America; rather, we should use these words to empower us to create new words that describe and counter what ails our culture, or our absence of culture. American ethnocide will attempt to suppress the creation of those words, especially when they originate from within the Black community. Black culture is often violently extinguished when it advocates for an equality that will challenge American ethnocide.

To adequately understand the horrors of ethnocide, we must examine the culture and new philosophies of mid-twentieth-century Europe, as the continent's best minds frantically worked to create words and ideas to educate Europeans how *not* to destroy their civilization in a matter of decades. European ideas are not superior to non-European ideas, but the first step toward articulating America's foundational problems can come from European intellectuals who have already articulated these problems and proposed solutions. Many of our answers have been lost in translation.

3

WAITING FOR LUCKY

For reasons unknown . . .

For reasons unknown . . .

For reasons unknown . . .

LUCKY,

From *Waiting for Godot* by Samuel Beckett

Once I'd settled on *ethnocide* and seen how it could clarify America's social, cultural, and political turmoil—which had been magnified by the ascension of Donald Trump to the presidency—I had to figure out how to explain the legitimacy of this word to everyone else.

Because *genocide* and *ethnocide* were forged during the destructive, chaotic terror of early twentieth-century Europe, I decided to examine other ideas that emerged from this period. When existence hangs in the balance, people become more inclined to develop ideas to sustain human life and to counter the destructive norms society has embraced.

The French philosophies of Existentialism and the Absurd are two of the most relevant for understanding the manifestations of ethnocide. At the most basic level, French Existentialism and the Absurd attempt to explain life without adhering to religious dogmas. If your continent is being destroyed to a previously unimaginable scale, and your God seems unable to intervene, it is logical for people to question the existence and necessity of God.

The complexity of Existentialism and the Absurd derives from finding purpose and explaining the legitimacy of one's actions without having a relationship to a God. For hundreds of years a Christian God had provided Europeans with meaning and had been the center of their lives and societies. If life no longer focuses on performing actions to obtain access to heaven or avoid hell, what is the purpose of any action?

French Existentialism's disregard of Christianity makes it a nonstarter with many Americans, yet despite being a God-fearing child, I grew up with a great appreciation of Existentialism before I was even formally introduced to the philosophy. My understanding of Existentialism stemmed from the oppressive racism of the South.

As a child growing up in suburban Atlanta in the 1980s and '90s, polite and subtle racism was the everyday norm of my existence. Initially, my parents wanted me to attend the local public school for elementary but decided against it after visiting because it did not appear welcoming to people of color. Instead, I attended a much more welcoming private school that was not far from my mother's job at IBM. Class sizes were small, everyone knew everyone, and I had a great time. But despite the joy I found at school, teachers or administrators often found ways to diminish my actions—comparing me unfavorably to white classmates, telling me that I wasn't as smart as I thought. But somehow these statements did not impact my confidence in the slightest, and I think our weekly math exams played an important role. I was very good at math as a kid, and during one school year I almost always earned a perfect score on those tests. Telling me that I was not smart or diminishing my accomplishments never stuck with me because my near-perfect grades proved otherwise. I even wondered how dumb someone must be to not think I was smart.

At this school, more often than not, I was not invited over to my white friends' houses. My friends explained how they could only invite a few people to sleep over, and I soon realized that I was being excluded not because I had done anything wrong. Something bad was happening to me without any rhyme or reason, and I was disappointed. When I realized that all of this stemmed from race, I responded in a way that now I see as Existentialist.

I did not internalize America's racism and wonder if something was wrong with me. Instead, I decided that it made no sense to dislike me because of my race, so these actions by white people had zero legitimacy to me. I remember thinking, "I did not pick my parents, I did not pick where I live, and I did not pick what I look like." It made no sense to judge me based on these variables. From there it hit me that if white people could make judgments about me based not on my actions, then they were capable of making any judgment about me at any time and without any legitimate justification. It seemed that the opinions of others could be formed and changed with no justification, so it made no sense for me to modify my behavior for anyone. I did not attempt to mold myself in response to receiving racist abuse—neither to make white friends nor Black friends. All I knew was that my society made no sense, and that I should not change myself so that I would embrace the nonsense. In the South—arguably throughout the entire United States—society is structured around the legitimacy of white people—their ideas, actions, and beliefs. But I had, in my own way, seen that legitimacy crumble before my eyes. Back then, of course, I was guided largely by feelings that I struggled to articulate. Still, those feelings were my guides, and my task then became figuring out how to navigate my environment and find a purpose for my actions.

—

During college I studied abroad in France, and this is when I was formally introduced to Existentialism, or the Absurd, through Albert Camus's play *Caligula*. Camus was a pioneer of the philosophy of the Absurd, and I eventually read many of his other books. They spoke to me. I understood the alienation, bleakness, and absurdity of his characters, and it reminded me of the America I saw but few others seemed to.

At the beginning of *Caligula* no one can find him, and everyone in the palace is panicking. He has been out chasing the moon because "well . . . it's one of the things I haven't got." Caligula defends his insane excursion to capture and own the moon as an act of daring and conviction, and he concludes his argument by celebrating his logic. No one questions his logic and his yes-men even embrace their inability to think. As the play unfurls, Caligula's logic remains insane and eventually leads to his demise. At one point, Rome's bank accounts run dry, and to replenish their coffers Caligula orders his supporters to kill all the nobles who do not support him and use their money and property to balance the budget. This was just one of many decisions that made those close to him question his logic, and eventually turn on him.

This play reminded me of the absurdity of American life—our constant pursuit of happiness, eternal youth, and the facility of going insane when surrounded by sycophantic yes-men. Caligula attempted to capture the moon, and no one could tell him that that was a bad idea. Attempting to capture the moon became a good idea, and Caligula's energy focused on using language to justify his good ideas that in fact were horrific.

A few months before I studied in France, I interned for then congressman Bernie Sanders in his Washington, D.C., office. Sycophantic yes-men wielded all the power in the capital as America pursued its deadly moon shot in the Middle East, but Bernie vocally opposed the war, which was one of the many reasons I wanted to work for him. America formally launched Operation Iraqi Freedom during my internship, less than a week after my twenty-first birthday. The Bush administration's disastrous logic and mangling of language to justify preemptive military action in Iraq had plenty of ardent defenders, and this logic extended to funding the war. Essentially, American funds would run low because of the war, but the wealth and oil of our dead enemies would pay for it.

The Iraq War and the Bush administration made me rethink the American concepts of good and bad. By the time he left the White House, George W. Bush was considered one of our worst presidents, but few would say that he was a bad person. Bush Jr. could do bad things—like invading a country and killing nearly half a million people—without becoming a bad person, because few would argue that he had malicious intent. Vice President Dick Cheney, however, is considered a bad person by many people because these people believe he had bad intent. The second Bush administration, for me, resulted in a profound examination of the importance of intent. Good intent does not make a good person.

During my internship in Washington, D.C., an anti-French tone consumed the district as Republicans developed a new strategy for demonizing then senator John Kerry and slandering any country that objected to America's unjustified invasion of Iraq. Rather quickly, the GOP decided to exploit the fact that Kerry spoke French, and he became open to ridicule. Republicans frequently would say that Kerry "looked French." The French had opposed our unjustified invasion of Iraq, so they had become the enemy. The fact that Kerry had voted to authorize the invasion of Iraq did not matter. He was the enemy of the GOP, so all other facts became subjective and prone to being redefined by the GOP.

The anti-French propaganda was not limited to Kerry. French fries were now called "freedom fries" in the congressional cafeteria. Once, when I asked for french fries, a Black cafeteria employee proudly proclaimed, "We serve freedom fries here!" as she put them on my plate. The expectedness of her response masked the dystopian nature of it all, but here was a Black woman defending the legitimacy of propaganda intended to justify America's right to invade a foreign nation, to plunder its resources and liberate its people by forcing upon them a white American concept of freedom: a freedom dependent on the exploitation of their culture and natural resources. Centuries ago, Black people were African natives, but ever since our captivity we have been forcefully indoctrinated with white America's ethnocidal freedom. This woman had probably never conceived of ethnocide, and I would not come to the word until fifteen years later, so there was nothing we could say to each other.

—

Camus emerged on the French philosophical and literary scene in the early 1940s, and he and Jean-Paul Sartre (the father of French Existentialism) embodied a fascinating shift in popular French philosophical life. Philosophers were beginning to be viewed as celebrities and World War II resistance fighters, not just stuffy theologians, academics, or recluses. They could write novels and plays as well as dense philosophical tomes. They were journalists and wrote their opinions for mass consumption. Philosophy became more accessible.

To Camus, life is absurd because life has no meaning, yet we must find or create a meaning for existence. His philosophy refuted the helplessness of nihilism—two world wars had left much of the continent feeling helpless within a meaningless and destructive world—and turned existence into a constant rebellion against life's meaninglessness. We have to create meaning within the meaningless, and cannot resign ourselves to a meaningless existence within a meaningless world.

Irish playwright Samuel Beckett, who lived in Paris and published his work mostly in French, became arguably the greatest figure in the Theater of the Absurd. His play *Waiting for Godot* references many themes in Camus's work. *Waiting for Godot* can appear to be a frustratingly simple play that obscures its complexity. The stage remains essentially barren apart from a tree, and the plot revolves around two characters, Vladimir and Estragon, waiting for a Godot that never arrives. The play ends without an ending. We get no satisfying resolution. The emerging Theater of the Absurd sought to break away from the orthodoxy of the theater. If plays normally had ornate sets, Absurd plays had hardly any set decoration. If plays had clear beginnings, middles, and ends, then Absurd plays had none and could start and end at any point. If playwrights were known for giving lengthy interviews detailing the message behind their plays, an Absurdist playwright might leave it to the audience to find their own meaning. This is what Beckett did. *Godot* was first performed on January 5, 1953, at the Théâtre de Babylone in Paris—less than nine years after Lemkin's coining of *genocide*, and long before *ethnocide* became known. Within this definitional and linguistic void, I see *Waiting for Godot* as a perfect example of one facet of ethnocidal inequality.

Much of the play focuses on Vladimir and Estragon's conversations about why they wait for Godot, yet as they wait, two characters, Pozzo and Lucky, interrupt them. Pozzo and Lucky do not wait for Godot, but Pozzo waits for Lucky, who is his slave. Lucky appears onstage first, with a long rope tied around his neck, carrying a heavy bag, a folding stool, a picnic basket, and a coat. The rope around his neck is so long that Lucky walks to the center of the stage before Pozzo enters. All Pozzo carries is a whip, and you can hear it crack as Pozzo demands Lucky follow his orders. Lucky does not speak.

Throughout the first act of the play, Pozzo refers to Lucky as "pig" and only communicates with him to order him around: "Closer! . . . Stop! . . . Coat! . . . Whip! . . . Basket!" After initially thinking Pozzo may be Godot, Vladimir and Estragon are soon consumed with examining Lucky and analyzing the relationship between him and Pozzo. They wonder to themselves what ails Lucky, and discover the "inevitable" sore from the rubbing of the rope around his neck. Lucky hesitates to speak, so Vladimir attempts to speak for him, but is unable to articulate exactly what about such inhumane treatment is a scandal, a disgrace. Vladimir's attempted defense of Lucky is both forceful and hollow, and soon his defense withers away. Vladimir and Estragon threaten to leave, but they don't. Lucky remains silent. Pozzo tells them that he intends to sell Lucky, who begins to weep.

Act 1 culminates—if *Godot* can have a culmination—in the moment Lucky finally speaks—as ordered by Pozzo, to satisfy Vladimir and Estragon's curiosity as to whether Lucky can think. First, Pozzo instructs Vladimir and Estragon to put a hat on Lucky's head, which will allow him to think. What follows is three pages of nonsensical rambling from Lucky, yet his words have all the meaning in the world. The purpose of his words is not what he does or does not say, but the reaction of Pozzo, Vladimir, and Estragon. Prior to Lucky's speech, everyone lived in an environment contingent on his silence. It did not matter whether one was forcing Lucky's silence or merely allowing others to compel his silence. Lucky's silence was their status quo, and now it has been shattered.

In the end, all three work together to silence Lucky, which is a core dynamic of an ethnocidal society. Lucky has been decultured through being denied the ability to speak. Pozzo works to deny Lucky of culture in order to make him his slave. Pozzo's ability to communicate, obfuscate, and present a humane façade entices Vladimir and Estragon to stay and commune with him even as he oppresses Lucky. Vladimir and Estragon had been merely waiting for Godot, but now they tacitly perpetuate Lucky's oppression.

Each independent word, thought, and action expressed by Lucky represents an acquisition of culture that could shatter their ethnocidal dynamic: If Lucky can think, then he is no longer dependent on Pozzo's orders. Pozzo projects himself as Lucky's master and the dominant person in their relationship, but Lucky's tirade demonstrates Pozzo's inescapable fragility. Any sign of a human life or any degree of culture in Lucky threatens to unravel Pozzo's parasitic ethnocidal existence. Pozzo expresses no enjoyment from Lucky's speech.

Vladimir and Estragon, however, fluctuate between attentive and angered as Lucky speaks, and only God, Godot—or whoever one chooses to wait for—knows what prompted their seesawing of emotions. Vladimir and Estragon could have been outraged like Pozzo during portions of Lucky's speech. They could have been confused and unable to fully process exactly what Lucky had to say and preferred to silence him instead of acknowledging the legitimacy of his words. Eventually, they both side with Pozzo and forcefully attack and silence Lucky. Once the hat is removed from Lucky's head, he does not say another word for the rest of the play. "There's an end to his thinking!" exclaims Pozzo after he stomps on the hat.

Lucky's role in the play highlights the destructive absurdity of the social divisions that separate Lucky from Pozzo, Vladimir, and Estragon. The audience does not understand what Lucky says, and we do not understand why Pozzo, Vladimir, and Estragon silence him, so it is easy to perceive

Lucky as the absurd person in this situation. Yet in *Waiting for Godot*, Lucky represents the dilemma of the Theater of the Absurd. The genre is not intended to be a light, Absurdist escape from reality, but a mirror upon the absurd reality we all live within.

As with Lucky, the initial responses to *Waiting for Godot*, especially in Britain and the English-speaking world, were those of horror, outrage, derision, and attempts to silence the play. Many people surely thought that they had stomped on Beckett's thinking cap, ending his insufferable gibberish. Yet as time passed, Beckett's and Lucky's words became comprehensible to those who could not listen. Today, *Waiting for Godot* is regarded as one of the most important plays of the twentieth and twenty-first centuries. Within American ethnocide, Black Americans and other communities of color see themselves in the role of Lucky, and our society's inability to confront the environment erected by the proverbial Pozzos, Vladimirs, and Estragons means that our articulated truth—i.e., Lucky's and society's as a whole—becomes incomprehensible and silenced.

In 1851, more than a century before *Waiting for Godot*, Mississippi physician Samuel A. Cartwright coined the term *drapetomania* in his report "Diseases and Peculiarities of the Negro Race" published in *DeBow's Review* to describe Lucky's yearning for freedom. *Drapetomania* derives from the Greek words *drapetes*, meaning "a runaway [slave]," and *mania*, meaning "madness, frenzy." According to Cartwright, an enslaved person attempting to free themselves from a white oppressor constituted a mental illness that needed to be diagnosed and treated. Cartwright stated that slave owners who became too friendly with their slaves and treated them as almost equals helped cause this mental illness. Similarly, slave owners who were too brutal also caused drapetomania. For Cartwright, slave owners needed to have the proper balance between friendly and brutal to prevent Black Americans from yearning to be free.

Additionally, the sight of an enslaved person acting "sulky and dissatisfied without cause" was the precursor to an attempt at liberation, and Cartwright's solution for a Black American's dissatisfaction with a life of enslavement was "whipping the devil out of them." According to Cartwright's soulless language, the yearning for freedom equated to a devil that needed to be beaten out of people.

In the same report, Cartwright also coined the term *dysaesthesia aethiopica*, claiming that Black Americans also suffer from a mental illness that makes them lazy and prone to criminality when not under white supervision.

Cartwright's language was popular in the South and ridiculed in the North, but even Northern ridicule gave the Pozzos of the South a line of communication with the Vladimirs and Estragons of the North that was unavailable to Lucky. Even in ridicule the absurd pseudo-science of Cartwright seeped into America's national discourse.

Following emancipation, Black Americans were ten times more likely to be diagnosed with a mental illness than white Americans, General Order Number 3 that officially ended slavery in America on June 19, 1865 advised Blacks "to remain quietly at their present homes, and work for wages," and during Reconstruction Southern states created black codes that effectively turned free Black Americans into criminals if they did not labor for white Americans. The narrative of a liberated Black existence equating to criminality, incivility, and indicative of an insanity that would destroy America's ethnocidal status quo still influences America today. Cartwright and his fellow Pozzos need to control the thinking hat, so that they can destroy thought and legitimize their soulless, destructive, pseudo-science.

In act 2, Vladimir and Estragon return to the same spot and wait for Godot for a second day. Eventually, Pozzo and Lucky reenter the stage, but now Pozzo is blind. The noose around Lucky's neck is shorter because it now guides Pozzo through his visionless world. Pozzo is completely dependent on Lucky, and Lucky's continued silence means we never get any clarity as to why he has not left blind, dependent, parasitic Pozzo to survive on his own.

Lucky demonstrates how a culture's commitment to ethnocide harms all parties. Pozzo believes he is strong, but his weakness emerges in act 1, and is on display in act 2. Prior to Pozzo and Lucky entering the stage, Vladimir and Estragon had found a meaning in their life. Their meaning was absurd, but in a barren world devoid of any discernible meaning or purpose, they found or created meaning from the simple act of waiting for Godot. This act gave them a reason to wake up in the morning, a place to go, and a friend to socialize with. In an American sense, their *job* consisted of waiting, and they appeared committed to waiting every day. However, Pozzo and Lucky changed their dynamic as they were forced to confront two dehumanized individuals, and when given a choice, they sided with the one they could communicate with.

Pozzo's life, purpose, and meaning derived from depriving Lucky of any semblance of independence or agency. Pozzo created nothing on his own, and he was not in search of meaning or purpose. He derived meaning from making Lucky's and his own life meaningless, and he actively stomped out Lucky's attempt at a meaningful life to sustain his parasitic existence. Only one-fourth of their four-person population was enslaved, but Lucky's enslavement influenced the actions of all of them. America was founded upon a similar ratio, where Vladimir and Estragon represent the North and Pozzo and Lucky the South. The South's commitment to slavery and the North's commitment to legitimize the opinions of slave owners made America's Vladimirs, Estragons, and Pozzos all committed to sustaining this oppressive status quo. America's ethnocidal quartet still influences our society today.

Despite not understanding anything that Lucky says, we do understand that he fights to keep on speaking as Pozzo, Vladimir, and Estragon attack him and seek to destroy his ability to think. So even if we do not understand the meaning of his tirade, we do understand that it is not meaningless to him. Lucky's tirade resonates with me as a Black man. Struggling to find your words and be understood without being silenced is a constant struggle in communities of color. An ethnocidal society does not benefit from educating the oppressed.

For centuries, the Black community has worked to create the opportunity to express ourselves, but our silencing has long been the inevitable outcome. Lynchings, assassinations, police brutality, and other iterations of murder or -*cide* have long been ethnocidal methods for silencing the oppressed. Trayvon Martin, Walter Scott, Sandra Bland, Philando Castile, Eric Garner, Michael Brown, Breonna Taylor, George Floyd, and the other faces of Black Lives Matter experienced the brutal and forced silencing of ethnocide. Their capacity to think and express their humanity threatened the status quo of ethnocidal oppressors. Civil rights activists, and indeed all Black Americans, have encountered this brutality once our humanity is on display.

The ethnocidal struggle that Lucky embodies demonstrates both the difficulty of obtaining the space to speak and the complexity of speaking without then being silenced by oppressive ethnocidal forces. Obviously, speaking and expressing thoughts that please ethnocidal oppressors—ethnociders—will result in their not wanting to silence your voice, but then the words of the oppressed only perpetuate ethnocidal oppression. Ethnocidees may even proclaim their continued oppression as a form of liberation because it may help them obtain the support of the ethnociders and a potentially greater degree of freedom within their existing parasitic ethnocidal relationship, but a loosening of chains is not an absence of chains.

America has long encouraged this school of thought and implored Black Americans to pursue this path toward freedom. Black Americans who unambiguously follow this path are often described as Uncle Toms. We are also encouraged to forgive white Americans for their transgressions against us, but without reciprocity forgiveness provides an excuse for continued oppression. Harriet Beecher Stowe's novel *Uncle Tom's Cabin* professed the supposed benefit of Black forgiveness, but the concept extends far beyond Stowe's work. The narrative of *uplift suasion* has been the primary vehicle, and white and Black Americans both have supported this path toward alleged liberation. *Uplift suasion* proclaims that Black people need to excel in the values of white colonizers to uplift themselves out of the alleged barbarism of African culture and prove that they belong and can excel in a white-dominated society. This philosophy's core tenet is legitimizing white culture, holding it above other cultures, and modeling one's life around obtaining an acceptable amount of whiteness. According to this idea, once Blacks achieve this white threshold, they can begin to live in a society governed by equitable relationships, but this is impossible within ethnocide, which depends on continuous oppression. Complimenting your Black friend by saying they are "white like us," is also a manifestation of *uplift suasion*.

In America we frequently hear stories about affluent Black Americans who live in predominantly white environments and attended Ivy League colleges who are shocked when they are unjustly assaulted or targeted by law enforcement. Their success in white environs cannot spare them from America's racism. America's racial distinctions are a by-product of the required social divisions of ethnocide, so unless and until ethnocide is confronted, racial inequality can never be surmounted.

The dilemma Lucky and other victims of ethnocide face requires them to find and create the language to describe their oppression while also empowering the ethnociders to dismantle ethnocide. Without words, both ethnocider and ethnocidee will be more inclined to resort to violence as their method for continuing oppression or gaining liberation. The Americas have witnessed countless rebellions from slaves and other ethnocidees in search of freedom. Likewise, authoritarian ethnociders have forcefully oppressed those cries for liberation. Concepts like *ethnocide* help alter the power dynamics of this crime against humanity, and can diminish the chances of violence as we seek liberation through equality. Lucky's capacity to think, however, cannot be the end goal in his search for freedom and equality. Once he obtains his liberation, he must also be able to find meaning in a world devoid of the ethnocidal structures of his oppression, the fight against which has thus far provided him meaning.

Camus's philosophy of the Absurd argued that people must rebel against a meaningless world by boldly creating a meaningful life. In "The Myth of Sisyphus," Camus says, "One must imagine Sisyphus happy" because he has dared to create a meaningful existence despite being condemned to roll a boulder up a hill only to watch it roll back down again. In 2020, as COVID-19 engulfed the planet, Camus's book *The Plague*, published in 1947, became a renewed source of interest as the events in his novel mirror the present. As a deadly disease attacks the large coastal city of Oran, Algeria, the hero of the story becomes the doctor who diligently fights to keep people alive. As destruction consumes his world, Dr. Bernard Rieux works to keep life meaningful.

America is inherently dependent on oppression, destruction, and exploitation as founts of meaning. As a Black man growing up in the South, the unjustifiable inequality of my environment pushed me to accept the meaninglessness of Southern society while daring me to create a meaningful life nevertheless. I have rarely found much meaning in the structures, norms, and expectations put before me. To this day I engage in the struggle of finding or creating meaning. For Camus and Beckett, colonization and World War II prompted their understanding of an absurd life. For me, it was American ethnocide and being tragically *Lucky*.

4

DESTROYING EXISTENCE

I was not leaving the South to forget the South, but so
that some day I might understand it.

RICHARD WRIGHT, Black Boy

I first started studying French in middle school, lured by the promise of
the annual eighth-grade trip to France. (None of the other language classes
offered such a trip.) The thousands of dollars this two-week trip would cost
was simply out of my parents' budget, but there was no way I was going to
learn French and then not go to France. So I got a job. Every weekend I
had a soccer match and my parents drove me to the park, so I decided to be
a soccer referee. I could schedule to referee other matches at the park every
weekend. My parents loved this plan, but still wondered if I could earn
enough money for the trip, so they made a deal with me. If I could earn
half the money, they would pay for the other half. For the next two years

I basically lived at the soccer park during the weekend. And it was worth every second, because in eighth grade I went to France, and left America for the first time.

This trip was back in 1996, so airport security was way less severe and my entire family could walk with me to the gate. My mother was nervous and scared—this would be the farthest I had ever been from home without my parents. My dad tried to remain stoic, which has always been his general demeanor, and my sister was both sad and fascinated. At the airport, I could tell that Rachel, who is three years younger, wanted to follow me to France. (In middle school she would also take French, and three years later she went on the trip herself.) I wanted her to come with me, but I also wanted to leave my family behind and experience someplace new on my own. My dad actually had to remind me to give my family hugs goodbye because I just wanted to run onto the plane—I was that excited to leave.

I first spent three days in Paris, and then a week and a half in Toulouse staying with a host family. Toulouse is one of Atlanta's sister cities—because Airbus's French headquarters are located outside of Toulouse, and Delta's headquarters are in Atlanta—and my school had created an exchange program with a school in Toulouse.

Our French teacher, Madame Bonnenfant, chaperoned the trip, and she had to wrangle about twenty middle schoolers. To her total dismay, I rebelled against all of her sensible recommendations. I constantly jaywalked, dodging cars left and right, and I once got on the Parisian subway without my class. I did not see the panic on her face as I hopped on *le métro* alone, but I witnessed her fury and relief when she caught up to me as I waited for everyone at the next stop. Honestly, it was a minor miracle that I left Paris in one piece.

I had fun in Paris, but Toulouse was the place that changed my perspective on the world. It wasn't sightseeing that changed my life, but walking down the street, playing pickup soccer, and visiting the post office affected me in ways that I never could have imagined.

Toulouse had a belief in public, communal space it seemed America did not. Growing up in Marietta, walking meant venturing from one person's private property to another's. Even on the sidewalk I was adjacent to someone else's property, and neighborhood subdivisions policed themselves. As a Black boy, I knew that common, public space did not exist for me in America, but it did in France. Trayvon Martin was born in 1995, a year before my trip to France, and on February 26, 2012—three weeks after his seventeenth birthday—he was killed by George Zimmerman because as a Black boy he looked suspicious walking in his own neighborhood.

Also, prior to leaving for France, I was warned that the French were cold, unfriendly, and that I needed to prepare myself for an environment where strangers would not greet me as we crossed paths in the street. This aspect of French society was troubling for my classmates since we came from an environment filled with superfluous, empty greetings where people marveled at our Southern hospitality and friendly disposition. But I found France's absence of incessant greetings to be liberating. By middle school, I had concluded that the South's culture of hospitality was perverse and oppressive. Our culture expected Black Americans to parade throughout society, enthusiastically and joyously greeting every white person we encountered. Our society was not concerned with how Black people greeted each other. A white person would never consider a Black child to be rude if he did not give another Black person the requisite nod, fist bump, or dap. Black children only became rude or problematic when we did not give white Americans the benevolent greeting they "politely" demanded. In France, strangers did not expect me to greet them so that I could tacitly proclaim my enjoyment of living within a systematically destructive ethnocidal society. The absence of hellos and a greater freedom of movement had a profound impact on me.

As one of the few Black kids playing soccer back in my hometown, I frequently encountered some form of racism as I played. Well-meaning coaches would focus on my "athleticism" and encouraged me only to outrun other players, but I enjoyed soccer because it was a large, complex puzzle. It was a tactical battle, and I wanted to figure out how to win. One coach had even called me a "head case" with talent who would be better if I just "put my head down" and followed his instructions. In middle school, a white friend's father coached a rival soccer team, and when our teams played each other, he instructed my classmates to kick me. My team won the match, but the conversation at school was not about how well anyone played. Instead, it was about how committed this grown man was to encouraging my friends to hurt me physically. This white friend was also one of the people who I was friends with at school, but was never invited into their home. In France, I ended up playing a decent amount of pickup soccer at the local school or on the street, and I exceeded the low expectations the French had of my American skills. They recognized that I could play and welcomed me. No one tried to kick me, and in fact, I was probably the most physical player. When you are accustomed to getting kicked, you anticipate having to kick back, and sometimes you even kick first. Playing the sport I loved without the expectation of abuse was a foreign concept, and playing pickup soccer in France helped rekindle my joy of playing the game.

Eventually I decided to send my family a postcard from Toulouse. One day, after picking out a nice postcard to send my family, I went to the post office to buy stamps, pretty excited to practice my French in a new place. When I approached the desk and asked for stamps, the postal worker said, "*Non.*" I asked her again, and again, "*Non.*" I assumed that I must have butchered my French and asked my host mother to help me. My host mother proceeded to get into a heated argument with the postal worker, and I eventually got the stamps that I needed. As we left, I asked my host mother what the argument was about, and she told me that the employee did not want to sell me stamps because she thought I was an African immigrant to France. My host mother yelled at her and told her that I was an American student visiting France, and the employee apologized. I had never experienced this iteration of racism before, and it stayed with me.

In America, the dominating narrative—particularly from the perspective of white Americans—is of Blackness without any nuance. If you look Black then you are Black, and there is very little concern about one's national origin or culture. As a Black child, I understood that the stigmas of American racism held no escape in my country, so it was fascinating how quickly I was able to escape France's racism to an extent. There was a kind of liberty in this greater nuance to Blackness in France, in that there existed at least a tenable method for obtaining relative cultural and social acceptance.

America was built around the hatred and dehumanization of *all* Black people, regardless of culture, as it built and sustained its ethnocidal society. Also, the cultural narrative for gaining acceptance in our white-dominated society was to become "white like them," and I had no desire to embark on that fruitless journey. As an eighth grader, this perspective was crystal clear for me without the need for much nuance, but as I got older many people challenged my perspectives on France and America. In a column for the BBC, I referenced my experience at the post office, and of course received both praise and pushback. African immigrants in France and other parts of Europe expressed that I had dismissed the severity of the racism they face, and Americans said that I was being too negative regarding America. However, the crux of the comparison—despite it originating from my limited personal experience—focuses on the systemic structures of the society and not necessarily the disposition of individuals.

As a middle-class child of the suburbs, my experiences with racism in America were far less severe than those of countless other Black Americans, but my relationship with American racism was focused more on America's systemically racist structures than on my experiences. The culture of America made it hard for a Black child's white friends to give him compliments, and our cities were built to deprive Black people of public space. France's culture did not have these same structures, and in comparison, it became an empowering place for me as a child. Years after this initial trip I learned about James Baldwin, and the other Black artists who were embraced by France, and I was heartened to know that other Americans also felt welcomed in France. I still received racist abuse on my trip, but it felt better than America nonetheless.

I returned home to Marietta a slightly different version of myself. I had left America and found a place that I enjoyed better than my home, mostly via minor things that could be easily overlooked and were hard to quantify. How could walking down the street in silence leave such a lasting impact? How could casual pickup games rekindle my passion for soccer? How could racism at the post office become a source of liberation? I had encountered more nuance in those two weeks than I found in my suburban existence, and this appreciation has stuck with me for decades. France's racism is of course destructive, but to my mind, the more immediate problem was the propensity for Americans to dismiss my reality in favor of an idyllic mythology. American freedom is spoken of as if it were a constant presence in the lives of all Americans. For years, I struggled to succinctly express my perspective, yet once I reached my thirties, I realized that I had now lived long enough to be able to adequately look back upon my life and more clearly understand and articulate my sentiments about the world. This maturity led me formally to Existentialism and Jean-Paul Sartre.

—

Jean-Paul Sartre, like Camus, was a French philosopher and celebrity who rose to prominence in the 1940s, yet despite being lumped together—much to their dismay—they could not have been more different. Unlike Camus, Sartre was raised in France in a stable middle-class family and attended l'École normale supérieure, one of France's best universities. But, like Camus, Sartre also articulated his work in essays, plays, and novels to make them more accessible to readers.

Sartre first spoke about *existence precedes essence* on October 29, 1945, at the Club Maintenant in Paris, in his lecture "L'existentialisme est un humanisme" (Existentialism Is a Humanism), and in 1946 his lecture was made into a book of the same name. *Existence precedes essence* revolutionized European philosophy, arguing for human purpose or meaning to be removed from the purview of a God. Beginning with the rise of Christianity, Europeans largely believed that God provided people with meaning and determined who they were. God created each person's essence, and since God created essence, then one's essence preceded their existence. For example, if God has the power to determine if a person is good or bad, then he has bestowed that essence upon them before that person physically manifests on earth through birth. That essence preceded that person's existence. As someone who had survived World War II, participated in the Resistance movement, and lost numerous friends during the war, Sartre—like Camus and Lemkin—needed a new method for understanding a world that could produce such destruction. For Sartre, a world without a God became his explanation. And if God did not exist, then existence must precede essence. But he went a step further and acknowledged that essence could exist without God.

The importance of *existence precedes essence* derives from the destruction during World War II, and the fact that competing European essences had nearly ended European existence. The Nazis propagated and believed in a superior Aryan essence that gave them the authority to obliterate the existence of other people who they deemed had a lesser essence. The Nazis targeted European Jews, as well as African people in Europe, those with disabilities, Eastern European Slavs, and anyone else who challenged the supremacy of their essence. Non-Aryan people challenged the essence of Aryan people not by being confrontational, but by merely existing. The presence of non-Aryan people made it harder for those with an Aryan essence to sustain the racial purity they believed they needed to survive. The existence of others challenged Aryan essence.

Similarly, the rise of nationalism represents another iteration of essence that is not necessarily derived from or dependent upon God, but invocations of God to legitimize nationalism remain a possibility. For example, in the United States "God Bless America" remains an integral part of American nationalism, patriotism, or identity, and represents a de facto coupling of God and non-God-dependent essence.

As Europeans colonized the Americas, they identified themselves not only by their European identifiers—British, French, Dutch, Spanish—but also new identifiers in the New World that distinguished them from Indigenous and enslaved people. With regard to the country that became the United States, this identifier was "white." White became a new European essence as they interacted with people outside of Europe. An alleged God-given purity or supremacy of this essence provided colonizers with a justification for mutilating the existence of non-white people.

White Americans, fueled by essence, waged a prolonged genocidal campaign against Indigenous people to occupy their land either by extermination or forced removal, and inflicted ethnocide upon African people as well. The attempts to reeducate Indigenous people, to make them conform to European customs in order to "Kill the Indian, Save the Man," are an ethnocidal agenda upon Indigenous people. American society encourages Americans, and the world, to legitimize the supposed necessity or benefit of white essence, but the foundation of this troubling demand stems from the fact that colonial or ethnocidal white essence, the American norm, derives from an embrace of white dominance and perpetual inequality. The demand is to prioritize white essence before existence, and that must never be a request anyone should feel comfortable asking. Demanding that essence must precede existence nearly brought about the destruction of Europe by Europeans, but this unjust demand has always been the foundation of America.

The destruction of culture is far less noticeable than the destruction of people, as the tragic impact of its destruction presents itself over years and generations, not in seconds and minutes like the destruction of bodies. The slow burn of ethnocide can allow people to believe in the legitimacy of an essence, a white essence, as society ignorantly waits for and lives within the catastrophic ramifications of an ethnocidal essence that will destroy its existence.

As Europeans set sail with grand ambitions to colonize and "civilize" the non-European world, they too often believed that they held a monopoly on the capacity to think and that non-Europeans were a sub- or lesser iteration of humanity. Europe's supposed ownership of the capacity to think has obvious parallels to the Cartesian philosophy put forward by René Descartes. His famous phrase "I think, therefore I am" gave Europeans and Pozzo ownership of the "thinking hat." Descartes's phrase is not racist, but since it does encourage people to determine their humanity based upon one's individual thoughts and not our shared humanity, these five words can actually strip people of their humanity. If Europeans and white people thought they owned the capacity to think, then they could be inclined to view the rest of the world as unthinking and subhuman. Those without a white essence supposedly did not think, therefore were not human. The ownership of the ability to think became the white essence that Europeans embodied and professed as they committed themselves to building new ethnocidal societies via global colonization. Cartesian philosophy prioritized essence ahead of existence because one's thoughts, or essence, allegedly proved their existence. Existentialism reversed hundreds of years of European philosophy by declaring existence precedes essence.

Europeans not only gave themselves a superior essence based on their alleged capacity to think and reason, but they also gave non-European people dehumanized essences based on their perceived inability to think. In America, African people became *niggers, coons,* and *negroes,* and the word *black* now had a negative connotation when applied to African people in America's ethnocidal society. As a people, Black Americans had to work to liberate themselves from these negative identifiers. *Uplift suasion*—the idea that Black people must prove they deserve freedom by living according to European ideals, places the responsibility for eradicating racist ideas on oppressed peoples themselves—became one method for attempting liberation. Some Black Americans who could pass as white found liberation by leaving their Black life behind. Other Black Americans opted to side with ethnocidal slave owners ahead of their fellow Black people to receive lessened terror from their oppressors. Slave rebellions, the Underground Railroad, and America's Great Migration were other attempts at liberation by Black Americans, either working to convince white ethnocidal society that their Black essence is in fact good, or removing ourselves from the judgment of white ethnocide. Proving the legitimacy of one's essence within an ethnocidal society will only adjust the power dynamics while sustaining ethnocide. By focusing on essence, we continue to overlook existence. This has always been the building block of an ethnocidal society.

—

It can be difficult to imagine abstract concepts such as *existence precedes essence* and the impact of a white American essence and understand how they manifest in everyday American life, but their most succinct representation may be found in the American application of the question "Where are you from?"

In America, this question is less about inquiring about a person's nation or culture of origin, but an inquisition about one's proximity to the white essence that dominates American ethnocidal society. In the Cartesian sense, it seeks to classify people as subjects who think due to their claim of some connection to a white essence, or as objects who do not think or exist and who now must be objectified, defined, and dehumanized by the subjects who claim the capacity to think.

For many American immigrants from non-European nations, this question can be especially troubling. Many of these Americans were born in the United States or moved to this country at such a young age that this has become the only country they feel comfortable calling home. When they are asked "Where are you from?" they feel affronted, denied their American identity. They are from America, but since they do not look white they cannot claim a white essence. Their inability to claim this essence inclines Americans indoctrinated in ethnocide to claim the power to objectify and define the existence of these non-white Americans. That feels like a removal or denial of one's American identity because the narrative of America—freedom, opportunity, wealth—consists of describing the supposed privileges that a white essence can provide while also obscuring the necessity of whiteness to obtain an American identity or pursue the American Dream. In a sense, people from across the world immigrate to America to obtain the privileges of a white essence—which are professed as innate human rights and not exclusive privileges—without becoming a white person. For people who cannot pass as white, being asked "Where are you from?" becomes an impediment to the freedom, opportunity, and wealth they were led to believe was accessible to all Americans, regardless of skin color.

Psychologists argue that most of America's reliance on "Where are you from?" derives from essentialist thinking, or believing that a person or community's value derives from their essence. Since America was created to value white essence ahead of the existence of non-white people, the existence of empowered non-white people will always pose a threat to white essence. Far too often this essentialist threat is misinterpreted as a threat to existence. Japanese Americans did not pose an existential threat to America during World War II, but their non-white essence meant that many white Americans always saw them as a threat. America sent our own citizens to internment camps because white Americans decided that some non-white Americans will always have a foreign essence.

I wonder about the essence-based social pressures people feel when they live in America, the lengths people are willing to go to obtain an American essence that extends to them the capacity to think and be a human instead of being defined as an unthinking object whose way of life may be stripped away in order to preserve white essence, and the various permutations of this struggle within America's many non-white cultures.

As a Black man from the South, I have been stamped with an essence from a white ethnocidal culture that devalues my existence and aspires to relegate me to the unthinking other that they can exploit and manipulate. Ethnociders depend on this essentialist inequality to justify and sustain their identity. They want me to feel lucky, or *be* Lucky, and celebrate the opportunity to live within their oppression. As a child I was lucky enough to leave American ethnocide—if only for two weeks—and experience existence without the full burden of American essence.

5

BAD FAITH AND THE FAÇADE OF FREEDOM

Those who deny freedom to others, deserve it not for themselves; and, under a just God, can not long retain it.

ABRAHAM LINCOLN,
"Letter to Henry L. Pierce," 1859

Existentialism has never been a static philosophy. Because existence is always in flux, people will yearn for something static to which they can attach themselves in the hope of finding stability. Many people turn to religion and/or philosophy for this stability, and in so doing expect them to be "perfect," devoid of flux and immune from evolution. Christianity and other religions thrive off this assumed essence and, unsurprisingly, religions frequently have had no problem with killing people who do not follow their beliefs, destroying existence in order to sustain the presumed supremacy of their essence.

Philosophy, however, should not rely on destruction *or* essence for survival and, in fact, must evolve with time and provide people with the tools to question and wisely navigate life. Existentialism speaks to the flux of existence, and, in *Being and Nothingness*, Sartre introduced the world to the Existentialist interpretation of *mauvaise foi* (bad faith). Understanding bad faith is necessary for navigating an ethnocidal world and combatting the stagnancy of essence.

Bad faith, or "acting in bad faith," is a concept that preceded Existentialism, as did good faith. Ideally, people aspire to forge "good faith," or trustworthy relationships with one another. A bad-faith relationship would be devoid of trust. Politicians and businessmen frequently are associated with bad faith when they do or say anything to win a vote or sell a product, but then fail to execute their end of the deal once the votes are cast and the products are purchased. The focus of bad faith within this context centers on one side's intent and awareness of their commitment to lie and deceive. This understanding of bad faith is well-known and precedes the Existentialist perspective. In *Being and Nothingness*, Sartre explores bad faith via one's capacity *to lie to oneself.*

"The one who practices bad faith is hiding a displeasing truth or presenting as truth a pleasing untruth," writes Sartre. "Bad faith then has in appearance the structure of falsehood. Only what changes everything is the fact that in bad faith it is from myself that I am hiding the truth."

In *Being and Nothingness*, Sartre famously gave the example of a waiter in a café whose movements were "a little too precise, a little too rapid," and it appeared as though the person aspired to define himself as *being* a waiter. The waiter's movements became almost mechanical and industrialized. The more proficient he was at being an idealized version of a waiter, the more money he could make. People are not paying him for his humanity. They are paying him to *be* a waiter. The more this person devalued his humanity and defined himself via the essence of being a waiter, the richer he could become. This person had convinced himself of the importance of prioritizing the essence of being a waiter ahead of his own existence. This is a lie that he told himself, and for Sartre it represented one of countless examples of *mauvaise foi*.

For Americans, this example of bad faith can be hard to grasp because American culture encourages all Americans to attach their identity and purpose for living to their professions. From an early age, we are asked about our "dream job" and are encouraged to be the proverbial waiter who is "a little too precise, a little too rapid." Taking vacations and working only forty hours a week is considered a sign of weakness. Work in America provides people with the opportunity to make money, and with that money we are told that we can purchase and consume goods and services that will provide us with happiness. America has intentionally structured its society so that one's wealth determines the quality of the health care and education they receive. Knowledge and health come after wealth in America, so *being* a "waiter" provides Americans the opportunity to be themselves during the fleeting moments when they are not waiting, serving, or working.

The more work you do in America the more money you can obtain, and through this money you are promised the opportunity to buy freedom and happiness. We devalue life in favor of the freedom and wealth that perpetual labor is supposed to provide. As Americans suffer from burnout, familial instability, and a persistent sense of meaninglessness, we talk about the importance of finding a healthy "work-life balance," but even when we attempt to liberate ourselves from soul-crushing work we still articulate that work precedes life. The gateway to American freedom reads "Work will set you free."

An individual or collection of people who engage in ethnocide must act in bad faith, or lie, because the people they are encountering would never interact with them if their true intentions were known. Ethnociders want to profit off the destruction of another's culture. This cultural destruction might also include the destruction of one's body or forced removal, at which point ethnocide becomes genocide. However, ethnocide and perpetual division may remain the ethnociders' agenda, and the ethnociders will work to establish an exploitative, dehumanizing, and parasitic relationship with those with whom they interact. In ethnocide, the first interactions must be a lie, and now the question shifts to whether the ethnociders know the truth and have decided to lie—pre-Existentialist bad faith—or have convinced themselves that the lie *is* the truth—Existentialist bad faith. In American ethnocide, both iterations of bad faith have shaped the trajectory of the United States, and the foundation of America's systemic deceit derives from our reliance on white essence.

The creation of the Carlisle Indian Industrial School in Pennsylvania, which aspired to indoctrinate Indigenous people with Anglo-Saxon Protestant values and culture—white essence in order to "Kill the Indian, Save the Man"—represents Existentialist bad faith. Brigadier General Richard Henry Pratt founded the school in 1879, and it remained America's primary boarding school for Indigenous people until it closed in 1918. Prior to the Carlisle School, America had other Indigenous indoctrination schools, but their primary goal had been to return Indigenous people to their tribes after they learned white American practices. At Carlisle, Pratt intended the program as the "ultimate Americanizer" and employed corporal punishment on "students" who practiced their Indigenous culture. However, the problem with Pratt and the Carlisle School was not that Pratt lied to the federal government or Indigenous people about his goals, but that his school was founded upon a lie he had convinced himself was true. Pratt, and countless other white Americans, had convinced themselves that Indigenous people were a subcategory of human being. The slogan of the school stated that Indian culture, or existence, needed to be killed for an Indigenous person to be considered a man or human being. The falsity of this belief is obvious to anyone who is not a racist, but in this way, denying the truth of our shared humanity shaped the founding of America. And to continue the many levels of bad faith that became the American norm, Pratt created an industrial school. To become a man in the eyes of a person governed by white essence, Indigenous people needed to become industrious and mechanical. Denying their humanity and culture and adopting the culture of white essence demanded that they, too, must live in bad faith.

During the late 1800s, Canada also wanted to indoctrinate Indigenous people with European values, and the creation of Canada's Residential Schools was modeled after the Carlisle School and their ethnocidal policy of "aggressive civilization." And while the Carlisle School closed in the early 20th century, Canada's system lasted for more than a century. From the 1880s to the 1990s over 150,000 Indigenous children were taken from their homes and forcefully indoctrinated in Christian, Euro-Canadian culture. Abuse was rampant throughout the schools as the Christian church and the Canadian government attempted to beat out Indigenous culture. Canada's first Prime Minister Sir John A. Macdonald considered this system of "industrial schools" the ideal method for exterminating Canada's so called "Indian Problem."

Following the closure of the last Residential School, Indigenous peoples have demanded recognition and restitution. In 2007 Indigenous peoples and the Canadian government agreed to the Residential Schools Settlement Agreement, and in it the Canadian government recognized the damage inflicted by residential schools and established a multi-billion dollar fund to help victims recover. In the subsequent years more information about the horrors of residential schools have become known. In May of 2021, at least 215 unmarked graves were found on the grounds of the former Kamloops Indian Residential School in British Columbia, and in June of 2021, at least 751 unmarked graves were found near the ground of the former Marieval Indian Residential School in Saskatchewan. It is estimated that over 10,000 Indigenous people died in Canada's residential school system.

Bad faith consistently governed the interactions between Indigenous people and white colonizers in the Americas as colonizers broke treaties and reneged on promises in order to take Natives' land and work to destroy their culture. And still today, the United States' annual Thanksgiving holiday perpetuates and normalizes American ethnocidal bad faith. During Thanksgiving Americans celebrate a feast between the Pilgrims and the Indigenous Wampanoag tribe, and we use this meal to symbolize equality and the sharing of culture in America despite this narrative's gross misrepresentation of the truth.

While it is true that the Pilgrims and Wampanoag shared a feast during the harvest season sometime around the beginning of the seventeenth century, this feast in no way demonstrated a sustained good-faith relationship between the two cultures. At the beginning of the century, the Wampanoag population was over ten thousand in what is now Massachusetts, Connecticut, and Rhode Island, but by the end of the century there were only about four hundred Wampanoag. At the beginning of the seventeenth century, Massasoit was the sachem, or leader, of the Wampanoag, and he worked to sustain a peaceful relationship with the colonists. In the spirit of good faith, Massasoit had even given his two sons both Wampanoag and English names. His eldest son, Wamsutta, was given the name Alexander, and his second son, Metacom (or Metacomet), was named Philip.

Everything changed, however, after Massasoit's death. Wamsutta became the next sachem and followed his father's philosophy. He frequently interacted with the colonists to sustain the peace, but after one trip to meet with the colonists, Wamsutta mysteriously fell ill and died. Many Wampanoag suspected poison. Metacom became the new sachem, and tensions between the Wampanoag and the Pilgrims increased as more colonists arrived and encroached on Wampanoag territory. Metacom, in response, made alliances with other Native tribes to push back against the colonial invasion. By 1675, the Native peoples could no longer tolerate the colonial attacks and they fought back. From 1675 to 1676 Metacom led what is now called King Philip's War. In just one year of this war, 40 percent of the Wampanoag population died. Combined with the thousands who had already died from exposure to European diseases, the Wampanoag numbered less than five hundred people by the end of the war. Metacom's widow Wootonekanuske and nine-year-old son were captured and sold into slavery in the Caribbean. Numerous other Wampanoag were sold into slavery in New England. Metacom was captured and killed in 1676. Colonists drew and quartered his body, and his severed head was shoved on a stake and put on display in Plymouth for twenty years.

After nearly wiping out the Wampanoag people, the colonists rapidly expanded throughout New England. Thanksgiving depicts one of the very few harmonious moments between Native peoples and colonizers, and America uses this image to present an objectively untrue narrative— one of equality and good faith—as the truthful or celebrated story of the Pilgrims and Indigenous peoples. Most Americans know that the purpose of Thanksgiving is to perpetuate a lie, but since it is a national holiday, one of the few times it is culturally acceptable to not work, and an opportunity to bring families together, most Americans prefer to continue the lie.

—

While I was growing up in the South, the public school system hardly spent any time educating my classmates and me about the prevalence of slavery in Georgia and the rest of the South. Of course, everyone knew about slavery, but we never spoke about its scale. We never discussed how the ratio of enslaved people to white people was nearly one to one in much of the South. Black people made up 40 to 50 percent of the population in many of these states prior to the Civil War, and even became a majority in some states after the war as thousands of whites had died fighting for the Confederacy. If a society consists of two groups of people for well over two hundred years, one might assume that there would be large amounts of mixing between the two groups unless the society was based on sustaining perpetual division. Throughout the South it remains unspoken, yet understood, that racial division has always been the bedrock of Southern society, but we also believe in the inevitability of white people living in the South.

If the South prioritized equality ahead of division and exploitation, the amount of mixed-race people would increase, and white people would decrease. This observation has nothing to do with any belief or opinion that a white person is good or bad, but simply the basic reality that it is hard to sustain a European appearance when you live in a society with large amounts of people from Africa, North America, and other parts of the world who have a darker complexion. Considering that Anglo-Saxon colonists neglected to make intricate racial mixing charts, as did the Spanish, and instead relied on the one-drop rule—where one drop of African blood makes one Black and no longer white—white colonists provided themselves with no lateral or semi-lateral racial or cultural identifier they could claim if they mixed with someone of non-European descent. Their identity, or essence, became zero-sum through the rules they crafted for themselves. The foundation for the culture, identity, and essence that primarily Anglo-Saxon European colonizers created for themselves in the Americas meant that their identity depended on sustaining racial and cultural division. Within American ethnocidal culture, white Americans created our societal division in order to perpetually exploit Black people, and if they were to cease exploitation and instead promote equality, this would result in racial mixing and the extermination of their white essence, their identity.

Here is the fragility of whiteness and white identity. It is easy, yet painful, for them to imagine a future where they no longer exist, yet the abyss they gaze into is of their own creation. Perversely, the response white Americans normally request is sympathy toward the "white anxiety" this realization generates. But the only way to relieve their anxiety is to allow them to continue their social division.

As a Black man, I realize this request demands that I go along with the continued cultural oppression of my people to placate the fears of white people. If one understands this stark truth, one will never acquiesce to this request. Therefore, America's ethnocidal state must indoctrinate people with a lie about the supposed authenticity of white essence, and society must work to convince everyone it is the truth. America inclines people to believe that whiteness remains inevitable and sustainable. Bad faith governs the society.

For a more contemporary example of bad faith and whiteness in America, we need look no further than President Donald Trump. His entire existence has been a uniquely American façade of authenticity to disguise the bad faith he depends on. Trump aspires to *be* a living business, and his business is his family name. Trump's family represents generations of human beings willing themselves into *becoming* a business. They exist as a brand. Trump *lives* as a façade and dares America to challenge his farcical existence. Trump's hair is fake, his tan is fake, his medical reports describing him as in "very good health" while being technically obese are fake, his claims of being a billionaire are fake, and he launched his presidency by demanding that his then press secretary Sean Spicer provide fake numbers for the crowd size of his inauguration. After losing both the popular vote and the Electoral College in the 2020 presidential race, Trump promoted unsubstantiated accusations of voter fraud and declared himself to be the winner of the election. On January 6, he elevated the danger of his lies and directed a mob of his supporters to attack the U.S. Capitol to prevent Joe Biden from becoming president. Lies are his power, and the normalization of "fake news" during his presidency demonstrates America's propensity to accept white lies. The list of fake or inauthentic characteristics attributed to Trump is lengthy, but Trump's bad faith is only part of the story. The issue is not merely Trump's bad faith, but how America's ethnocidal reliance on bad faith helped propel Trump to the White House.

—

White ethnocidal dominance in America requires a democratic façade. For a culture based on exploitation, there can be no greater lie than "all men are created equal." People pay taxes to governments under the good-faith promise that they will receive government services in return (roads, safety, education, equal protection under the law, health care, voting rights, etc.), yet America has always worked to deprive communities of color of these services.

America's reliance on bad faith makes our government less capable of fulfilling its good-faith obligations, which leads to Americans losing faith in government. When government fails to work, which it inevitably does in America, Americans turn to business leaders to solve the problem. Americans want governments to function like a business. Yet, for non-white people in ethnocidal America, work was never intended to provide them with purpose or meaning, but rather to distinguish between whites and non-whites.

The threat of equality and the inability to distinguish between white and non-white Americans has always been a source of anxiety for white Americans who prioritize their white essence before existence. Historically, poor whites have always felt this anxiety the most because their precarious financial position puts them in a situation where the possibility of being considered equal to Blacks—the perpetually oppressed within ethnocidal America—remains a constant fear.

When one is dependent on good faith coming from bad-faith actors, good faith becomes untenable. When the American government, which has always operated under ethnocidal bad faith, attempts to work in equitable good faith, white Americans who are accustomed to the preferential treatment of ethnocidal bad faith will view good faith as a threat that deprives them of services. The Affordable Care Act (ACA) implemented under President Barack Obama required Americans to participate or face fines when it came time to pay taxes. For the program to work, it needed to create a large pool of Americans signing up for health insurance to provide people with affordable health-care rates. For the ACA to succeed, it required that you trust the government and your fellow Americans. The ACA's good faith was misrepresented as a denial of freedom, and it became an *essentialist* threat to countless Americans. Many of the former Confederate states refused to adequately implement the ACA, and some of the most vocal objectors to the ACA were the poor white Americans who needed it the most.

Bad faith prioritizes essence before existence, and when confronted with the opportunity to receive improved health care, many white Americans chose their essence ahead of their existence. Sociologist Jonathan Metzl describes this dynamic as "dying of whiteness." They would rather let their whiteness kill them to sustain whiteness, but no culture can survive if its adherents believe death is their best option for survival. For eight years, large swaths of white America lived in constant fear of the looming equality and good faith that Obama professed, and it is no surprise that these same Americans chose to support Trump, a Svengali of bad faith committed to destroying Obama's legacy, as our next president. The promised destruction of the ACA was a pillar of Trump's presidency that galvanized his base of uneducated white voters. They championed the lies, false promises, and bad faith of Trump over the good faith of America's first Black president.

Donald Trump is as American as slavery and systemic oppression. Trump is a rich, landowning white male who mixes business with politics, unabashedly prefers white Americans, revels in demonizing and exploiting non-white Americans, and lives in a world of his own making governed by bad faith. Trump demands loyalty from his collaborators, convinces them that a shared loyalty exists, yet never hesitates at being disloyal himself. His platform consisted of destroying the work of America's first Black president, dismantling services that prioritized good faith and equality, exploiting and extorting non-whites for money, and implementing policies that prioritized white wealth and employment above everything else. As president, he worked to solidify his base and power by steadfastly being ahead of the truth by perpetually disseminating lies. His white ethnocidal base loves his lies because they believe his lies will work in their favor, and they embrace his lies because they know the truth will undermine the essence that they value ahead of their existence.

This is the total expression of ethnocide, bad faith, and essence before existence. Trump is a human machine fueled by this dystopian trifecta.

—

"There is no determinism—man is free, man is freedom . . . We are left alone, without excuse. That is what I mean when I say that man is condemned to be free. Condemned, because he did not create himself, yet is nevertheless at liberty, and from the moment that he is thrown into this world he is responsible for everything he does," said Sartre in *Existentialism Is a Humanism*.

To Sartre, freedom comes with an immense responsibility. One must build one's existence, and nothing is preordained. No one is born good or bad; we make ourselves into either based on our actions. Freedom is not the liberty to do whatever you want with only a marginal concern for the repercussions. Freedom is instead an acknowledgment that we are always free to make our own decisions and be held responsible for our actions. Sartre's existence-based concept of freedom flies in stark opposition to America's essence-based understanding. We use the same word but have diametrically opposed understandings.

In America, essence precedes existence; therefore, we are encouraged to believe unsubstantiated and absurd nationalistic propaganda such as "America is the best country in the world" or "People are inherently good." If a nation focuses more on "being" or presenting as the "best," it is probably neglecting the existence of its own people to project a supreme essence rather than focusing on better serving its own people. As Donald and Melania Trump ignored the needs of the American people, the first lady decided to name her signature initiative "Be Best."

Americans also like to believe that people are "good," and this absurd idea greatly distorts our understanding of freedom, because if people are "good," then they will naturally exercise America's freedom in "good" ways. In America, we don't often consider ourselves as "condemned" to be free, and spend even less time considering the negative outcomes of our actions. We are supremely confident in our "goodness."

As a Black man from the South, I grew up in a society that was anything but good or free. Yet Southerners, especially white ones, desperately need to feel and proclaim that they and the South are "good." The barometer for good or bad derives from one's expressed or perceived intent rather than the result of one's actions. People want you to know that they mean well. In the South, someone can have clearly racist beliefs and feel comfortable defending them because they do not believe that their ideas are racist, and they are confident that they themselves are "good." The focus on articulated intent instead of impact provides cover for racists who disguise their racism and thrive on the normalized bad faith of the society. The impact of their beliefs or actions play almost no part in determining if they are or are not "good." Facts are irrelevant because their essence has already determined their goodness. To them, freedom is their capacity to do whatever they please with the presumption that good things will inevitably occur. In the South, and much of America, white freedom has also depended on the denial of freedom to non-whites.

White America's essentialist understanding of freedom does not extend to me or other people of color. A person of color's simple act of exercising any form of freedom might prompt an essentialist crisis in white Americans. As people of color gain more agency in America—running businesses, obtaining elected office, earning advanced degrees—Americans actively discuss the growing anxiety white Americans face as they confront a changing America. Obama's presidency prompted much anxiety as we acknowledged the horrible consequences of white America's negligent exercising of its freedom. Addressing existence and reality becomes a traumatic experience for countless white Americans whose entire lives have been shaped by essentialist understandings of "good" and "freedom."

As American ethnocide results in a rise in white anxiety due to non-whites' exercising of any iteration of freedom, we must embark on a brief examination of the Existentialist work of Danish philosopher Søren Kierkegaard, and his understanding of freedom and the Danish word *angest* that translates as either *angst*, *anxiety*, or *dread* in English.

Kierkegaard's work influenced Sartre and Camus, and he is frequently described as the "Founder of Existentialism," even though the word was not invented until nearly a hundred years after his death. Kierkegaard's book *Begrebet Angest* fascinated twentieth-century Existentialists as it discussed the relationship between *angest* and freedom. It was first published in Danish in 1844 but was not translated into English until 1944 under the title *The Concept of Dread*. Today, the English translation is titled *The Concept of Anxiety*. The English word *angst* derives from the Danish *angest* and the German *Angst* and did not exist in English until the publication of Kierkegaard's and Sigmund Freud's work (specifically Freud's book *Hemmung, Symptom und Angst*, or in English: *Inhibition, Symptoms and Anxiety*) in the 1940s.

In *Begrebet Angest*, Kierkegaard describes anxiety as the "dizziness of freedom" and states that "anyone not wanting to sink in the wretchedness of the finite is obliged in the most profound sense to struggle with the infinite." American anxiety within ethnocide struggles not only with the infinite but also the inevitable. White anxiety emerges once actual freedom presents itself in our society and white ethnocidal culture struggles to sustain its *laissez-retenir* grasp on existence. *Retenir* means "to hold" in French, so instead of letting (*laisser*) existence naturally unfurl or do (*faire*), ethnocide must hold on to and dominate life, destroying existence and nature. *Laissez-retenir* holds on to life and turns the infinite into the finite. With *laissez-retenir*, the philosophy is to control or take hold of life and promote a culture of ownership and individuality instead of one focused on sharing, which I am calling *communeship*, and accepting the constant uncertainty and flux of existence. America's application of this idea has always focused on allowing white Americans to hold and own existence.

America's obsession with ownership stems from before the founding of our nation. Thomas Jefferson's famous phrase in America's Declaration of Independence from the British describing "certain unalienable Rights, that among these are Life, Liberty and the pursuit of Happiness" has been widely celebrated since America's inception. But American society frequently ignores the fact that the "pursuit of Happiness" was a last-second amendment by Jefferson to modify the trinity of "life, liberty, and property" professed by British philosopher John Locke. At first glance, this amendment represents a massive ideological leap, when in fact it only made Lockean ideals more palatable to the newly liberated white American ear. At the founding of the United States of America, the U.S. Constitution allowed each of the thirteen original states to determine who could vote, but generally voting was only extended to white male property owners. Jefferson—as a major slave owner in Virginia—literally owned the existence of hundreds of people. The denial of their freedom provided Jefferson with the "freedom" to help found a nation reliant on the continuation of denying their freedom and supporting their perpetual oppression. Property and ownership became the precursor to freedom, the "pursuit of happiness" and democracy in America, and freedom and democracy only extended to white men. Despite obvious improvements in American voting rights, America still views property and ownership as the foundation for freedom and happiness.

As a Black man, my community has systematically been denied equitable opportunities to own property and obtain American freedom, and far too often we have been treated as the property of white Americans. Yet despite the illegitimacy of the relationship between freedom, happiness, and property, the language of American English still professes the necessity of ownership to obtain freedom and pursue happiness. We are encouraged to own this thing and that thing, and revel in the supposed liberty that ownership should provide. Asking a Black person whose ancestors were bought and sold during the slave trade to employ the language and ideals of ownership as a pathway to freedom and happiness should be considered absurd and insulting to anyone who is not dependent on *mauvaise foi*.

To counter America's embrace of ownership, I champion *communeship* instead, which professes the sustainable freedom of equitable shared spaces, communing with others, and forging community. America, thus far, shuns *communeship* because it jeopardizes white essence, and we rely on a *mauvaise foi* understanding of freedom. As a Black man in America, my existence consists of either avoiding the grasp of white ownership/power or encroaching upon territory white ownership considers its own. The holding of existence to sustain an essence creates a suffocating stillness and lack of culture.

In *Begrebet Angest*, Kierkegaard speaks about how societies can create a spiritless environment as they dominate life to avoid anxiety and the infinite: "In spiritlessness there is no anxiety. It is too happy for that, too content, and too spiritless . . . Spiritlessness is spirit's stagnation and ideality's caricature."

When I think about Sartre and Kierkegaard's understanding of freedom, I think about the horror I have felt while walking down some streets in America, and the empowerment of the phrase *l'appel du vide*, the "call of the void." When my brain tells me to do something that could end my existence, I silence that voice not just because I value my existence as an individual, but because I value my connections to other people that make my life meaningful. By silencing the voice in my head, I reaffirm the importance of other people and silence the call of the void. Tragically, America's individualistic and essence-focused ideology advocates the inverse.

America prioritizes private space so that each person can *hold* their own slice of freedom. But for Blacks in the South, this sense of private space means an almost complete denial of freedom. Our freedom exists when we are beyond the scope of white ethnocidal Americans. Our hold is barely allowed to exist. Spaces that might reasonably be considered communal come with the expectation that our presence will generate some form of anxiety for white Americans. We could potentially disturb the "spiritlessness" of this white-dominated society, and there is pressure to project ourselves as "happy" or "content" in order to sustain the "spiritless" status quo.

Lastly, when Kierkegaard examined *angest* and freedom, he used the analogy of the fear one encounters when standing on a cliff. In this position, one has the fear of falling off the cliff to his death and also the fear of his own impulse to jump off the cliff. In this situation, the immediate ramifications of rejecting one's existence and choosing to jump to one's death bring the aforementioned "dizziness of freedom" and highlight the difficulty of choosing life while free. The "dizziness of freedom" is the precursor to the call of the void, and philosophers and cultures who genuinely prioritize existence and freedom devote time to discussing the difficulty and complexity of freedom.

America is not one of those places. We do not have these discussions. America's freedom depends on essence and not existence; it thrives on bad faith and depends on the denial of freedom to others. Initially, ethnocidees have their freedom taken away, but soon thereafter ethnociders lose their freedom too. Their dependence on denying the freedom of others becomes increasingly important as the inevitability of existence threatens their finite world. Now they are only "free" to take away freedom. We live in a spiritless society that only survives via the lies we tell ourselves. America lies to itself because we are afraid of our existence.

6

THE DIALECTIC OF
GEISTMORD

Whoever can make you believe absurdities can make
you commit atrocities.

VOLTAIRE, Questions on Miracles

The Germans, and their glorious compound words, have many words to describe the collective, cultural process of reconciliation that transpired in the decades following the Nazi regime. *Vergangenheitsaufarbeitung* means "working off the past." It was created in the 1960s. *Erinnerungskultur* means "memory culture" or "culture of remembrance," and implies that the debt the German people must repay due to the evil of the Nazis can never be repaid, but that the work of reconciliation must still continue. *Erinnerungskultur* is the more recent of the two, and I am interested in how it acknowledges that the damage may never be adequately fixed, even while *Vergangenheitsaufarbeitung* expresses the belief that you can "work it off." A sobering realization, but one that in no way implies a futility in reconciliation and confronting the past.

On a flight some years ago, the white American sitting next to me struck up a conversation, and after learning of my work, asked me how long I thought it would take for race issues in America to get better. I cannot remember if he said that we should "move on" from the past, but his questions spoke to that idea. He told me that he grew up in Florida and was not alive during segregation, so he felt that it was unfair for him to be "blamed" for the past. He made sure to tell me that his parents or grandparents were not like the other racists in Florida. His family had some sort of restaurant that served Black people, and this family felt it was okay to associate with Black people. He told me how he had Black friends, too. He insisted that he was "good," but he did not want to be held responsible for the past. He wondered when things would get better without him having to do anything differently, since he was confident that he was already doing the right thing.

I grew up around these types of people, and the absurdity of their arguments intrigues me. Eventually, though, I stopped him and politely said that even if his family members were "good" for the South, they were still racist. They did not see Black people as equals, and they treated them differently due to the color of their skin. This isn't complicated. Even if, in comparison to the other racists in the South, they were less racist, that does not equate to not being racist. Less racist is still racist. He did not like that answer but saw my point; and then he wanted to talk about what he could do to make things better and whether he would be able to see the equality he wanted during his lifetime. I replied that the equality he envisions might not be as equal as he thinks it is. He did not understand my point.

To elaborate, I asked him if it was easier to break or to make something. He agreed that breaking was easier than making, and acknowledged that repairing what you have broken can take more time than it took to make it, and even then it might not be fully fixed. I told him that Europeans had broken civilization through the slave trade; they continued to break it during Jim Crow. Europeans have been breaking civilization and destroying non-European cultures in the New World since the fifteenth century, and he wondered if these problems would be solved during his lifetime without having to accept any responsibility.

This white guy sitting next to me had good intentions, but it did not take long to highlight the profound problems with his ideas, and he didn't like the revelation. The idea that it could take multiple generations and consistent effort from white Americans to undo the damage of ethnocide was not something he was comfortable hearing, and he ended the conversation. His notion of equality would probably result in the continuation of sustained division and racial tension because he wouldn't be able to cope with the amount of work needed to reach his desired outcome.

—

A little while later, I was introduced to the work of the Institute for Social Research at the Goethe University Frankfurt, or the Frankfurt School. It is a school of thought that focused on the social or cultural aspects of life, and it was the first Marxist institute affiliated with a major German university. The Frankfurt School inspired my journalistic work and explorations that would lead me to ethnocide. It rekindled my appreciation for German philosophy and culture in new ways that soon would prove essential for understanding ethnocide.

The Frankfurt School was founded in 1923 by Felix Weil, a young, affluent German Jew. The original members of the Frankfurt School were primarily German Jews whose families had recently become part of the growing bourgeoisie that had emerged in Europe following the French Revolution and the growth of industrialization. They had economic opportunities that were previously unknown to many Jews in Europe, yet the Frankfurt School saw bourgeois life as a threat to their Jewish identity. The Frankfurt School did not believe that money provided the same security and stability as their Jewish culture. Instead of embracing capitalism, they embraced Marxism, but their application of Marxist ideals distinguished them from the numerous other Marxist revolutionaries across Europe. From the French Revolution to the twentieth century, Europeans had latched onto many different ideas to justify toppling the monarchy and creating new nations, and by the late nineteenth and early twentieth centuries, many European revolutionaries had combined the philosophical ideas of Marx with the widespread governmental instability to urge for the creation of Communist nations.

The Frankfurt School did not adhere to this application of Marxist ideas. Instead of professing the need for utopian Communist nation-states, the Frankfurt School professed the importance of the Marxist, or Hegelian, dialectic as the best application of Marxist ideas. Early on, this reluctance to merge Communist ideas with warfare to create Communist utopias made many Marxist revolutionaries view the Frankfurt School as passive and disconnected from the turmoil engulfing Europe, yet that could not be further from the truth. Their writings focused on the social changes remaking Europe as they adhered to the Marxist, or Hegelian, dialectic. Their method resulted in the creation of critical theory. Critical race theory derives from critical theory, and some of America's preeminent Black intellectuals and civil rights champions have studied the work of the Frankfurt School. The dialectic and critical theory are essential for understanding and combatting ethnocide.

The dialectic is the quest to obtain knowledge through conversation, or dialogue, and the critic, in critical theory, asks the difficult, probing questions that help us uncover the truth. The dialectic forces us to find truth not just within our minds and thoughts, but also through our experiences with one another. The Hegelian dialectic argued that conversations or social events commence with a thesis and that it is essential for an antithesis to emerge; however, the end goal is not for either the thesis or antithesis to prevail and be the dominant force. Instead, the end goal would be the creation of a synthesis.

In German, Hegel and Marx used the verb *aufheben,* or the noun *Aufhebung,* to describe the action and relationship between the thesis and the antithesis that creates the synthesis. *Aufheben* cannot be directly translated into English, but the closest translation is the word *sublate,* which means "for a smaller entity to assimilate into a larger entity." But this does not work exactly, because this would imply that the thesis and antithesis are not two equal forces. However, despite *sublate* being the most adequate, yet still inadequate, word for *aufheben,* Engels approved the usage of *abolish* for *aufheben* in the English translations of Marx's work.

Aufheben can also be translated as to "preserve" and "transcend," and at first these definitions appear contradictory. How can you preserve and abolish at the same time? And how does transcendence fit into the mix? This is what a synthesis should do. Certain aspects of both the thesis and antithesis are abolished and preserved, and through the creation of something new their limitations are transcended. However, if *aufheben* is translated as "abolish," it is easy to think that either the thesis or the antithesis will abolish the other, and one side of the argument will prevail. This perspective would have no synthesis and no *Aufhebung.* Misdefining *aufheben* as "abolish" has undermined the dialectic and created a toxic relationship with the antithesis. People unfortunately believe that the creation of an antithesis is for the purpose of destroying or abolishing the thesis instead of engaging in

Aufhebung and creating a transcendent synthesis. Societies and governments can become authoritarian, regardless of whether they embrace capitalism or Communism, as they work to prevent the emergence of an antithesis.

Hegel's dialectic also speaks to the inevitability of conflict. The thesis and antithesis clash with each other. Hegel viewed the decapitation of Louis XVI in 1793 as a thesis. In response, other monarchies in Europe attacked France with the goal of putting a new king on the throne—this was an antithesis. He knew the end goal would not be one side defeating the other. Instead, *Aufhebung* would create a synthesis in the form of Napoleon and the citizen. Napoleon was both a king and a man of the people, while also being neither. He created the Napoleonic code and elevated the role of the citizen. Prior to this revolutionary era the word *citizen* was not commonly used, and European revolutionaries resurrected the word from the Greek city-states of the past to describe the new roles of people in the present. Significantly, the French had to infuse new words into their discourse in order to create a synthesis. The Declaration of the Rights of Man and the Citizen and many of the other radical changes that remade France consisted of unearthing neglected and wise language from the past, creating brand-new words, and using these words to alter how people think in order to transcend their destructive present.

Marx applied a dialectic approach, with a focus on economics since industrialization was remaking the fabric of European life. The drive to remain competitive meant that factory owners cared little for the well-being of their workers, focusing only on production and revenue. Working in factories was incredibly dangerous; severe injuries and death were common. People had become disposable within this capitalistic system driven by wealth, and Marx's creation of Communism served as the antithesis of capitalism. Marx published *The Communist Manifesto* in 1848 during a time when impoverished European peasants were revolting against aristocrats and overturning feudalism from Ireland to Hungary, even as Italy was consumed with the volatile Risorgimento that destroyed the Italian nobility and created a unified Italy. The notion of a proletarian uprising was the norm of the continent at the time. The proletariat would need to rise up and challenge the bourgeoisie and other landowners who controlled the means of production, but this uprising's purpose was to commence *aufheben* and create a new synthesis, and not the abolishing of capitalism with Communism remaining. The denial of *aufheben* results in authoritarianism since the antithesis cannot exist, and the state uses its authority to destroy any actions that might challenge the state's thesis.

The Frankfurt School believed in the dialectic and *aufheben*, and this distinguished them from numerous Marxists whose understanding of Communism was lost in translation. America as a capitalist society sees Communism as an antithesis that wants to abolish our thesis, and not as an opportunity to transcend our present limitations and create a better synthesis.

The capitalistic foundations of ethnocide are also abundantly evident as European colonizers monopolized the means of production, took African people from their home continent, and forced them to work in inhumane conditions for the entirety of their lives in America. However, a key distinction between Europe and the New World focuses on how Europe's industrialization derived from the creation of machines that destroyed and maimed Europeans and the New World's version derived from notions of "race" that resulted in Europeans working to turn Africans into human machines.

As Black people have worked to obtain liberation from these oppressive ethnocidal structures by professing our humanity, we have proposed many antitheses. But since American culture never existed without ethnocide, all Americans struggle to imagine what a synthesis could look like. Far too often we imagine an existence where the thesis and antithesis live side by side harmoniously, but all this does is abolish *Aufhebung*, prevent synthesis, and deny the inevitability of the struggle that will exist between the thesis and antithesis. The notions of "separate but equal" and segregation speak to this absurdity. We desire for things to remain the same and for ethnocide to continue while also sustaining the comforting and hypocritical belief that things have changed and progress is inevitable.

—

Prophetically, Hegel also spoke to the dynamic of a potentially untranscendent dialectic in his book *Phänomenologie des Geistes* (*The Phenomenology of Spirit*). In the *Herrschaft und Knechtschaft*, or master-slave dialectic, the master controls the slave, yet this domination over the slave only enfeebles the master. In this relationship, the slave does all the work that the master demands; therefore, the slave has become responsible for his—which is also "their"—work, but he has no authority in their relationship. The master has the inverse. He has all the authority, yet none of the responsibility. As the relationship progresses, the slave is supposed to grow stronger because, although he despises his work, the act of labor makes him more aware of his physical and mental self. As the slave grows stronger and more self-aware, the master grows weaker and less self-aware as he remains dependent on the work of the slave. He is only responsible for the action of the slave; therefore, his main purpose is to sustain the master-slave dialectic. Through knowing himself and having the responsibility of his society on his shoulders, the slave eventually becomes strong enough to overthrow the master. Likewise, the master may become so enfeebled that he is dependent on the slave for every aspect of his life. Pozzo and Lucky in *Waiting for Godot* are a theatrical representation of the master-slave dialectic, but with a nearly 150-year delay. The surprise of act 2 in *Waiting for Godot* is not the fall of Pozzo, but the fact that Lucky has not abandoned or killed Pozzo.

Historians speculate that Hegel was inspired to create the master-slave dialectic due to the Haitian Revolution as peoples of the African Diaspora defeated French colonial forces on January 1, 1804, creating the first nation of liberated peoples of the African Diaspora in the Americas. Few Europeans had even imagined that it could be possible for enslaved Africans to defeat the mighty French. The Haitian Revolution sent shock waves through the United States, as white Americans feared that its success could galvanize enslaved Blacks to launch their own rebellions. Ethnocide's exploitative relationship between the ethnocider and ethnocidee is a manifestation of the asymmetrical, unequal relationship of the master and the slave. This dynamic obviously applied to the slaveholding South, but it also applies to the rest of America and has continued long after the end of slavery in America. The master-slave dialectic is a discourse and way of life that destroys freedom because its purpose is to sever the inherent connection between freedom and responsibility. Paraphrasing Sartre: Human beings are condemned to be free, because despite not creating ourselves we must endeavor to live free lives in which we are responsible for our actions. The unfree perspective of the master instead embraces the destruction of our shared humanity and connection to the earth, and considers irresponsible destruction as the source of their power. The master-slave dialectic creates an irresponsible society devoid of freedom that perversely celebrates the benevolence of an irresponsible "freedom."

When Americans talk about democracy and freedom, we articulate these ideas from the perspective of the master. Slave owners have always had a disproportionate role in shaping American society and freedom, and unsurprisingly, Americans often express "freedom" as an ability to be free from responsibilities and the opportunity to own whatever you please. Owning property and/or people has been foundational to American "freedom."

America's relationship with guns adheres to the master-slave dialectic, since our ethnocidal society has always encouraged white gun ownership but discouraged Black Americans from exercising their Second Amendment rights. As gun ownership increases in America and domestic terrorist attacks become the norm, America also fosters a dialectic that removes the responsibility of gun-related fatalities from white gun owners and pro-gun politicians. Pro-gun Americans have argued that gun-related deaths are the price Americans must pay for "freedom," and that "guns do not kill people, people kill people." The former equates freedom with terror and death, and the latter both professes the inevitability of people killing each other while removing all responsibility from the implement of terror. America celebrates guns so that white Americans can have the irresponsible power to enact terror.

Ethnocidal Americans who revel in being the ethnocider do not want to limit their freedom to be irresponsible. Unsurprisingly, Black Americans and other Americans who have been forced to be responsible yet without authority are far more in favor of gun regulations and work to implement them once they obtain authority.

Gun control is just one of many American examples of how the master-slave dialectic manifests in America today. America's rhetoric of religious freedom presents itself as a symmetrical relationship where all religions are free to coexist equally in America, but America's religious right, who influence and shape the Republican Party, interpret religious freedom as the right for Christianity to dominate other religions and shape the moral fabric of American society and government. Their notion of freedom is an extension of the master-slave dialectic as well. It is asymmetrical and exists via having total authority and zero responsibility. If the religious right dislike any facet of American life, the responsibility lies with another group who, in relation to the religious right, occupies the role of the slave in its dialectic. Muslims, Jews, homosexuals, atheists, secularists, immigrants, minorities, etc. are responsible for America's problems according to them, despite having hardly any capacity to shape American society.

The irresponsibility of American ethnocidal freedom derives from our cultural celebration of the master. The American Dream is a narrative extension of our democracy, and it professes that America provides all people the opportunity to become the master. This Dream is not true—more American bad faith—because for there to be a master there must be a slave; therefore, the American Dream only exists via denying the Dream to certain Americans.

The United States has had countless liberation movements, but the size of the country and comparatively small percentage of Black people has made it much harder for Black people to liberate themselves from the ethnociders. Liberation from the master-slave dialectic consists of abolishing the asymmetrical relationship. Throughout much of the Americas this liberation has resulted in the removal of European colonizers back to Europe and the forging of a symmetrical relationship among the liberated people who remain. However, this scenario does not apply to America, due to both the geographical and the numerical obstacles that Black people would face if they were to aspire to remove white people from the continent. Additionally, the fact that white Americans have already severed their ties to Europe adds a further complication. They too do not have a home that they can go back to. Thus, American liberation must focus on dismantling the master-slave dialectic and encourage a traditional dialectic with a thesis, antithesis, *Aufhebung*, and synthesis. However, since ethnocidal culture in America derives from a static, un-shareable white identity, the prospect of *Aufhebung* and synthesis across racial divides would result in the abolishing of white essence, or whiteness.

White Americans have always engaged in a traditional dialectic with European immigrants. At first new European immigrants—Irish, Italians, Poles, Catholics, etc.—clash with white Americans as they confront bigotry and terror because their presence in America represents an antithesis to the thesis of white Americans. However, over time *aufheben* occurs. Facets of white America are abolished and preserved, and the same applies to the cultures of the European immigrants. The synthesis is a changed whiteness. The European immigrants have now become white, and have altered what "white" means while sustaining their European physical appearance. The European immigrants can now exist as the master, or ethnocider, within the neo-feudal *Herrschaft und Knechtschaft*, or master-slave, dialectic that is the foundation of American society and ethnocidal culture. This dialectic also applies to European Jews, which is why Jews who fled the oppression of Europe can embrace white essence, the ethnocidal culture of America. They synthesize into an oppressive culture after being oppressed, and many American Jews combat this assimilation by remembering their history. Preserving their culture provides them with at least a partial escape from a culture committed to the destruction of culture.

Many immigrants move to America to obtain or capitalize on the authority of becoming a master. They believe the narrative of America disseminated from the perspective of the master, and either consciously or subconsciously aspire to obtain the irresponsible wealth and "freedom" that the master presents as the American Dream. Due to the horrors of building a society around the master-slave dialectic, America will remain in a destructive cycle that is dependent on fragile white essence until we learn how to cultivate the liberating language for symmetrical, equal conversations—a dialectic that transcends America's ethnocidal discourse.

—

Geist is another German word that is hard to directly translate into English, but it is commonly translated as meaning "ghost," "soul," or "spirit." In German, people have a *Geist* that exists within them, and when they die their *Geist* remains as their bodies fade away. *Geist* also means "mind" or "intelligence," so there is a nuance and complexity to the word that does not exist within the English "soul" or "spirit." Additionally, *Geist* also applies to a group of people. A collection of people can have a shared *Geist*. The word *Zeitgeist* means "spirit of the time" and speaks to the idea of a culture having a shared collective spirit during a particular moment in time. Artists or leaders who have a spiritual connection to the *Zeitgeist* of their people can create art or cultural movements that speak to their people. However, a collective spirit is not dependent on a particular time, or *Zeit*, in order to exist. Distinct cultures have a *Geist* that exists within their people, so when *Geist* is applied to a collection of people, it also means culture.

With regard to ethnocide and the Americas, the crushing of African *Geist* is a foundational aspect of our society. Slave owners aspired to "break" slaves. This was not a physical break, which would prevent the enslaved person from working. Instead, they wanted to break the slave's spirit. A person devoid of spirit is easier to oppress. The destruction of African culture extended beyond the removal of slaves' bodies from Africa, and included the severing of familial and communal bonds, the denial of native languages and religion, and the erasure of African cultural items. In other words, the attempted destruction of an entire cultural spirit. America has a dialectic committed to killing one's spirit, or a dialectic of *Geistmord*. *Mord* means "murder" or "-cide" in German; *Geistmord* is the linguistic sibling of *Völkermord*, German for "genocide." *Geistmord* also refers to the "spiritlessness" Kierkegaard speaks about within societies devoid of freedom.

It is clear that *Geist* plays an important role in the culture of the Black community because we define many of the things that are unique to our culture via the word *soul*. We eat "soul food," listen to "soul music." We compliment each other by saying that so-and-so has "soul." When given the chance to have our own music and dance television show, we called it *Soul Train*. And when we needed to elect America's first Black president, "souls to the polls" boosted Black voter turnout. W. E. B. Du Bois's celebrated book about the lives of Black people in the South was titled *The Souls of Black Folk*. The motto of Martin Luther King Jr.'s Southern Christian Leadership Conference was "to save the soul of America." The reverence of a collective soul that connects Black people as we work to survive and liberate ourselves from the soul-crushing nature of ethnocide remains a key aspect of our existence, and as we preserve our soul we also work to save the soul of America. As the ethnocidees within ethnocide, we cannot survive via parasitic relationships and the destruction of culture, so we in turn must cultivate our culture and strengthen our collective soul. Yet the ethnocidee also must work to save the soul of the ethnocider because our soul will always be under attack as ethnociders propagate *Geistmord*.

The ethnocider, on the other hand, has a culture dependent on the justification of destroying *Geist*, where the greatest destruction would be the end of their white essence. White Americans will gladly engage in soul-destroying, alienating work if they believe it will sustain their essence. As unregulated capitalism and industrialization swept across Europe, Marx observed a cultural alienation consuming European people. As people worked in factories, they became merely cogs in an assembly line with very little connection to the products they created or the labor they exerted, so they became alienated from their work. They also spent the majority of their day engaging in this alienating labor, so their life became the continuation of meaningless, soul-crushing work, and now they were alienated from themselves. Lastly, as they worked in these factories, Europeans sat alongside each other, but not with the purpose of forming communal bonds. Instead, their proximity was in order to maximize the productivity of their alienating work, and now people were alienated from their fellow human. In the United States, our ethnocidal society perpetuates this industrialized *Geistmord* by encouraging white Americans to perceive work as a preservation of white essence. White Americans are encouraged to bond over their shared alienation and the erasure of their *Geist* as their soul, mind, and intelligence are destroyed to sustain their white essence. Cultural destruction has now become interpreted as cultural preservation, and white Americans will fight for the freedom to destroy their own *Geist*.

The lives of those brought to America to be destroyed have never mattered in our bad-faith discourse (a.k.a. our master-slave dialectic). And by ignoring the destruction of the other, ethnociders only become aware of the destruction they have wreaked when they begin destroying themselves. Yet the paradox of the ethnociders' new awareness of their own destruction centers around the fact that they have spent their lifetimes both justifying the destruction of the other and articulating this destruction as a beneficial form of creation. For example, slave owners had long argued that slavery was good and necessary because the slave could not survive without a master. The ethnociders had essentially convinced themselves that their cyanide-laced drink was a thousand-dollar bottle of wine that benefited both the ethnocider and the ethnocidee. The ethnocidee knows that the drink is poison, so they liberate themselves by abstaining from ethnocidal culture, but the ethnocider needs to believe that their poison is wine in order to believe that their culture is legitimate. Thus, when ethnocide becomes threatened, the ethnocider drinks even more poison, and they grow progressively despondent, depressed, anxious, and angry as they become sicker and sicker. They only recognize the existence of a poison once they have become sick, yet it will remain difficult for them to recognize that the poison is something they have long consumed and defined as a privilege that only they have access to. Due to this difficulty, it becomes much easier for American ethnociders who depend on bad faith, sustaining white essence, and the master-slave dialectic to blame their illness on the ethnocidee whom they work to enfeeble.

For example, since the 2008 financial crisis, economic hardships have hit lower-income white communities pretty hard, but still not as hard as they have hit Black communities. The instability that can come from no longer having employment has created a culture of despair, resulting in increased alcohol and drug consumption, as well as suicide. The blame for this instability is not directed toward banks and financial institutions or large corporations who have crashed the American and global economy; instead, the blame is placed on the immigrants who have "taken" jobs, or the foreign countries American businesses have relocated their factories to. This too is part of the master-slave dialectic, but in this case, the capacity to be the master is not based on wealth or owning the means of production; it is solely about essence. The master in this scenario is supposed to be white essence, yet white essence is divided between the white owners and the white workers. White workers will gladly work in soul-crushing, alienating jobs if they believe it will sustain their white essence, and they will believe that the capitalist white owners have their best interests at heart because of their shared whiteness. The threat to their way of life from their perspective does not come from the poison they consume, but the existence of people trying to take their poison away. The ascension of Donald Trump—a white male landowning businessman—derives from the Americans dependent on consuming ethnocidal poison doubling down on their destructive way of life.

The *Geist* of these people was and continues to be eliminated via the soul-crushing society they created, and when tasked with rekindling their spirit they reverted to all they have ever known. The prevalence, inevitability, and inescapability of this deadly scourge within poor communities has been termed "deaths of despair" by Nobel Prize–winning economist Angus Deaton and fellow economist Anne Case, who also happens to be his wife. America is waking up to the reality that our ethnocidal society, with our master-slave dialectic, creates an environment so devoid of meaning that it encourages white people to kill themselves via the terror and alienation they intended to inflict upon others.

Yet despite the significance of these observations, they too will be meaningless without addressing the normalized destruction that precedes observing the self-inflicted destruction of white communities. We cannot have a national campaign to address the opioid epidemic without readdressing the continued impact of America's War on Drugs, and how crack addiction and even casual marijuana use became *crimes* because they were more common in Black communities. Opioid and methamphetamine addiction, on the other hand, became *illnesses* that need treatment because they exist within white communities. America cannot make systems of destruction and then act surprised when they destroy more than the ethnociders' intended targets. Unless we dramatically reshape our discourse, American ethnocidal society will continue to ignore and legitimize the crimes it inflicts upon the ethnocidees, and then remain gobsmacked when white society inflicts those crimes upon itself.

The irony of this dialectic of *Geistmord* is that the solution to this soul-sucking way of life derives from the ethnocidees, because they have spent their lives cultivating their individual and collective soul. Communities of color are the soul of America, but a soul-destroying white essence still dominates our society. Obama's presidency represented a kind of elevation of soul to the pinnacle of American life. Some Americans embraced this reality, and ethnocidal Americans saw it as the end of their way of life. This has always been the reality of the master-slave dialectic.

Not only does the call of the void call everyone's name every second of the day within the dialectic of *Geistmord*, but the asymmetrical participant gleefully jumps into the void—plummeting to their death—to find meaning in life. The dizziness that freedom can bring when standing at the edge of a cliff will never occur if you jump off the cliff. However, with genocide and murder, the death is almost instantaneous. Your free fall lasts only seconds and you can see the ground. You know the end is near. You know you have been pushed off, and the last thing you would ever do is encourage someone to join you on the way down. Those who have not been pushed off the ledge can feel the void that the person's death has left in their soul and culture, and in response they might create practices to strengthen their soul and find meaning in their lives despite the looming prospect of being shoved to their death. The work of Viktor Frankl and other Holocaust survivors speaks to this reaction. The original English title of Frankl's famous book *Man's Search for Meaning* was *From Death-Camp to Existentialism*.

Yet the end of freedom and meaning within ethnocide is entirely different than within genocide. With ethnocide an entire society collectively jumps off the cliff, and can plummet for decades or centuries before hitting the bottom. Ethnociders forcibly pull ethnocidees off the cliff because they need to fall together for the ethnociders to derive meaning from their homicidal plunge into the abyss. The descent can last for so long that one can forget there is a bottom, and that people are falling. Our all-consuming nothingness as we plunge into the abyss could even be described as a freedom. One is attached to nothing, one is responsible for nothing, one has become nothing, and we have been falling for so long that we could even convince ourselves that we have been flying and not falling all along.

7

THE BANALITY OF
AMERICAN EVIL

As a black male living in Mississippi in 1960 I was already a walking dead man . . . It takes no great courage for a dead man to want to live.

JAMES MEREDITH

At the National Portrait Gallery in Washington, D.C., hung a series of photographs by American artist Ken Gonzales-Day titled *Erased Lynching*. Each photograph depicts a lynching that took place in America in the late nineteenth or early twentieth century. In the photos, Gonzales-Day excises the corpse of the lynching victim, redirecting our attention from the terrorized to the terrorist. The demeanors of the lynch mob are startlingly casual. Devoid of context, they look like a group of white men gathered recreationally in the forest or relaxing on horseback. Some have their gaze fixed on the blank space above their heads; others look directly into the camera.

During this period in America, photographing lynchings was common, and white Americans frequently mailed these photographs to their friends and family, like you would to commemorate a party. Gonzales-Day's series exists today because these photos from as recently as 1935 were both widespread and preserved. *Erased Lynching* forces us to look at the banality of American terror. The men in these photographs do not immediately appear "evil."

For centuries, white Americans have killed, tortured, and terrorized non-white Americans without suffering any legal recourse. Historically, white Americans have been more likely to be punished for aiding Black Americans than for murdering them. The first two Americans executed for treason were the abolitionists John Brown and Aaron Dwight Stevens, who in 1859 attempted to launch an armed slave rebellion in the South.

In contrast, Roy Bryant and J. W. Milam were never convicted for killing and mutilating the body of fourteen-year-old Emmett Till in 1955. Images of Till's mutilated face shocked and horrified much of America and ignited the Civil Rights Movement, but American justice, or injustice, condoned their terrorism. The all-white Mississippi jury stated after the trial that they knew that Bryant and Milam committed the crime, but that they believed that life in prison or the death penalty were too severe a punishment for the crime of killing a Black boy. In 2008, Carolyn Bryant, the wife of Roy, allegedly admitted that she had made up the story about Till spewing obscenities at her that prompted the men to kill him. For the rest of their lives, several decades, Carolyn and everyone else connected to Till's murder lived quiet, peaceful lives.

As I closely observed each of the photos in Gonzales-Day's series, I stopped at a photo that read *Marietta, GA (Leo Frank) 1915*. My hometown. This photo was different than many of the other photos because Leo Frank was not Black; he was of German Jewish ancestry.

Leo Frank was born in 1884 and raised in Brooklyn, New York. Around 1910 he moved to Atlanta, Georgia, to work at the National Pencil Company. Around noon on Saturday, April 26, 1913, thirteen-year-old Mary Phagan returned to the pencil factory to collect her pay from Frank, and he paid her. At 3:30 a.m. the next morning, Phagan's raped and brutally murdered body was found in the basement of the factory. Initially, the police did not consider Frank a suspect, but on April 29 the public outcry, fueled by rising anti-Semitism, reached a fever pitch, and Frank was arrested later that day and charged with Phagan's rape and murder. Frank's trial drew national attention. Throughout the trial, publisher Thomas E. Watson spewed anti-Semitic propaganda in his newspaper, *The Jeffersonian*, that enraged and emboldened the white terrorist mobs hungering for Frank's death. That same year the Anti-Defamation League was formed in Chicago.

The prosecution's key witness, Jim Conley, a janitor at the pencil company, had also been arrested on May 1 in connection to Phagan's murder after he was found washing a red-colored substance—some accounts claim it was blood and others say it was rust—out of his clothes. Today, historians believe that Conley, a Black man, was probably the murderer, but that he agreed to be the state's key "witness" in order to save his life. Essentially, either a Jewish American or a Black American was going to die for Phagan's murder, and Conley chose to save himself. This trial pitted Blacks against Jews in the American South so that white Americans could erect a façade of justice and legitimacy. Despite Conley's inconsistent and contradictory testimony, the all-white Atlanta jury found Frank guilty, and sentenced him to death. Soon thereafter, Frank's attorneys filed three appeals to the Supreme Court of Georgia, and two more to the United States Supreme Court. All of their appeals were denied, so in a last-ditch attempt to save their client they reached out to Georgia's governor John M. Slaton to commute his sentence.

Throughout the trial and numerous appeals by Frank's lawyers, Watson's *Jeffersonian* continued to promote anti-Semitism. The more hate he spewed the more popular his paper became. By the time Governor Slaton reviewed Frank's case, many Georgians were enraged that Frank had not already been executed. Slaton conducted a judicious review of the case, looked at over ten thousand pages of documentation, and visited the pencil factory. Upon completing his investigation, he concluded that Frank was innocent, and commuted his sentence to life in prison. If Slaton had released Frank from jail, the two of them would have been dead men, and this was the best he could do. When Slaton's term ended in 1915, he left the state and did not return for a decade.

Slaton's decision enraged white Georgians. Soon thereafter, Frank was attacked by another prisoner who slit his throat. Prison doctors thankfully reached him in time and saved his life, but Frank's escape from death only further enflamed the growing mob. On August 16, 1915, a mob of men from Marietta calling themselves the Knights of Mary Phagan drove the 120 miles from Marietta to Frank's prison in Milledgeville, Georgia, abducted him from his cell, and drove him back to Marietta, where they lynched him. Later that year, the Knights of Mary Phagan gathered with other anti-Semites and racists from across the South at Stone Mountain, one of the largest monoliths in the world, to relaunch the long dormant Ku Klux Klan. These are the men documented in Gonzales-Day's photo.

In the 1960s, during the height of the Civil Rights Movement, the United Daughters of the Confederacy raised money to carve images of Confederate "heroes" Robert E. Lee, Jefferson Davis, and Thomas "Stonewall" Jackson into the face of Stone Mountain. The men in Gonzales-Day's photos aren't a relic of history, but a continuation of a cultivated cultural evil that is passed down from generation to generation. As with the men in Gonzales-Day's photos, these "heroes" of the South might appear as upstanding citizens in a photograph or monument—if you erase or forget the terror they inflicted upon others.

Growing up in Marietta, I was never taught about Leo Frank's lynching in school. There was no memorial or day of remembrance commemorating his murder. Despite learning about the horrors perpetrated against Jews in Europe, I was never taught about the horror that took place less than twenty miles from the house I grew up in. In fact, during my formal American education I learned more about the Dreyfus affair in France—where Alfred Dreyfus, a Jewish French military officer was falsely accused of treason around the turn of the twentieth century—than about the lynching of a Jewish American in my own hometown. Similarly, Americans learn about Anne Frank and it is often compulsory to read *The Diary of a Young Girl* during school. We learn about the horrors that other societies commit, as we ignore and make our domestic horrors appear banal.

When our past is filled with records of white terror, large swaths of America proclaim that the past needs to be forgotten. We do not have a culture of working off the past (*Vergangenheitsaufarbeitung*) or one of remembering the past (*Erinnerungskultur*). For far too long, we have had a culture of erasing the past and filling the void with propaganda celebrating white essence, but this is starting to change.

—

Under the corrupting influence of the Nazi Party, *Übermensch*, and the plural *Übermenschen*, took on an entirely different meaning than in Existential philosopher Friedrich Nietzsche's *Thus Spoke Zarathustra*. According to Nietzsche, an *Übermensch* was essentially a guru who left his enlightened solitude to share his wisdom with the common man. Not everyone could become an *Übermensch*, but learning from one would improve our lives. In

Thus Spoke Zarathustra, the townsfolk ridicule and chase away the *Übermensch*, and embrace a notion of superiority whose only requirement is an elevated sense of self. Nietzsche's *Übermensch* calls these dangerous people *letzter Menschen*, or "Last Men."

The Nazis corrupted Nietzsche's idea and turned *Übermensch* from a state of existence that required effort and mastery of self into a status of essence that required zero effort or mastery. Germans and Aryans became "supermen" purely from birth. Hitler's Third Reich proclaimed itself to be a race of "supermen" who were destined to dominate Europe, and their reign would last a thousand years. The essence-based philosophy of the Nazis extracted meaning from Nietzsche's *Übermensch*, and used it as a justification for terrorizing the world. They behaved as *letzter Menschen* while proclaiming that they were *Übermenschen*.

According to the Nazis, their new definition of an *Übermensch* could not exist alongside an *Untermensch* or "underman"; the Nazis used this horrific logic to commence their Final Solution, and proceeded to kill six million Jews. Any group of people that they chose to classify as other could become *Untermenschen*. The Nazis employed their essentialist worldview to commit genocide, but European colonizers likewise used an essentialist philosophy to justify genocide against Indigenous people in Africa, Australia, Asia, and the Americas, as well as the creation of ethnocidal societies. European colonizers needed to find room for themselves to live outside of Europe, and their room to live existed at the expense of the rest of the world. Indigenous people outside of Europe were killed and enslaved to support the expansion of a *letzter Menschen* way of life. Europe condoned this *letzter Menschen* expansion until it spread across Europe. Declaring the non-European world to consist of *Untermenschen* has been foundational to European thought for hundreds of years. Using the language of the Nazis to describe colonization is predictably frowned upon by the Western world, but this dismay does not make these descriptions less accurate. Disturbing their essence-based happiness represents wisdom, and the outrage only reinforces the legitimacy of the perspective.

At the beginning of the twentieth century, the idea of *Lebensraum* (or "room to live") grew in popularity across Germany as a way of coping with population growth. Germans felt that they did not have enough room to live in Germany, so they determined that they needed to colonize or conquer more land to address population growth. Germany had fallen behind their European neighbors—England, France, the Netherlands, Spain, and Portugal—in conquering the globe. And this makes sense since the country is nearly landlocked, and it only became a unified Germany in the nineteenth century. As its population grew, Germany sought to engage in colonization to obtain wealth from exploiting the colonized and their land, and to provide more "room to live." Germans often referenced British and French colonization and American "Manifest Destiny" to justify *Lebensraum*.

However, Germany's defeat in World War I meant that Germany had to give up its newly conquered territories. The loss of these colonies, no longer being able to exploit them, added to the humiliation many Germans felt after losing the war. The Nazi Party was fueled by this anger and resentment, and a key part of its agenda was to apply *Lebensraum* to Europe and conquer the European lands occupied by Slavs and Jews, whom the Nazis considered *Untermenschen*. (Western Europe has a long history of dehumanizing Eastern Europe, and the intra-European slave trade dating back to Ancient Greece was driven by enslaving Eastern European Slavs to such a profound degree that the word *slave* derives from *Slav*.)

During World War II, the Nazis' policy of *Lebensraum* turned traditional soldiers into genocidal implements of terror. Victory was no longer the goal. Extermination became the goal. *Lebensraum* did not focus exclusively on Jews, but on any *Untermenschen*, or "underpeople," who occupied a space in Europe where Aryan *Übermenschen* wanted to live. When we talk about World War II and extermination by the Nazis, America primarily focuses on the estimated six million Jews killed by the SS, or Schutzstaffel (Protection Squad), in the Holocaust, but we cannot forget how *Lebensraum* turned Germany's entire armed forces, the Wehrmacht—the army, navy, and air force—into an army of genocide. On the Eastern Front, the Wehrmacht consisted of ten million soldiers, and Hitler's Barbarossa Decree on March 30, 1941, ordered that the war on the Eastern Front against the Soviet Union would be a war of extermination that included the eradication of Russia's political and intellectual elites. Later that year, Hitler described "Judeo-Bolshevism" as the deadliest threat to Germany.

As the Germans conquered territory on the Eastern Front they also felt the need to protect German women from these so-called *Untermenschen*, so if any Russian or Slavic male was found guilty of intercourse with a German woman they were punished by death. The Wehrmacht in the Eastern Front killed millions of innocent men, women, and children, and sent millions of Jews to concentration camps. Nearly six million Soviet soldiers were taken prisoner and over three million died in captivity. Prisoners were subjected to human experimentation—including various pseudoscientific treatments to cure homosexuality. Wehrmacht soldiers raped millions of Soviet women. The Wehrmacht created an elaborate brothel system made up of widespread sexual slavery. Wehrmacht soldiers regularly corresponded back home describing the supposed nobility and necessity of the Wehrmacht's terror, and the alleged inhumanity of the Jews and Slavs. Often these letters included photographs of lynched Soviet citizens and other manifestations of the murder, torture, and terror of the Wehrmacht. Germans at the time, just like their ethnocidal American brethren, would gaze at these photos and feel pride, not outrage or horror. Germany's and America's bond over their belief in a superior white essence inclined both

cultures to celebrate their actions as divine, and fondly gaze into their dystopian abyss.

The actions and correspondences of Wehrmacht soldiers mirror the
normalized terror that has always been foundational of American society,
and the racist, ethnocidal policies of America helped provide a justification
and template for many of the terrorist policies of the Nazis. (The raping
of Black women and the killing of Black men in order to protect white
women had been an unabashed American norm until at least the 1960s,
in addition to the persistent threat of lynching.) In fact, the emergence of
the Nazi term *Untermenschen* has been attributed to America's Ku Klux
Klan. In 1922, only seven years after the KKK's rebirth at Stone Mountain, Harvard-educated Massachusetts native Lothrop Stoddard, who was
a KKK member, published *The Revolt Against Civilization: The Menace of
the Under-Man*. In 1925, it was published in German as *Der Kulturum-
sturz: Die Drohung des Untermenschen*, and the success of Stoddard's book
in Germany brought *Untermenschen* into mainstream German discourse.
During World War II, Stoddard traveled to Germany as a journalist and
developed friendly relationships with high-ranking Nazi officials and even
met Hitler. After the war, although his published work continued his syn-
ergy with Nazi ideals, Stoddard's ideas were no longer socially acceptable in
America, and he fell into obscurity. The Nazis' defeat shattered the façade of
America's essence-based ideology, so in order to remain legitimate, America
needed to erase Stoddard.

The horrors of Nazi terror could no longer remain hidden or so easily
erased; thus their evil—unlike America's—became apparent to the world,
bringing shame to German culture. Stoddard needed to disappear so that
America could hide its shame and remain respectable in the eyes of the
world. Yet America continues without shame for our atrocities because
America believes that it can erase or obscure our crimes. America, in its

present state, has neither capacity nor space for shame, because our ethno-cidal culture is founded upon forging shameless bad-faith relationships with our fellow man and the world. Allowing for shame would equal the end of America as we know it, since our collective shame would not be confined to a decade of insanity, as the Nazis were to Germany. America's shame would encompass its entire existence. Working off the past becomes even more daunting when you must work off the entirety of your past. Likewise, "memory culture" becomes even more difficult when much of your history consists of bad memories. America hides itself—both its atrocities and the culture that commits them—because it needs to hide its true self from not only the world, but also from itself. *Mauvaise foi* helps hide the shame of America's toxic essence.

Stoddard, the KKK, and the Nazis have an essentialist interpretation of *Übermensch*, and their corrupted interpretation of the word actually inclines them to behave as *letzter Menschen*. I think it would be fair to describe their actions and ideology as those of *Untermenschen*. Their celebrated barbarism should be considered the basest manifestation of human existence. Their actions should be considered beneath human dignity. The essentialists who project the idea of the *Untermensch* on the other are, in fact, the real *Untermenschen*.

As a Black man from the American South, my family, along with the Jews in the South, have needed to survive by escaping the terror of *Untermenschen* who exist in order to describe us as subhuman. When our *Übermenschen*—Dr. Martin Luther King Jr., Medgar Evers, James Chaney, etc.—and those of our Jewish brothers and sisters who have fought alongside us for freedom—Andrew Goodman, Michael Schwerner, and more—challenge the oppressive, ignorant happiness of the American *letzter Menschen*, it is normal for them to be murdered in order to sustain the reign of the Last Men. When the Last Men tell the stories of their atrocities, they do not regard themselves as such, so it is unsurprising that in some of the English translations of *Also Sprach Zarathustra*, *letzter Mensch* is translated as "Ultimate Man," completely disregarding the intent of the word and the fact that *letzter* can also be translated as "worst." America's dependence on placing essence before existence, like the Nazis, results in our corrupting Existentialism, albeit in a more subtle, slower-burning methodology. It is easier to convince people to jump into the abyss when they believe they are the "Ultimate Man" and not the Last, or worst, Man.

—

On January 6, 2021, President Trump spoke at the "Save America" rally in Washington, D.C., where he implored his supporters to "Stop the Steal" and prevent Congress from "stealing" the presidential election Trump had dangerously and erroneously claimed he had won. Upon the completion of the rally, American *letzter Menschen* stormed the U.S. Capitol and attempted a futile coup d'état. They proclaimed that they were the Ultimate Men and "patriots" as they plunged into an abyss of inevitable failure.

Trump's supporters stormed the U.S. Capitol as Congress was certifying the Electoral College votes that would confirm Joe Biden as the next president of the United States. They believed that if they could stop the voting, Trump could remain president. These "patriots" wanted to destroy our democracy to demonstrate their fidelity to Trump. As Trump's brigade of *letzter Menschen* attacked Congress, the Capitol was evacuated and the counting of Electoral College votes delayed as senators, representatives, and staffers were ushered to secure locations away from the terrorist mob. Trump's supporters attacked numerous police officers including Brian Sicknick, who died the following day, as they laid siege to the Capitol: breaking into Speaker of the House Nancy Pelosi's office, storming the Senate floor, looting the building, and parading the Confederate flag through the halls of Congress. Hours later, after law enforcement successfully secured the U.S. Capitol, members of Congress returned to finish certifying the votes and Joe Biden officially became the president-elect. The coup d'état failed and delayed the inevitable only by a handful of hours, yet it succeeded in displaying America's white ethnocidal terror that had long been concealed and made to appear banal.

In the days and weeks that followed, historians and political experts began comparing this failed coup d'état to the Nazi Party's Beer Hall Putsch in 1923, when Hitler and approximately two thousand Nazis attempted to overthrow the regional government in Munich, Bavaria, and use it as a strategic base to launch a larger coup d'état against Germany's Weimar Republic. Hitler was captured and sentenced to five years in prison following the failed coup d'état. However, he received favorable treatment while in jail and was able to de facto run the Nazi Party while incarcerated. In jail he wrote *Mein Kampf* and in December 1924 the Bavarian Supreme Court pardoned Hitler. He only served a little over a year in jail. Germany underestimated the danger Hitler posed, and they are still paying the price for this mistake.

On January 6, most Americans responded with shock and horror because they believed that this type of attack could not occur in their own country. The memory of American terror had been erased from their minds. Gonzales-Day's work erases the victims, but America seeks to erase the knowledge of the perpetrators of white ethnocidal terror. I did not have this reaction, and following the results of the Georgia senatorial elections on January 5, I was bracing for the worst. I anticipated a backlash from America's *letzter Menschen*.

To the surprise of most Americans, and especially Donald Trump, Biden won Georgia in the presidential election, and neither of Georgia's

two incumbent Republican senators, David Perdue and Kelly Loeffler, obtained a majority of votes on election night to prevent either of their races
from going to a runoff. Since the 1960s, as Jim Crow began to unravel
and more Black Americans were able to vote, Georgia has mandated that
statewide races require that a candidate must obtain a majority of the vote
to win. If no candidate earns more than 50 percent of the vote, a runoff
election is held between the top two candidates. Georgia's system of runoff
elections was created by racist segregationists who feared that the rising
Black vote would reconstruct Georgia politics. Essentially, white voters
might have many candidates they could vote for, but Black voters would
most likely have only one major candidate. White segregationists feared
that white Georgians would split the white vote and open the door for Black
Georgians to become senators or the governor. To reduce the power of the
Black vote, the state adopted the runoff election system that is still in effect
today.

After all of the votes were counted in the national elections in November, Biden and his running mate, California senator Kamala Harris, had
won the presidential race, the Democrats kept their majority in the House
of Representatives, and the Democrats held forty-eight seats to the Republicans' fifty in the Senate. Georgia's two Senate runoff elections would
decide who controlled the Senate. If the Democrats won both races, the
Senate would be a 50–50 tie with Vice President Kamala Harris acting as
the tiebreaker, giving the Democrats control over both Congress and the
White House.

On Tuesday, January 5, Democrats Rev. Raphael Warnock and Jon Ossoff won Georgia's two contested Senate seats, defeating incumbents David
Perdue—the cousin of Georgia's former governor Sonny Perdue—and Kelly
Loeffler—America's richest senator with an estimated net worth of $500
million. Neither Warnock nor Ossoff had any political experience prior to

winning the election, but they represented the Georgia that Georgians who prioritized existence and equality hoped to create.

Warnock is the reverend of Ebenezer Baptist Church where Martin Luther King Sr. and Jr. were both ministers. Warnock represents the soul of Georgia's Black community and is a continuation of the legacy of the King family and their ministry. Warnock's parents, Jonathan and Verlene, were both ministers, and as a teenager in the Jim Crow South, Warnock's mother picked cotton and tobacco on plantations owned by white people. "Because this is America, the eighty-two-year-old hands that used to pick somebody else's cotton went to the polls and picked her youngest son to be a United States senator," said Warnock in a speech following his victory. Warnock is Georgia's first Black senator, and his election speaks to the changing face of Georgia that has been long delayed by segregationist *letzter Menschen*.

Ossoff, who was thirty-three years old when elected, is both Georgia's first Jewish senator and the youngest senator currently serving in Congress. Ossoff's political career started in 2017 when he ran for Georgia's Sixth Congressional District after Republican congressman Tom Price became the secretary of the Health and Human Services Department in the Trump administration. Marietta—where Leo Frank was lynched—is in Georgia's Sixth Congressional District, and for the majority of my life it has been the epicenter of Republican political power in the state. Newt Gingrich represented this district for twenty years from 1979 to 1999, and he was succeeded by Johnny Isakson. Isakson held that seat until 2005 when he became a U.S. senator, and he held that Senate seat until illness forced him to retire in 2019. Loeffler was then appointed to his Senate seat. Likewise, Price took Isakson's seat in the House in 2005 and held it until he joined the Trump administration in 2017.

In the 2016 presidential race, Hillary Clinton shocked the state of Georgia when she won Cobb County, the county that includes Marietta and much of the Sixth District. Ossoff had a lot of momentum in his 2017 race, but he lost to Republican Karen Handel. However, in 2018, Handel had to run for reelection and she lost her seat to Lucy McBath, a prominent Black Lives Matter activist. McBath, who is Black, tragically rose to national prominence in 2012 after her seventeen-year-old son Jordan Davis was shot and killed by Michael David Dunn, a forty-five-year-old white male, at a gas station in Jacksonville, Florida. Dunn believed that Davis and his high school friends were playing their music too loud, so Dunn fired ten bullets into their car and drove away, killing Davis and injuring his friends. On October 1, 2014, Dunn was sentenced to life in prison. Four years later McBath turned her tragedy into triumph and now a Black woman represents the people of the county that used to be the epicenter of Republican politics in Georgia. Ossoff's political career was launched from the area where a Jewish man was lynched a century earlier, and now he represents the entire state.

Georgia's Black voters helped propel Barack Obama's vice president to the White House and gave Democrats control of the Senate in 2021. If you know anything about America's ethnocidal culture, it was obvious that a backlash would occur. In 2021, the backlash occurred the day after a Black man and a Jewish man became Georgia's senators. And to no one's surprise, Georgia's ethnocidal Republican *letzter Menschen* had by the end of January 2021 taken a page from the oppressive playbook of the 1960s, which had created runoff elections, and began formulating legislation that would make it harder for people of color to vote. "[Election officials] don't have to change all of [the election laws], but they've got to change the major parts of them so that we at least have a shot at winning," said Alice O'Lenick, a Republican on the Gwinnett County, Georgia, board of elections. In March 2021, Georgia's Republican-controlled state legislature signed into law new voting restrictions that limited absentee voting, required strict ID requirements, reduced polling locations, made it illegal to give people water as they waited in line at the polls, and numerous other oppressive requirements to corrupt our democracy. In June 2021, the Department of Justice led by Attorney General Merrick Garland—Obama's Supreme Court nominee in 2016—sued the state of Georgia over the voting legislation, claiming that it demonstrated an "intent to deny or abridge" Black citizens' access to voting. *Letzter Menschen* cannot exist without *mauvaise foi* and oppressing others.

Also, *Mensch* is German via Yiddish—the Nazis used a Yiddish word to proclaim their Aryan supremacy—and the word is not gendered. It is frequently translated as "man," but it is more accurate to translate it as "person" or "human." Additionally, a *Mensch* is considered a person with integrity. It is a personhood that requires consistent effort and not a fixed identity based on one's birth or skin color. Lucy McBath and Stacey Abrams—whose work to increase Black voter turnout in Georgia helped turn the state Democratic—are also *Übermenschen*. Likewise, David Perdue, Kelly Loeffler, and Alice O'Lenick are *letzter Menschen*. (The true meaning of *Mensch* disappears when it is attached to the Last Man.) America's *letzter Menschen* steadfastly work to delay progress and equality, but America's *Übermenschen* can still prevail.

—

The chaos of World War II prompted a wellspring of philosophical concepts and moral reckonings, such as Existentialism and criminalizing genocide, to hopefully prevent Europe from again devolving into a continental hellscape set ablaze by the base desires of essence-driven *Untermenschen*. The chaos of the continent also resulted in an exodus of some of its brightest minds. When I think about the Germanic cultural paradox that balances creation and annihilation, I think about the Frankfurt School and about what it must have been like to witness what was arguably the cultural heartbeat of a continent destroying itself, and for many of its greatest minds to either die during the war or seek refuge in an ethnocidal society like America. The Frankfurt School relocated to America during World War II, but not all of its members made it out of Europe alive. For those who did, their focus on culture resulted in many of their members loathing their time in America.

Prior to their forced exile to America, adherents of the Frankfurt School arose during a revolutionary time for Jewish European culture. European Jews now had access to wealth and opportunity that had been largely impossible for them to obtain in the past, but their Jewish identity meant they still were not fully accepted into Christian European culture. In France, there was the Dreyfus affair; in Austria, Sigmund Freud created psychoanalysis; and in Bohemia, Franz Kafka was writing masterpieces that would only be celebrated after his death in 1924. The profound cultural influences of Jewish soldiers, intellectuals, and writers all influenced the work of the Frankfurt School and its focus on cultural analysis. European Jews were equal parts celebrated, ignored, and exiled. The Frankfurt School's disdain for bourgeois capitalism was based in knowing that they had a vibrant Jewish culture that preceded their inclusion into the bourgeoisie. Their cultural and Marxist analysis stemmed from having a culture that could serve as the antithesis to the destructive industrialization, capitalism, and tyranny that had consumed Europe. America tragically does not have an attachment to a culture that precedes ethnocide, and instead we rely on consuming foreign cultures to satiate our need for culture.

Frankfurt School member Theodor Adorno, while living in exile in America, famously described Walt Disney as "the most dangerous man in America" because many Disney creations derived from German fairy tales, but Disney had extracted the German culture and meaning from the stories and disseminated them through America's "culture industry." In the 1800s, Jacob and Wilhelm Grimm recorded German and European oral folktales and compiled them into a series of books that became *Grimms' Fairy Tales*. Jacob and Wilhelm were also lexicographers, and in 1854 they published the first volumes of the *Deutsches Wörterbuch* (German Dictionary). The *Deutsches Wörterbuch*, or DWB, is the largest and most comprehensive dictionary of the German language in existence. It is the German equivalent of the Oxford English Dictionary. Beginning in 1838, the Grimm brothers worked on the dictionary for over two decades, until their deaths—Wilhelm died in 1859 and Jacob in 1863.

The DWB continued publishing new volumes and updates after their deaths, and it still exists today. The brothers were intellectuals and academics, and their work to preserve language and stories was for the public good. Documenting oral traditions and language in order to preserve culture has always been an essential practice for sustaining any culture. These folktales provided Germans with purpose, so the sight of Disney extracting the cultural meaning of these fables for profit rightfully angered Adorno. Disney was not an evil man in the conventional sense, but he was an American who only knew ethnocide. Within an America devoid of culture, Disney needed to extract the culture of another people to create meaning, purpose, entertainment, and wealth. The desecration of language and stories destroys culture.

In 1947, Adorno and Max Horkheimer, a fellow member of the Frankfurt School, published the *Dialectic of Enlightenment* that asserted the modern age represented a failure of the Age of Enlightenment, and that our reliance on or interpretation of reason had led us astray. How can a society obsessed with reason be defined by unreasonable men and ideas such as colonization, Nazism, and fascism? In this book, Adorno and Horkheimer also coined the phrase "culture industry" to describe how capitalism and industrialization had created an industry devoted to creating mass-produced, sterile, and sanitized "culture." The supposed progress of modernity resulted in both the absence of what they considered culture, and the mass consumption of the absence of culture masquerading as culture. In the view of some members of the Frankfurt School, Americans lived off an inauthentic substitute of culture that they considered authentic culture.

In 1947, Adorno, with the support of the U.S. government and the University of California, developed the F-Scale to determine an authoritarian personality type. The "F" stood for "fascist." In 1950, he published *The Authoritarian Personality*, which described his findings. According to Adorno, the authoritarian personality included traits of anti-intellectualism, a dislike of imagination, an embrace of power and toughness, destructiveness, both authoritarian aggression and submission, and a predilection to project one's own flaws onto the other. The goal of the F-Scale was to measure prejudice and anti-democratic tendencies in people, but America never seemed too interested in applying the F-Scale to the still-segregated Jim Crow South of the 1940s and '50s. America wanted the F-Scale to identify Communists and Nazis who brought foreign threats. America could be consumed with fascists, have a test for fascists, and never feel the need to use it on the evil that America creates. America's fascists during Jim Crow were the progeny of slave owners and Redeemers, and America's Republican fascists today derive from a GOP formed when segregationists left the Democratic Party in the 1960s. America has a type of fascism that originated before and has lasted longer than its authoritarian Italian and German siblings. We have always lived with this type of fascism, and we believe it is normal.

—

Hannah Arendt was born in 1906 in Prussia, and in the mid-1920s she moved to Berlin, where she read Kierkegaard and studied under German

Existentialist philosopher Martin Heidegger. The rise of Nazism in the 1930s eventually forced Arendt into exile. In 1933 Arendt fled Germany with her mother to avoid the Nazi Gestapo who wanted to silence her writings in support of the Jewish people. Eventually, they settled in France after stops in Prague and Geneva. In 1940, following Germany's invasion of France, Arendt was captured and held in an internment camp for nearly six weeks. Soon thereafter she escaped and left Europe for America in 1941 via Portugal. In 1951, she shot to fame after publishing *The Origins of Totalitarianism*, which discussed the rise of totalitarianism in both Nazi Germany and Stalinist Russia, yet her writings for *The New Yorker* on the trial of Adolf Eichmann might be her most celebrated work. Her articles for *The New Yorker* were then compiled into the book *Eichmann in Jerusalem: A Report on the Banality of Evil.*

The provocative appeal of the book focuses on the idea that evil can appear banal. Some critics question whether Arendt meant to say that evil itself could be banal, but it is obvious, based on her depictions of Adolf Eichmann, that she viewed him as a banal man who orchestrated unimaginable acts of terror. Eichmann was a Nazi SS officer who oversaw the logistics of forcefully removing Jews from their homes and sending them to concentration camps. After the war he fled to Argentina, assumed the name Ricardo Klement, and lived a quiet peaceful life before he was captured by Israel's Mossad and Shin Bet and taken to Jerusalem to stand trial for war crimes, crimes against humanity, crimes against the Jewish people, and other charges. Upon seeing Eichmann in court, Arendt was reminded more of a boring bureaucrat than the living embodiment of evil he was projected to be.

During his trial Eichmann insisted that he was only guilty of "aiding and abetting" in the commission of his criminal charges, and that he never committed any overtly criminal acts. He did not personally kill any Jews.

Also, the sadistic nature of Nazi death camps meant that "it was usually the inmates and the victims who had actually wielded 'the fatal instrument with [their] own hands,'" said Arendt in *Eichmann in Jerusalem*. Thus, as with ethnocide and the master-slave dialectic, the masters sought to distance themselves from the responsibility of their terror by blaming the oppressed for their own oppression.

The judgment of the court responded to Eichmann's defense as such:

> In such an enormous and complicated crime as the one we are now considering, wherein many people participated, on various levels and in various modes of activity—the planners, the organizers, and those executing the deeds, according to their various ranks—there is not much point in using the ordinary concepts of counseling and soliciting to commit a crime. For these crimes were committed en masse, not only in regard to the number of victims, but also in regard to the numbers of those who perpetrated the crime, and the extent to which any one of the many criminals was close to or remote from the actual killer of the victim means nothing, as far as the measure of his responsibility is concerned. On the contrary, in general *the degree of responsibility increases as we draw further away from the man who uses the fatal instrument with his own hands* [Arendt's italics].

This judgment is provocative because obviously those who commit crimes with their own hands are responsible for their actions, but it injects the belief that those who are further removed from the crime have a greater responsibility to see the horror. Their relative distance from the atrocity gives them a greater degree of freedom, and therefore obligation, to denounce the terror. Eichmann's defense argued that he should not be punished for "acts of state." Eichmann's last statement proclaimed that he did not hate Jews or will the murder of human beings, and that he was only guilty of being obedient to a Nazi Party that led him astray. He said that he was merely a victim, and that only the leaders deserve punishment. "I am not the monster I am made out to be," Eichmann said. "I am the victim of a fallacy." He was found guilty on fifteen counts of crimes against humanity, war crimes, crimes against the Jewish people, and membership in a criminal organization. He was sentenced to death, and on June 1, 1962, Eichmann was hanged.

In America evil continues to take banal forms. The men in Gonzales-Day's photos got away with evil. The men who killed Emmett Till got away with it too. In 2020, Ahmaud Arbery, a Black man, was chased down in Brunswick, Georgia, by a white father and son, Gregory and Travis Mc-Michael, in their pickup truck and shot to death in broad daylight. They thought he looked suspicious as he jogged through their neighborhood. After the murder, local law enforcement attempted to cover up the crime and not prosecute these white men because the father used to work for the police department. The McMichaels were on their way to living a quiet life in the American South after killing a Black man in cold blood, but the Black Lives Matter protests following Arbery's death drew national attention, and Georgia law enforcement were compelled to prosecute. When interviewed by reporters, Gregory McMichael, like Eichmann, claimed to have no ill will or hatred toward Black people and that he "would never have gone after someone for their color." Today, America still combats an ethnocidal evil made to look banal.

American society has a history of excusing white evil, and allowing the perpetrators to live banal, seemingly normal lives. Jewish American novelist Philip Roth even coined the phrase "indigenous American berserk" to describe the inevitability and numerous permutations of white American violence upon the other. Yet even this phrase contains a lie because white Americans are not indigenous to America.

America condones the evil of the American ethnocidal berserk because America needs to live the *mauvaise foi* of American Exceptionalism and thus sustain white dominance. America exists as a society governed by a white essence that proclaims the false promise that everyone except the other is born an *Übermensch*. The American Dream promises the opportunity to be a master. Yet as our irrationality drags America further and further into the abyss, we yearn for the lie to be true because we do not know any other way to live. America does not know existence before ethnocide.

In the end, Eichmann proclaimed that he was not a monster, only the victim of a fallacy. In fact, he and America are both.

8

CULTURAL VULGARITY AND DESTROYING DIGNITY

Nothing in this world is harder than speaking the truth,
nothing easier than flattery.

FYODOR DOSTOEVSKY, *Crime and Punishment*

Before COVID-19 I had recently joined a co-working space, and this environment allowed me to regularly spend time in conversations about my work and the idea of ethnocide. Through these regular conversations I learned a Russian word that succinctly articulates the normalized immorality of American society.

Poshlost (пошлость in Cyrillic) loosely translates as "vulgarity," but this definition does not do the word justice. In his book about Ukrainian Russian author Nikolay Gogol, Vladimir Nabokov spent eleven pages attempting to define the word for English speakers. To his dismay, despite the popularity of Russian literature with English-speaking audiences, neither Gogol nor the concept of *poshlost* had become as well-known as he felt they deserved. At one point, Nabokov defined *poshlost* as "not only the obviously trashy but also the falsely important, the falsely beautiful, the falsely clever, the falsely attractive." Additionally, to make *poshlost* more digestible for the English ear and tongue, Nabokov proposed changing *poshlost* to *poshlust* to emphasize the vulgar, unrefined sexual lust that often accompanies *poshlost*. *Poshlust*, however, did not catch on. An American journalist for *The Moscow Times*, Michele A. Berdy defines the adjective *poshlyi* as "1) vulgar, crude; 2) a mix of pretentious, superficial, philistine, false, banal, soulless, hackneyed, mediocre, saccharine, tasteless, clichéd, all served up with a fine sense of moral contempt."

Within America's dialectic of *Geistmord*, the embrace of a soulless existence has long been our social norm. America aspires to make our persistent ethnocidal terror appear banal so the terror can continue unabated. Trump embodies this soulless, banal, and false existence, but he is also tasteless, clichéd, mediocre, hackneyed, saccharine, pretentious, superficial, philistine, crude, and vulgar. Alongside his perpetual fake tan, elaborate comb-over, and inflated sense of self, Trump is "obviously trashy but also the falsely important, the falsely beautiful, the falsely clever, the falsely attractive." America's Muscovite Candidate embodied an existence that Russians intimately understood but Americans had never articulated.

Poshlyi is normally used to describe a vulgar person you might find in a nightclub wearing revealing clothes, and it is less common to describe a rich person as *poshlyi*, but it can be applied to a mobster who has just been arrested. Either during or after the arrest the public can view the opulent lifestyle the mobster funded with their criminal enterprise, and the sight of the gaudy, tacky aesthetic they chose for their home more often than not is undeniably called *poshlyi*. Their vulgarity is less in your face and away from public view, but once you see it you know it is *poshlyi*. Trump, as of 2020, is not yet a criminal who has been arrested, but his real estate properties are notorious for being bought by Russian mobsters and millionaires. Trump cavorts with criminals, but he utilizes negligence as his defense against criminality. In an environment without responsibility, there are no requirements that people follow the proper procedures, and America has always been a society that encourages the merging of white power and irresponsibility. Due to America's reliance on a master-slave dialectic, sustained white ignorance is a viable business model as it works to blur the line between illegal and legal.

Trump's lifestyle is a crude joke against decency, yet America does not truly have the language to adequately laugh at him. During the 2011 White House Correspondents' Dinner, President Barack Obama mocked Trump, exposing his *poshlyi* lifestyle. Obama ridiculed Trump's rumored presidential aspirations, and even relayed a comical depiction of how Trump would modify the White House to suit his *poshlyi* aesthetic. To no one's surprise, when Trump became president, he promptly redecorated the Oval Office by adding gold-colored curtains.

Trump has a long history of cavorting and engaging in business with mobsters, and he has an aesthetic that matches theirs, but since he was not officially a part of a criminal enterprise, my friends were still hesitant to use the P-word. However, their opinions started to change when I asked them about Viktor Yanukovych, the former president of Ukraine.

—

Yanukovych fled Ukraine on February 21, 2014, and has been living in exile in Russia ever since. His whereabouts in Russia remain unknown. Yanukovych was born in 1950 when Ukraine was still part of the USSR.

He was born in the eastern part of Ukraine in what is now called Donetsk Oblast, which borders Russia, and his political career focused on strengthening Ukraine's relationship with Russia.

Since the fall of the Soviet Union, Ukraine has gradually worked to integrate itself with Europe and the European Union, and for the last two decades the tug of war between Europe and Russia has dominated Ukrainian politics and society. Yanukovych was at the center of this battle for nearly two decades. From 2002 to 2004, Yanukovych served as Ukraine's prime minister under the pro-Russia government of President Leonid Kuchma. In 2004, Yanukovych ran against Viktor Yushchenko, and the election pitted the pro-Russia and pro-Europe factions of Ukraine against each other. During the presidential campaign, Yushchenko fell ill and was rushed to the hospital. Analysis confirmed that he had been poisoned with dioxin, and as a result his face was greatly disfigured: covered in pockmarks, bloated, and jaundiced. Dioxin is a primary ingredient in Agent Orange, which the United States used during the Vietnam War. (An estimated four million Vietnamese were exposed to Agent Orange during the war.) Despite being poisoned, Yushchenko stayed in the race, and today he is alive and fully recovered. During his recovery, Yushchenko claimed that he was poisoned during a dinner he had with Ukrainian government officials.

Just under two months after his poisoning, the first round of Ukraine's presidential election took place. Yushchenko came in first place with 39.8 percent of the vote, and Yanukovych came in second with 39.3. Yanukovych's support primarily resided in the Donetsk Oblast and other eastern regions that wanted strong ties with Russia, while Yushchenko's support resided in the central and western parts of Ukraine that favored closer ties with Europe. Since neither candidate won more than 50 percent of the vote, the election went to a second round of voting. There were reports of Yanukovych supporters voting multiple times and casting votes long after the polls had officially closed. Most polls gave Yushchenko a significant lead heading into the election, but the final results had Yanukovych winning by 3 percent. International election observers denounced the results of the election, and soon protests consumed the nation, launching what would be called the Orange Revolution. The revolution took the name "Orange" because the protestors wore the color of Yushchenko's campaign. (It is only a coincidence, or maybe a perverse joke, that the man leading a campaign whose official color was orange was poisoned by Agent Orange.)

On November 23, five hundred thousand people peacefully protested in Kyiv's Maidan Nezalezhnosti (Independence Square) denouncing the election results. Protests continued for two weeks, until the Supreme Court overturned the election results and announced a date for a re-voting of the second round, which was an unprecedented de facto third round of voting. On December 26, Yushchenko won the re-vote with 52 percent to Yanukovych's 44 percent. Yushchenko's presidency lasted only one term and was marred by conflicts with his former ally Yulia Tymoshenko.

In the 2010 election, the three most prominent candidates were Yushchenko, Tymoshenko, and, of course, Yanukovych. During the first round of the election, Yanukovych came in first place with just under 36 percent, Tymoshenko came in second with nearly 25 percent, and Yushchenko came in fifth place with less than 6 percent. Prior to the second round of voting Yanukovych refused to debate Tymoshenko, frequently used sexist language in reference to her, and even told her to "go to the kitchen." Yanukovych's and Trump's rhetoric toward and treatment of women have obvious parallels. The celebrated sexism of two *poshlyi* men prevented both the United States and Ukraine from electing their first female presidents. Yanukovych won the second round with 48.95 percent, and Tymoshenko finished with 45.47 percent. Despite Tymoshenko's protests of the results and a history of election fraud, Yanukovych was sworn in as the president of Ukraine.

Following his victory, one of his first acts as president was to investigate Tymoshenko over the alleged corruption she engaged in during her time as prime minister. Tymoshenko was now being painted as crooked and untrustworthy, and for the entirety of Yanukovych's presidency she was either mired in litigation or in jail. In May 2010, numerous criminal cases were levied against her by the Ukrainian Prosecutor General's Office, and on October 11, 2011, she was found guilty of abuse of power and sentenced to seven years in prison in relation to an energy deal she had agreed to with Russia's state-owned gas company, Gazprom. The international community denounced her conviction. While she was in prison, she was also charged with two murders but never convicted. Tymoshenko remained in prison until Yanukovych fled the country.

In addition to imprisoning his political adversaries, Yanukovych also worked to align Ukraine closer with Russia, and his actions increasingly frustrated the Ukrainian people. The tipping point occurred on November 21, 2013, when he backed out of the Ukraine–European Union Association Agreement that would have put Ukraine on a clear path toward joining the European Union, and instead opted to strengthen ties with Russia. That same day protestors gathered in Maidan Nezalezhnosti in the heart of Kyiv, and Yanukovych found himself once again at the center of national protests. This protest grew into the Euromaidan Revolution that resulted in Yanukovych fleeing the country on February 21, 2014. The revolution is also known as the Revolution of Dignity because as more became known about Yanukovych's corruption and cronyism, it became obvious that he lived a vulgar, undignified life, and that Ukrainians needed to oust him in order to live in a dignified society.

As president, Yanukovych allocated disproportionately large amounts of government funds to the Donetsk Oblast and neighboring pro-Russia regions, and his cabinet was dominated by eastern pro-Russia politicians.

Yanukovych also worked to consolidate Ukraine's economic power into a cabal of fellow oligarchs, with his son Oleksandr being one of the largest benefactors. Yanukovych's disastrous economic policies reduced the value of numerous Ukrainian businesses, and now his son and other oligarchs could buy them on the cheap. At one point, Yanukovych had an estimated net worth of $12 billion, and he has been accused of misappropriating $70 billion from the Ukrainian treasury. After less than four years in office, Yanukovych's corruption had finally reached the breaking point, and the Euromaidan protest refused to end until he left office. Yanukovych treated Ukraine and its people as subjects he could exploit or manipulate for personal gain, and not as citizens he was elected to serve.

Immediately after Yanukovych fled, Russia invaded the Crimean Peninsula along the Russia-Ukraine border despite widespread condemnation from the international community. After taking control of the Crimean parliament, Russian installed a pro-Russia government in Crimea. On March 16, the Russian-controlled government of Crimea declared its independence from Ukraine, and on March 18, Crimea became part of Russia, or a federal subject of Russia. In Russia, a federal subject is essentially the equivalent of being a state in America, but the distinction between the language of subject and state is important. As democracy spread across Europe in the 1700s and 1800s and monarchies collapsed, Europeans rebelled against a life of being the subject of a monarch without rights or political influence in their society, and they drew inspiration from the language and ideas of the ancient Greeks who lived as citizens in a democratic city-state. The life of a citizen had more freedom and dignity than that of a subject. Today, Russia still considers Crimea as part of its country despite international objection.

After the annexation of Crimea, Russian-backed separatists and Yanukovych supporters in the Donestk and Luhansk Oblasts along the Russian border launched protests against the new Ukrainian government. These protests evolved into armed military conflicts between Ukraine and Russia for control of the region, and as of 2021 the conflict has continued to rage with no end in sight. Yanukovych might have left, but the fight for dignity and the catastrophic ramifications of his *poshlyi* existence remain.

On November 30, 2013, Ukrainian students in Maidan Nezalezhnosti were attacked by the government's Berkut riot police, and the outrage of seeing government soldiers attack civilians spread the protests across the country. In response, Yanukovych increased the militarization of the police and passed various laws outlawing protests, which the protestors dubbed the "dictatorship" laws. From December through February, the protestors engaged in violent clashes with Yanukovych's government. Peaceful protests quickly turned violent as Berkut officers attempted to forcefully disperse the protestors. Berkut snipers even fired into crowds of protestors from the roofs of government buildings. During the revolution, over a hundred Ukrainians died from violent encounters with the police, but despite the terror the revolution showed no signs of slowing down. The unrelenting pressure from the protestors effectively forced Yanukovych to leave the country because his government had been made powerless by the people. On February 21, 2014, Yanukovych signed official documents ending the political crisis, and later that day he fled Kyiv, traveled south through Crimea, and left the nation, never to return. Upon leaving Ukraine, Yanukovych had to abandon many of his possessions, including his elaborate estate, Mezhyhirya, on the outskirts of Kyiv. His *poshlyi* existence was laid bare for all to see.

Mezhyhirya is a luxurious, over-the-top compound situated on 350 acres and enclosed by a sixteen-foot fence. On the property there is a large wooden main clubhouse that is also called the Honka house (after the Finnish log-home manufacturer), and there are also tennis courts, hunting grounds, an equestrian club, a shooting range, a yacht pier, a golf course, an ostrich farm, a dog kennel, man-made lakes, a helicopter pad, and a small church. Despite the unholy nature of Yanukovych's kleptocratic cabal, a church remained among such vulgar opulence because Mezhyhirya had been an Orthodox Christian monastery for nearly a thousand years until 1922 and the rise of the Soviet Union. After Yanukovych escaped Ukraine, the public swarmed Mezhyhirya to get a peek at how he lived. Today, Mezhyhirya is an official government museum, but its function is not to celebrate Yanukovych or marvel at his opulent lifestyle. In fact, it is the opposite. Visitors gawk at the tacky, crude, "falsely important, falsely beautiful" lifestyle Yanukovych lived as he plundered Ukraine's money and exploited its people. The people finally got to see into his house, view his gaudy aesthetic, and recoil at the criminality that paid for the unnecessary excess. A revolution of dignity forced him to leave the country, and now his undignified life is on public display. His former home is now known as the "Museum of Corruption."

One friend, who had been unsure if Trump was *poshlyi*, now believed that the Trump International Hotel in Washington, D.C., represented the epitome of *poshlost*. At first, they hesitated to describe Trump as *poshlyi* because it is rare for such a weak, vulgar person to become the head of state. It is common to not want to see the vulgarity, and instead search for more dignified language, but once you see the "falsely important, falsely beautiful," you cannot ignore it. The president of the United States owns a hotel blocks from the White House, and makes it the de facto destination for any individual who aspires to engage in business or policy with the Trump administration, and as he politely forces people to stay in his hotel, he charges above market rates for everything in it. The hotel exists to extract as much money as possible from the people who aspire to work with him. This is not a dignified relationship. It is a blatant temple of vulgarity.

To continue the alarming connection, Paul Manafort, Trump's former campaign manager in 2016, even worked for Yanukovych and was paid millions to produce a smear campaign against Tymoshenko to turn Western Europe and the United States against her and in favor of her illegitimate prosecution. When Manafort worked for Trump, he also helped orchestrate a smear campaign against Hillary Clinton. However, in 2016, Manafort struggled to conceal his own corrupt, vulgar lifestyle, and soon his *poshlyi* existence was laid bare for all to see. During his trial for bank and tax fraud, it was revealed that Manafort attempted to hide $30 million in income and spent over $1 million on clothes in five years, including $15,000 on an ostrich leather jacket, $9,500 on an ostrich vest, and $18,500 on a python-skin coat. In 2018, Manafort was found guilty of bank and tax fraud, and pled guilty to conspiracy against the United States and conspiracy to obstruct justice. In 2019 he was sentenced to over seven years in prison. In December 2020, President Trump pardoned Manafort.

The garb of a head of state is the perfect attire to conceal vulgarity, and many people believe that the dignity of the office compels one to become dignified if they reach such a rarefied status. As Trump's vulgarity propelled him to the White House, countless Republican political pundits professed that the office of the president would fix his crude, philistine nature. Throughout Trump's presidency, Republican political experts yearned for the moment when Trump would transition from *poshlost* to dignified and act "presidential," but that moment never came. And it will never arrive. After losing the 2020 presidential race, Trump's corrupt vulgarity only increased as he proclaimed the election to be a "fraud" and engaged in both overt and covert attempts to disregard the will of the people and stay in office. On January 6, 2021, he implored his supporters to storm the Capitol to prevent the Democrats from "stealing" the presidency from him, but his wrath also extended to Republicans who agreed to uphold their constitutional duty and confirm Joe Biden as the next president of the United States. Trump's mob wanted to find Vice President Mike Pence and Senator Mitt Romney, who had broken ranks with Trump. A gallows with a noose attached, allegedly intended for Pence, could be seen on the Capitol grounds. Trump viewed the American people, even his close allies, as subjects he could condemn or compel to do his bidding, and not as citizens equitably working together to lead dignified lives. This is how a *poshlyi* president governs, and they never let go of power quietly.

People want to believe that the occupant of the office matches the dignity of the office, but when a *poshlyaki* obtains this position, the desire to believe that he is dignified only emboldens his vulgarity. People do not want to believe the vulgarity before them, and this gives him more opportunities to be *poshlyi*. Trump is the rarest and most destructive iteration of *poshlost*. Trump may not have been forced to flee to Russia prior to the end of his term like Yanukovych, but he left the White House as a reviled, vulgar figure who most Americans would like to disappear and finally face prosecution for the crimes he has been alleged to have committed. Since his last day in office, Trump has essentially lived in domestic exile in his trashy, falsely important, falsely beautiful Florida estate, Mar-a-Lago. Twitter has permanently banned him from their platform, so his dangerous, vulgar speech has been harder for him to spread, but as demonstrated by his impeachment trial, Trump's influence within the Republican Party remains just as strong. Trump sent his mob to attack disloyal Republicans, and a majority of Republicans in the Senate still voted to absolve him from any responsibility for the attack. When their lives were on the line, the Republicans chose to support the man who endangered them. They exist to be Trump's subjects within his master-slave dialectic. Unlike Yanukovych, whose exile has resulted in a life of obscurity in Russia, Trump's domestic exile after a failed coup d'état has alarming echoes of Hitler's Beer Hall Putsch as Trump allegedly plans for a 2024 presidential campaign and a dangerous return to power.

A vulgar person in a club is relatively harmless. A mobster is definitely dangerous to society, but a *poshlyi* president can destroy a country.

—

Ukrainian Russian novelist Nikolay Gogol was born on March 31, 1809, in Ukraine, which was part of the Russian Empire at the time. In 1836, Gogol shot to fame via his play *The Government Inspector*, which lampooned the corrupt bureaucracy of Russian society. The success of his play made him unpopular with the corrupt government officials who controlled St. Petersburg, and he soon left Russia for Rome. While in absentia he published *Dead Souls* in 1842.

The plot of *Dead Souls* is brilliant and simple, and displays how easy it is for one to live in a world consumed with vulgarity while also believing that your life represents the pinnacle of existence. In the novel, which Gogol also described as a poem, the main character Pavel Ivanovich Chichikov arrives in an unnamed Russian village with a sinister get-rich-quick scheme. As Western Europe saw various revolutions and rebellions topple monarchies and provide human rights to the people, serfdom was still going strong in Russia. In Russia, you were either a serf or a person who owned serfs. The richer you were, the more serfs you could afford to own, but owning serfs came at a price. The wealthy had to pay a tax for each of their serfs, and this tax was determined by the decennial census, but a serf population can change a lot over ten years. The only way to adjust your serf tax would be by buying or selling serfs and officially registering this transaction with the government. Also, if a serf died, you still had to pay the tax, because it would be far too easy for dishonest landowners to falsely claim the deaths of serfs to avoid paying the taxes.

Russia's serfdom economy and social structure was certainly crude and philistine, but compared to America's chattel slavery system it might be considered progressive. Americans did not need to certify the selling of slaves with the government, and slave owners did not have to pay a slave tax based on the number of slaves they owned. George Washington and Thomas Jefferson were two of the largest slave owners in Virginia, and they had no desire to impose a tax that would take away their own money. Instead, they created the Three-Fifths Compromise that counted three-fifths of the enslaved population for congressional apportionment and Electoral College delegates. Slaves in America were not a tax on the rich, but a tool for the rich to gain political power within a "democracy."

In *Dead Souls*, Chichikov, who is nothing but a smooth-talking con man, notices a flaw in Russia's serf taxation system since landowners are still paying taxes on dead serfs. The winter has been especially harsh, and a lot of serfs have died. More and more landowners have turned to booze and playing cards to relieve their stress, but they lose more and more money at the card tables. These rural landowners have been flocking to St. Petersburg in hopes of finding a government job that can help pay their bills, which still include taxes on the serfs who have died. Chichikov's ingenious, *poshlyi* solution is to purchase the dead serfs from the aristocracy, so that on paper he appears to be a rich aristocrat with an abundance of serfs. Chichikov hopes that these despondent landowners will sell him their serfs for next to nothing, so that he will take on the responsibility of the tax. On paper the serfs are alive, and he will "resettle" them in a distant rural province where the government is giving away the land for practically nothing. He plans on calling his new estate Chichikov's Hamlet or the Village of Pavlovsk, and then selling the serfs, who only exist on paper, to the government for a hefty profit. Due to the many serfs who had died that year, the government would jump at the chance to buy serfs from Chichikov so that they could be used for various government projects. If the Russian government ever found out that Chichikov's serfs did not exist, he could always claim that they died after the government bought them.

Despite being Russian, Chichikov's scheme has clear American undertones, since innumerable towns across the South are named after the white men who founded them. My father's family hails from Prattville, Alabama, and my ancestors were some of the first enslaved Black Americans Daniel Pratt took to Alabama in the early 1830s when he founded his eponymous town. With the aid of slave labor Pratt turned his town into the industrial capital of Alabama. Prattville specialized in building cotton gins to process the cotton harvested by enslaved Black Americans. Pratt is still regarded as Alabama's first and greatest industrialist, and the biggest distinction between his endeavor, and those of countless other white enslavers in America, and Chichikov's immoral scheme is that Chichikov's victims had already died, but in America's ethnocidal society Black Americans were kept alive and nearly worked to death.

As with *The Government Inspector*, *Dead Souls* caught the ire of the government censors. In order for the novel to see the light of day, the title had to be changed to *The Adventures of Chichikov*. This was because the two words of the original title, *Dead Souls*, succinctly described the depravity of Russia's serf-based society and economy. In Russian, the measurement word for counting serfs is *soul*. If a landowner owns forty serfs he would say that he has forty souls of serfs. When one landowner transfers ownership of a serf to another person, he is linguistically transferring the soul of the serf to another person. Chichikov aspired to traffic in the buying and selling of souls, and could there be a more soulless existence? *Dead Souls* is a Russian depiction of normalized cultural *Geistmord*.

In his biography of Gogol, Nabokov described Chichikov as "the ill-paid representative of the Devil, a traveling salesman from Hades." He was not the devil incarnate, merely one of his *poshlyi* pawns. America has hordes of people both present and past who would sell out their own family if it would make them a buck. Chichikov is an eternal con artist, a self-proclaimed genius who has found a way to make money that no one has ever imagined, yet throughout the novel he makes moronic mistakes that clearly disprove his genius, but never shatter his confidence. He is a con artist who has conned himself into believing that he is the opposite of what he is. *Dead Souls* made the foundation of Russian society appear vulgar and *poshlyi*, and its protagonist was the embodiment of *poshlost*.

The Russian censors did not approve of the brutal, accurate distillation of Russian society articulated in *Dead Souls*, but they could approve of the singular adventure of a man who visits an unnamed Russian village with a sinister scheme. Focusing on the individual and not the system made the *poshlyi* system palatable. It was no longer the system that was the problem, but merely a singularly immoral antihero. Likewise, Gogol had to tone down various parts of the novel that unabashedly attacked the system that governed Russian life, and instead direct our ire toward Chichikov. In the original version of *Dead Souls*, the censors did not approve of Chichikov because he was too unsavory a fellow to be considered a hero, so clearly making him an antihero earned their approval. After these changes and altering the title, *The Adventures of Chichikov*, with "dead souls" now relegated to a subtitle, was published on May 21, 1842.

Dead Souls further catapulted Gogol to literary fame in Russia, and today he is considered one of the fathers of Russian realism. His work influenced Nabokov, Leo Tolstoy, Anton Chekhov, and especially Fyodor Dostoevsky.

—

When I read *Dead Souls* I thought of Trump, but, most significantly, I could not help but think of the antebellum South and its social norms that continue throughout much of America. In *Dead Souls*, the wealthy complain about the supposed laziness of their serfs, and much of what fills their days are trivialities. When you have subjugated an entire segment of the population so that they can provide your necessities for survival, your attention will no longer focus on the essential aspects of life. The aspects of life essential for survival become relegated to the lowest caste on the social ladder. A wealthy person has no problem berating a serf who did not perfectly prepare their master's favorite meal, and he will not hesitate to decry the serf's stupidity or laziness while also being completely incapable of making the same meal for himself. There is an obvious vulgarity of proclaiming someone else incompetent due to their inability to perfectly execute something you also are incapable of doing, but this is the norm of a *poshlyi*, master-slave dialectic. Additionally, when the essential has become insignificant in the eyes of the wealthy, the wealthy make the trivial the height of existence. Their days are filled with gossip and the purchasing of cultured items from afar so that they can cloak themselves in a culture they do not have. This is a façade of culture to mask their emptiness.

Growing up in the South, I felt the oppression, racism, and division of ethnocide, which has obvious parallels to the *poshlyi* division of landowner and serf, but I also felt the triviality of everyday life. The South wanted a lightness of existence. Much of what determined if you were considered a good or bad person consisted of how well you embraced Southern politesse. Likewise, it was easy to have an abundance of white friends so long as you kept things light, trivial, and fun. Once a conversation of substance manifested and you might learn what the people around you actually believed, the vulgarity of their beliefs became so clear that it made you wonder how it was even possible to be friends with them in the first place. As my understanding of the world grew and my opinions took shape, I knew I needed to leave the South. One of the main reasons I moved to Washington, D.C., was the comparative absence of triviality.

The lightness of the South, and much of America, does not derive from freedom, but the absence of freedom. It is a lightness created at the expense of another. The projected lightness of Southern existence can be seen in its celebrated "hospitality" and the leisurely pace of Southern towns. There is an aura that someone else will casually take care of your needs. You just get to relax and embrace the lightness. The name *antebellum* literally means "before the war," but it has long come with a connotation that projects a harmonious relationship between slave owner and slave. The South has corrupted language to make a hellscape where nearly half of the population were enslaved sound like an idyllic, light, and carefree environment.

The lightness of American life quickly unravels once race becomes part of the equation, when it is much easier to see the vulgar, immoral destruction ethnocide is willing to create in order for people with a white essence to live a light existence. America's racial divide may actually make America's *poshlost* far more severe than Russia's. *Poshlost* is not supposed to be a vulgarity exclusive to a race of people. It is a common vulgarity that any person at any status of society can have based on their actions. In *Dead Souls* the wealthy and the con artist are both *poshlost*. However, in America colonizers created a "race" of white people forged from a culture of ethnocide. White Americans could live as the American equivalent to *poshlyi* European landowners, and America would never invent the words to describe this crude existence. Instead, we create language to celebrate the heroism and entrepreneurial spirit of Chichikov, the morality of Yanukovych, and the business acumen of Trump. We profess that governments should run like businesses, where they prioritize profit ahead of the people, and hardly flinch as *poshlyi* businessmen use the American government as a get-rich-quick scheme.

To extricate, liberate, and emancipate ourselves from American *poshlost* maybe we too need a revolution of dignity.

9

THE LANGUAGE
OF AMERICAN
FASCISM

"The first step in liquidating a people," said Hübl, "is to erase its memory. Destroy its books, its culture, its history. Then have somebody write new books, manufacture a new culture, invent a new history. Before long the nation will begin to forget what it is and what it was. The world around it will forget even faster."

MILAN KUNDERA,
The Book of Laughter and Forgetting

As Trump's dangerous presidential campaign continued, it became more common for people to describe Trump and his rhetoric as fascist, yet the language never stuck. By late 2015, journalists and scholars had begun to focus on a 1995 article by Italian philosopher and novelist Umberto Eco for *The New York Review of Books* titled "Ur-Fascism" that aspired to articulate the features of an eternal fascism. A fascism that was not regionally specific. Eco understood that Germany's Nazis and Franco's authoritarian regime in Spain had fascist attributes but were not exactly fascist in an Italian sense. To articulate how they could be both fascist and not fascist, Eco used philosopher Ludwig Wittgenstein's example of a game and the idea of a "family resemblance." Games can be vastly different. They can be competitive or not. They can require skill or no skill. They can involve money or no money. It is hard to describe exactly what constitutes a game, but you know it when you see it because there is a "family resemblance." With Ur-Fascism, he wanted to articulate the "family resemblance" of the fascist games of various cultures and countries, and it is abundantly clear that Trump and his supporters check all of the Ur-Fascist boxes.

According to Eco, Ur-Fascism has fourteen features, but you do not need to check all fourteen to be Ur-Fascist. You just need to have enough to create a "family resemblance." America's eternal fascism checks all of the boxes, but numbers 5 and 7 may be the most obvious today.

5. Besides, disagreement is a sign of diversity. Ur-Fascism grows up and seeks for consensus by exploiting and exacerbating the natural *fear of difference*. The first appeal of a fascist or prematurely fascist movement is an appeal against the intruders. Thus Ur-Fascism is racist by definition.

7. To people who feel deprived of a clear social identity, Ur-Fascism says that their only privilege is the most common one, to be born in the same country. This is the origin of nationalism. Besides, the only ones who can provide an identity to the nation are its enemies. Thus at the root of the Ur-Fascist psychology there is the *obsession with a plot*, possibly an international one. The followers must feel besieged.

—

At a campaign rally in January 2016, Trump said, "I could stand in the middle of Fifth Avenue and shoot somebody and I wouldn't lose any voters, okay? It's, like, incredible." That statement is the embodiment of Ur-Fascism, but as we know it did not harm his campaign. Hillary Clinton referring to his supporters as "deplorable" only emboldened and galvanized Trump's base. They felt besieged by Hillary Clinton and the Democratic Party. The *Access Hollywood* video in October 2016 also did not harm him, and his supporters dismissed his vulgarity as "locker room talk." Trump's vulgarity was no longer problematic in the eyes of his supporters because Trump's campaign found the language to articulate his *poshlyi* actions as trivial, meaningless statements that many Americans supposedly say when they believe no one is watching. Being vulgar became a new American norm, and this regressive dialectic made vulgarity socially acceptable and excusable. Trump appeared to be a "Teflon Don" for most of 2015–16, and none of his dangerous, inflammatory statements stuck to him despite having a blatantly fascist campaign. The reason Trump's fascism never became a problem was because America had never created a word for our culturally specific manifestation of Ur-Fascism. We did not have a domestic word that condemned America's unique brand of fascism. In Italy Ur-Fascism is Fascism, in Germany it is Nazism, in Spain it is a Francoist dictatorship, but in the United States of America, it is just a linguistic void. There is a root language without the actual spoken language. Trump could thrive because America was unable to culturally articulate the danger he presented. Trump's criminality did not have a name; therefore, it became incredibly hard to combat, and far too easy to grow. Trump's ascension aligns with what I describe as the American Cycle.

—

The American Cycle consists of four stages: Founding, Abolition, Recon-struction, and Redemption, and America is now experiencing the second iteration of this cycle. The American Cycle represents our society's desire for the inhumanity of ethnocide to coexist with the humanity of democracy. During the Founding stage, America's leaders attempt to forge this unholy alliance.

At its founding, America aspired to exist in two halves, with the Northern states being "free" and the Southern states having slavery. To sustain the "balance" between the North and the South, our Founding Fathers at the Constitutional Convention agreed to the Three-Fifths Compromise and the Electoral College, giving the South a dispropor-tionate influence over the trajectory of our democracy. Allowing slave owners to count three-fifths of their slaves for both House of Represen-tatives seats and Electoral College delegates gave the South greater in-fluence than the North in shaping the future of America. Around the founding of America, Pennsylvania and Virginia had roughly the same amount of eligible white male voters, but Virginia dominated American politics because of slavery.

The Founding eras of the United States, both the first and second iter-ations, consist of trying to find a compromise between the inhumanity of ethnocide and the humanity of democracy, but the end result will always be the empowering and normalization of the inhumane. The immorality of slavery has a greater influence in American society and government than the morality of human life.

During the Abolitionist era, parts of America worked to abolish eth-nocidal oppression. Since America's founding, Black Americans—both free and enslaved—have fought to end slavery or liberate themselves via slave rebellions and the Underground Railroad. Segments of white America also aspired to abolish slavery.

As America grew and expanded west, the debate about whether to expand slavery into the new territories consumed the nation. In the 1850s, the Republican Party emerged from the northern, abolitionist faction of the Whig Party, and grew into one of the most powerful political parties in America. The northern outrage from the *Dred Scott* decision emboldened the abolitionist movement, and increased tensions with the ethnocidal South. The election of Republican Abraham Lincoln to the White House meant that the potential for abolition became increasingly possible, and soon thereafter the South launched the Civil War. The deadliest war in the history of America was the inevitable culmination of the growing tensions between ethnocide and democracy, and the Union's victory presented an opportunity to create an America without ethnocide. Thus far, the American Cycle presents a narrative of progress, optimism, and the potential for transcending our limitations; but the second half of the cycle shows how regressive and dependent on ethnocide American society remained.

The North's victory in the Civil War and Lincoln's issuing of the Emancipation Proclamation signaled the success of the Abolition era, and now America had the opportunity to create an equitable society. This next stage in the American Cycle is represented by Reconstruction. For twelve years after the war, the Union attempted to remake the South into an equitable society. As part of this process, America added three amendments to the U.S. Constitution between 1865 and 1870, and before we discuss the radical impact of these amendments, we must highlight that these amendments expanded the number of amendments to the Constitution by 25 percent and that the Twelfth Amendment had been passed in 1803, over sixty years earlier. If America aspired to make an equally radical constitutional change today, it would equate to between six and seven new amendments.

The Thirteenth Amendment abolished slavery and involuntary servitude except as punishment for a crime. The Fourteenth Amendment granted citizenship to emancipated people, and the Fifteenth Amendment prohibited the denial of voting rights based on race, color, or previous conditions of servitude. According to the 1860 U.S. Census, enslaved and free persons of color made up 40 percent of the population in the states that would form the Confederacy. In South Carolina, enslaved people were nearly 60 percent of the population. Today conservatives bemoan the Deferred Action for Childhood Arrivals (DACA) created during Obama's presidency, but that program only protects less than a million people from deportation and does not give them citizenship or voting rights. Additionally, at most, there are about twelve million undocumented people in America, and granting them a path to citizenship has long been a political nonstarter. Undocumented Americans make up about 3 percent of the population. To have a radical change on par to Reconstruction, America today would need to grant citizenship and voting rights to all undocumented Americans, and then do the same for at least another thirty million people.

Despite the progress of Reconstruction, the South never stopped fighting to preserve slavery and ethnocide. John Wilkes Booth killed Abraham Lincoln less than a week after General Ulysses S. Grant met Robert E. Lee at Appomattox Court House to formally end the Civil War on April 9, 1865. Despite the end of the war, slave-owning states refused to free their slaves unless ordered to by the Union military. The official end of slavery in the United States was not the issuance of the Emancipation Proclamation on January 1, 1863, but on June 19, 1865, when the Union Army finally arrived in Texas, the last holdout state, and forced them to free their slaves.

Despite the end of slavery, the South was still unrelenting in its desire to reinstate the institution. Former Confederates created militias such as the Ku Klux Klan to terrorize enfranchised Blacks and their white allies, and they used the "except as a punishment for a crime" clause in the Thirteenth Amendment to force Black people into de facto enslavement. Black codes were created throughout Southern states that effectively criminalized Black existence and gave white Southerners ample opportunities to incarcerate Black people. Vagrancy laws were a key aspect of black codes because they effectively made it illegal for a Black person to exist outside of their home unless they were in service of a white person. If a Black person was merely sitting outside in a white part of town while not working, they could be classified as a vagrant. They could be arrested, and bail would be set at an amount that they could not afford to pay. Soon thereafter they could find themselves being forced to work the land of their old plantation without pay, but now they were a prisoner and not a slave.

—

The Redeemers movement was an unofficial group of Southern elites who wanted to "redeem" the South during Reconstruction by returning it to the pre–Civil War norms. Redeemers were business leaders, politicians, and others who ran Southern society. They destroyed progress and sustained ethnocide by any means necessary, but they had to sustain a façade of legitimacy and dignity while they did so. A redeemer could be an influential business leader who was also secretly part of the Ku Klux Klan, or at the very least collaborated with the KKK to obtain power. The KKK not only terrorized Black people, but they prevented Black people from voting and terrorized the white Republican politicians who won elected office. Voter suppression, intimidation, and demonization of the opposition became the political norm in the South, and this dynamic could only be sustained if the Redeemer candidates could appear above and disconnected from the terror while they actually orchestrated all of it.

Reconstruction lasted for only twelve years, but with each passing year it became increasingly obvious that Republicans in both the North and the South were growing weary of the effort required for Reconstruction to succeed. Many Republicans underestimated and dismissed the severity of Redeemer Democrat opposition, and believed that they had already done enough for Black people. In 1877, Reconstruction ended with the election of Republican Rutherford B. Hayes and the removal of federal troops from the South. During Reconstruction, a constant military presence was required in the South to suppress the terror orchestrated by Redeemers and implemented by the KKK. When the federal troops left, the Redeemers won.

The Redemption era consisted of the South actively working to dismantle the Reconstruction Amendments and return Black people to a life akin to slavery, to "Make America Great Again." The Redemption era lasted until Jim Crow, when the Redeemers and KKK had succeeded in their mission. The black codes of Reconstruction became the foundation of Jim Crow. The Supreme Court's "separate but equal" ruling in *Plessy v. Ferguson* legalized segregation and America's apartheid state. However, arguably the most significant impact of this era is the total corruption of language. Redemption was not the act of repairing a defect for the good of society, but the normalization of an atrocity. Redeemers also professed the narrative of the Lost Cause of the Confederacy, which aspired to rewrite the history of the Civil War to paint the South in a positive light. Robert E. Lee became a brilliant and noble military leader, and the war was a battle of "states' rights" and not slavery. Monuments were erected across the South to celebrate Confederate "heroes" and eventually textbooks were rewritten to espouse this false narrative. America allowed traitors and criminals to define the nature of their actions, and now their evil became associated with positive words, and the actions of anyone trying to prevent their terror had a negative meaning.

When Americans use the word *carpetbagger*, it means an untrustworthy outsider who has moved to an area for political gain and not the benefit of the people. This definition, which is now the American norm, derives exclusively from the perspective of former Confederates during Reconstruction. Carpetbaggers were Northern Republicans who decided to leave the comfort of the North to implement Reconstruction in the South. Many of them on the journey south carried their belongings in large carpetbags. Carpetbaggers held elected office, started businesses, and helped freed Blacks survive in the South. Many Northern women who could not fight in the war moved to the South as part of their civic duty and became teachers. Less than a decade earlier it had been illegal to teach Black people how to read, and many carpetbaggers uprooted their lives to help educate freed Black people. Carpetbaggers were the most progressive and democratic people in America, and as they lived in the South, they too were terrorized by the KKK. America should celebrate carpetbaggers as heroes who risked their lives to spread democracy to Black Americans, but instead America has chosen to see them how the white terrorists of the South framed them.

By the start of the twentieth century, Jim Crow had become the new American norm. Black Americans were not legally enslaved, but they de facto lived without the rights they had earned during Reconstruction. Many Blacks in the South worked as sharecroppers who lived on and worked the land of a white landowner, and they paid rent to their white overseer from the crops they harvested. Sharecropping was economic enslavement. Jim Crow was America's second attempt at balancing democracy with ethnocide. It was America's second Founding era.

—

The 1800s saw Black Americans embark on the treacherous journey on the Underground Railroad to escape the terror of the South, and the 1900s had the Great Migration in which Black families fled the South in droves and relocated to all of the major cities in the North, Midwest, and West. Yet America's Ur-Fascist discourse and linguistic commitment to erase the cultural experiences of Black people inclines all Americans to articulate the journey of America's domestic refugees as they fled terror with a palatable, benign, and quasi-uplifting title. The "Great Migration" encourages people to believe that the journey was "great," as in wonderful, or that the reception Black people received in their new homes was also "great," yet there was nothing great about the journey apart from the hope of leaving the terror of the South behind, and a great, or large, number of Black Americans left the South. From the 1910s to the 1970s, more than six million Black Americans fled the terror of the South in search of safety in the rest of America. Renaming the Great Migration the Overground Railroad would be more apt, since it harkens to the mass exodus of the previous abolitionist movement, but neither name fully articulates the terror of the South nor the dangers of the journey.

The Overground Railroad demonstrated the collective will of Black people to escape American terror, and the Civil Rights Movement existed to abolish Jim Crow and ethnocide. As with Dred Scott in 1857, the murder of Emmett Till in 1955 again demonstrated how the inhumanity of ethnocide could not coexist alongside democracy and Black freedom. Till's family was originally from Mississippi, but left on the Overground Railroad to Chicago. Till was murdered in Mississippi when he went back to visit his family over the summer. The horror of Till's mutilated body outraged and emboldened the Black community, and contributed to the growing abolitionist movement of the twentieth century that Americans refer to as the Civil Rights Movement. Actively working to escape and end ethnocide defined abolition in the 1900s and the 1800s, but what we all must understand is that America's second abolitionist movement did not end with the Civil Rights Movement of the 1960s, and in fact it continued into the twenty-first century.

The reason that America's second abolitionist movement lasted longer than the first is that the objective of the first was far less complicated. The first abolitionist movement aspired to abolish slavery, and winning the deadliest war in American history allowed Black Americans and abolitionists to accomplish that goal. The passage of the Thirteenth Amendment during Reconstruction appeared to accomplish that core goal. The Fourteenth gave Black people citizenship, and the Fifteenth the right to vote, and now Black people supposedly had the opportunity to live as equals in America. Jim Crow is far less straightforward, and this is why abolition has taken over a century and we still confront its horrors today.

Once Black people earned the right to live as human beings, and not merely subjects for white ethnocidal oppression, the South set about creating new laws that appeared objective, fair, and not in violation of the Reconstruction Amendments, but whose real objectives were to "redeem" the South and return Black people to a life akin to slavery. Black codes are a perfect example, because none of the laws that we refer to as black codes were officially designated that way. A law that made vagrancy illegal could outwardly appear to be a perfectly reasonable law. However, in the dystopian, Ur-Fascist reality of the South, vagrancy laws almost exclusively targeted Black people, and the clause in the Thirteenth Amendment made it incredibly easy to turn a Black vagrant into a prisoner who is forced to engage in unpaid labor on a former plantation that is now a prison. Jim Crow targeted each and every facet of existence and tried to make each of them illegal for Blacks and other people of color, so that white Southerners could sustain their white essence.

The Civil Rights Movement and the passage of the Voting Rights and Civil Rights Acts in the 1960s allowed Black Americans to technically reclaim the rights they earned in Reconstruction, but now we also had to abolish the myriad laws disguised as just, yet created intentionally to negate the earned freedoms of Black people. Laws to prevent redlining and predatory loans needed to be created. America had to dismantle the prison industrial complex, and reconstruct policing. We had to ensure equal opportunities to education, employment, and housing. We had to combat new attempts to prevent Black Americans from voting or obtaining political power, such as Georgia's runoff elections. The ethnocidal philosophy of Jim Crow and the founding of America permeates every facet of American life.

—

The Ur-Fascist corruption of American language and laws continues today, and the best example may be the name of one of our major political parties. In the 1800s the Republicans were the abolitionists, but in the latter half of the 1900s the Republicans became the progeny of Jim Crow segregationists. The Civil Rights Movement of the 1960s prompted Jim Crow segregationist Democrats to flee the Democratic Party, and the Republican Party welcomed them with open arms. The Republican Party, the party of Abraham Lincoln that was forged from the desire to abolish slavery, absorbed Southern white racists into their party in order to become a dominant political force. America chose to perceive this shift as racist Southerners joining forces with the non-racist Republicans from outside the South, and assumed that racism might represent only a small sliver of the party, not the dominant ideology. The palatable façade of passive racists does not absolve the terror of the active racists, but I can see why white Americans would prefer the non-racist narrative for the Republican Party. Richard Nixon in the late 1960s helped usher in a new era of concealing racism and perpetuating ethnocide.

Richard Nixon's 1968 presidential campaign employed dog whistles to appeal to white voters in the South. (Strangely, Americans are not repulsed by the terminology of dog whistles despite Republicans claiming that their obfuscated racist language can only be understood by their racist supporters, who in this analogy would be considered dogs.) Nixon spoke about "crime," the need for "law and order," and the necessity to decentralize the federal government. As Black Americans protested for their rights, Republicans called them "criminals" and denounced the central role the federal government played in making sweeping national changes to end Jim Crow. Nixon's language signaled to whites who embraced segregation that he was on their side. Nixon's dog whistles were echoed in Ronald Reagan's championing of "states' rights" and demonization of "welfare queens." George H. W. Bush's "Willie Horton" ad demonized Black Americans as dangerous criminals, and used the language of criminality and public safety to appeal to racist conservative voters. During the 2000 South Carolina Republican primary, South Carolinians received phone calls asking, "Would you be more or less likely to vote for John McCain ... if you knew he had fathered an illegitimate black child?" McCain had just won the New Hampshire primary and was in South Carolina actively campaigning with his adopted daughter from Bangladesh. Victory in South Carolina would have nearly ended George W. Bush's chances of winning the presidency. Bush Jr. went on to win South Carolina and the White House. Republicans still employ similar tactics and dog whistles today, and their vulgar, racist discourse helps them obtain political office. Part of what makes Trump unpalatable, yet still successful, is that he expresses the ideals of Redeemers without any obfuscation. Republicans agree with what he says, but they would prefer if he expressed his beliefs in a way that did not make them look so bad.

The idea of publicly saying one thing while meaning something completely different has been firmly entrenched in ethnocidal American politics since the Redeemers movement. Vagrancy laws were not created to stop vagrants, but to fabricate a reason to incarcerate Black Americans. "Separate but equal" never intended to extend equality to Black Americans, but to again legalize a system for perpetual subjugation, oppression, and exploitation. Since Nixon, the Republican Party has consistently engaged in dog whistles and race-baiting practices. They intentionally obfuscate their intent.

American racists have always worked to conceal their true intentions, and their goal is for people to believe that their lies are the truth. A war over slavery becomes a war of "states' rights." This is a manifestation of both traditional and Existential bad faith because in the first iteration the intent is to conceal a lie, but in the second the intent is to believe that the lie is true. Today, many Republicans probably know that they are lying to the public and obfuscating the truth, but it is also likely that many of them genuinely believe the intentional lies of previous generations are actually the truth. They now exist to obfuscate the truth and sustain lies, and they genuinely believe that they are moral arbiters of the truth. In both manifestations the lie continues, but the awareness of the lie differs.

—

In a society based on the corruption of democracy in order to sustain white dominance, you cannot have a more profound political and cultural shift than having a Black man become the president by fairly winning both the Electoral College and the popular vote. Obama's presidency focused on extending the promise of democracy to all Americans and empowering communities of color and marginalized people. Marriage equality for the LGBTQ community, the Deferred Action for Childhood Arrivals (DACA), and the Affordable Care Act are all policies that align with the philosophy of Reconstruction. Additionally, Obama's presidency is often criticized for not accomplishing enough, sharing a criticism of Reconstruction. This criticism derives from dismissing the severity of the obstructionism waged by the Redeemers of the nineteenth and twenty-first centuries. Obama's presidency is America's second attempt at Reconstruction. Both the nature and profound impact of America's conservative obstructionists and the structure of Obama's Democratic Party have obvious similarities to the 1860s.

From the beginning of Obama's term, Republicans vowed to make him a one-term president. Most famously, Republican Senate majority leader Mitch McConnell refused to hold Senate hearings for Obama's Supreme Court justice nominee Merrick Garland. McConnell's unprecedented obstruction allowed Republican Redeemers to politicize the Supreme Court, and following Trump's victory conservative jurist Neil Gorsuch became our next justice. Gorsuch's nomination was vetted by the conservative Federalist Society, which adheres to an "originalist" interpretation of the law that desires to interpret the meaning our Founding Fathers intended. It is a cult of tradition akin to a tenet of Ur-Fascism. The subsequent confirmations of justices Brett Kavanaugh and Amy Coney Barrett also adhere to this Ur-Fascist doctrine, and now due to the Supreme Court's 6–3 conservative majority, America's highest court is guided by the regressive ideals of an era that aspired to find common ground between ethnocide and democracy. Much like Reconstruction, those blamed for the lack of hoped-for progress during Obama's presidency are the ones who worked for the progress and not the political party and their derivative movements who exist to thwart progress and implement regression. Additionally, the disastrous long-term ramifications of the obstruction receive far less attention than the failure to achieve our hoped-for progress.

From the beginning of the first Reconstruction, white and Black Republicans staunchly opposed President Andrew Johnson. The influence of Black activists and politicians during this era, and the virulent opposition to their influence by Redeemers, also mirrors the impact of Obama's presidency. During Reconstruction, sixteen Black Americans served in the U.S. Congress—fourteen in the House and two in the Senate. Reconstruction would have had a third Black senator, but the Democrat-controlled Congress of 1872 refused to seat Louisianan P. B. S. Pinchback. During the 1872 Louisiana elections, the Redeemers were hell-bent on taking down Republican control of the state, and the elections were marred with fraud, corruption, and voter intimidation. The political alliance formed between carpetbaggers and freed Blacks gave the Republicans political control of the state. To take control, the Democratic Redeemers unleashed the White League, an American paramilitary group similar to the KKK, to inflict terror and swing the election in their favor. Due to the systematic terror, corruption, and fraud, the election resulted in no clear winner. Democrats and Republicans in Louisiana both claimed victory in the Senate and gubernatorial elections. The U.S. Congress refused to seat Pinchback, and within the state the Democrats and Republicans went to war. On Easter Sunday 1873, the White League attacked freed Blacks in Colfax, Louisiana, killing at least a hundred innocent people. The Colfax massacre was one of the deadliest white terrorist attacks of Reconstruction.

The Redeemers had no problem implementing terror to claim control, and in 1873 they even attempted and failed a coup d'état in Louisiana. However, their failure did not deter them, and in 1874 they attacked and captured the state capitol and the New Orleans police station. The Democrats took control of the state by force, and only relinquished control when President Grant sent down Union troops who defeated them in battle. Typical of America's eternal fascist discourse, the failed coup became known as the Battle of Liberty Place, and in 1891, during Redemption, a monument was erected to celebrate the Democratic "heroes" that fought for "freedom." That monument remained in New Orleans until 2017, when Democratic mayor Mitch Landrieu removed it.

Ironically, during the chaos of 1872, Pinchback, who was also the lieutenant governor, became the governor of Louisiana for six weeks, and America's last Black governor until the 1990s. During Reconstruction more than six hundred Black Americans were elected to state legislatures, and hundreds more held local offices in the South. The end of Reconstruction resulted in the gradual erasure of Black elected officials, but Obama's presidency resulted in an obvious uptick. Obama was America's fifth Black senator; America has only had eleven.

In the 1860s, President Johnson staunchly opposed equitably incorporating freed slaves into the newly unified Union, and the House of Representatives impeached him because of his opposition to Reconstruction. Johnson believed granting freed slaves voting rights and equality would result in them forming a "slavocracy" where the freed Blacks would form an alliance with former slave owners to dominate the South. Johnson's hypothesized slavocracy would result in poor whites becoming the bottom rung of the Southern caste system. Johnson grew up as one of those poor whites, and his decision to support the Union and become a "scalawag," instead of supporting the Confederacy, propelled him to national prominence. He supported the Union because he believed their policies would help poor whites, and not because he was a champion of racial equality. Johnson essentially represented the "swing voters" of the South who cared about economics ahead of race and did not consider themselves to be as racist as their fellow Southerners. The Union in the 1860s and the Democrats since the 1960s have needed to win these swing voters, and they have long been an obtainable demographic so long as economic opportunity precedes racial equality. Once race trumps economics, they are likely to side with the Redeemers.

The Union knew they would need to work with the South, so Union sympathizers in the South became a valuable political commodity. As a scalawag, Johnson became Lincoln's vice president, and after Lincoln's assassination he ascended to the White House. Despite supporting the Union, Johnson's ethnocidal, white supremacist ideology meant that common ground could never be found. During his presidency, Johnson's popularity among Republicans plummeted so severely due to his persistent obstruction of Reconstruction that in the 1868 election he ran as a Democrat. Johnson then embarrassingly failed to receive the Democratic nomination despite pledging to pardon all Confederate soldiers and politicians except a select few including Jefferson Davis. Before he left the White House, he went through with his promise and pardoned the treasonous Confederates.

—

From the beginning of Reconstruction, the Republicans believed that they would have unassailable control over America's democracy because of the enfranchisement of freed Blacks. The Republicans were obviously the dominant party in the North, and now they had just enfranchised about 40 percent of the population of the South. Demographics and diversity meant that racial equity, progress, and Republican political control were inevitable, and this narrative echoes the narrative of Obama's presidency. During Reconstruction, the active presence of Black voters and politicians surfaced racial tensions that Republicans had been able to ignore when Black people had no role in America's democracy. Believing that Black people should be free was a theoretical and philosophical belief that was easy to support, but believing that their freedom should allow them to "take" a white person's job or that white people should allocate funds and resources to improve Black life became hotly contested issues. President Andrew Johnson was against slavery in theory, but wanted to execute zero policies that would allow Black people to live their lives without being a perpetually subjugated people. One way to understand the dynamics of the tensions within the Republican Party is by examining the unofficial names the white Southerners gave them.

Northern Republicans who relocated to the South during Reconstruction were *carpetbaggers*, and Southerners who sided with the Union were *scalawags*. Scalawags were considered traitors to the South. Southerners had already given Black people a slew of hateful and demonizing names. This triumvirate of perpetually demonized people formed the new cultural and political fabric of American progress, and from the 1860s to today America still applies a hateful rhetoric to all three parties. The continued demonization of this triumvirate defined the 2016 presidential race.

Not all scalawags are as incompetent and racist as Andrew Johnson, but the ones who are normally defect and join the Redeemers. The ones who stay and fight for equality suffer the perpetual scorn of Redeemers and today's Republicans, but they also have the capacity to make change. President Lyndon Johnson was a Southerner from Texas who championed civil rights. In 1965, he signed into law the Voting Rights Act that allowed Black Americans to reclaim the voting rights they earned during Reconstruction that were then taken away from them by the Redeemers. Johnson's support of civil rights resulted in segregationist, Redeemer Democrats leaving the party to join the Republicans. The policies of Johnson's Great Society also radically changed American society, making it more equitable, diverse, and open to more immigrants from around the world. Our current political dynamic derives from ethnocidal Americans protesting against a scalawag fighting for racial equality. And following Lyndon Johnson, every Democratic president prior to Obama was a scalawag. Jimmy Carter hailed from Georgia and Bill Clinton from Arkansas. During America's second abolitionist era, Democrats needed scalawags to win the White House because the remnants of Jim Crow still systematically disenfranchised Black voters. A scalawag presented the chance of winning at least one state in the South. This subtle shift could swing an election and potentially signal the end of Redeemer Republican power.

Obama's presidency signaled the end of scalawag Democrats winning the presidency, and now a Black American controlled the White House. This trajectory posed an even greater threat to Redeemer, ethnocider political control, and Republicans existed entirely to either obstruct or remove Obama. They failed at removing him, but their obstructionism resulted in progressives and other segments of the Democratic Party growing frustrated at the lack of progress. Because America has a language built to demonize progressives and not obstructionists, it became much easier for infighting to dominate the Democratic Party. By 2016, scalawags, enfranchised Black Americans, carpetbaggers, and Northern progressives were all fighting each other within the Democratic Party, and to the myopic surprise of the American public, the Republican Party coalesced around their Redeemer candidate.

During the 2016 presidential race, Hillary Clinton, who was born and raised in the North but launched her political career in the South, became the Democratic nominee. The narrative of her campaign was largely one of female empowerment and that a woman president would be the next iteration of American progress. Liberals overlooked the fact that she was a carpetbagger and that her obstacles mirrored those of carpetbaggers during Reconstruction. In the 1860s, Northern carpetbaggers did not initially have a relationship with Black people prior to relocating to the South. Therefore, many of their ideas for how to advance the South were based on ignorant ideas about Black people and not an intimate knowledge of their community and culture. One of the major missteps by carpetbaggers was that they did not expect Black people to be so passionate about running for elected office. Many carpetbaggers had a paternalistic racism, and they expected Black people to want a white person with more political experience to represent them. Additionally, carpetbaggers underestimated the obstruction they would face from white Southerners. Their efforts to compromise and find common ground with Redeemers further undermined their credibility with Blacks, scalawags, and Northern progressives because Redeemers always operated under bad faith. It became easy to paint carpetbaggers as incompetent because Redeemers perpetually undermined their governance, but their efforts to reconstruct the South represent arguably the most progressive and ambitious endeavor in American history.

In 2016, Black voters did not want to vote for Clinton because they would have preferred to vote for another Black person who better understood their community. Clinton's political experiences as first lady of Arkansas and then the United States resulted in her supporting bipartisan policies that disproportionately harmed communities of color. Clinton's "superpredators" statement from 1996 harmed her with both progressives and people of color in 2016. Essentially, Clinton's track record of collaborating with anti-abolitionists made people question her ability to implement the progress she professed to want. To add fuel to the fire, conservatives have spent decades proclaiming the Clintons untrustworthy, but this rhetoric is the same thing they have said about scalawags and carpetbaggers for 150 years. Their rhetoric has been so successful that America still identifies the progressive radicals of Reconstruction via the demonizing language that racist Southerners foisted upon them. The Obama coalition of enfranchised Blacks, progressives outside the South, scalawags, and carpetbaggers began to fall apart when a carpetbagger became the candidate.

As the Democrats found reasons to splinter, the Republicans coalesced around their Redeemer candidate who found no problem with supporting corruption, voter suppression, and white terrorism to win the election. The KKK and the alt-right were emboldened by Trump's rhetoric. Trump encouraged foreign interference in our elections if it helped him win. The Supreme Court's gutting of preclearance in the Voting Rights Act made voter suppression easier for conservatives to implement. Now all Trump needed to do was find a way to win enough white swing voters and he had a viable shot at the White House. His chances were very, very slim, but the path was clear; and to the dismay of most Americans, he found that path via Pennsylvania, Michigan, and Wisconsin. He won those three states by a combined total of less than one hundred thousand votes, and these states allowed him to win the Electoral College and the White House without winning the popular vote. Trump used the Electoral College—an instrument of oppression, division, and exploitation created by America's Founding Fathers—and the playbook of the Redeemers to end America's second Reconstruction just as the first ended.

I do not believe that Trump, his campaign, or advisors are brilliant students of history who studied Reconstruction, but I do not believe that they even need to. All they needed to do was speak to the American people in the language they are conditioned to embrace and trust, and that is a dialectic of *Geistmord*. Trump's campaign openly embraced a populist movement modeled after Andrew Jackson and his Jacksonian Party that was a cult of personality, popular elitism, and selective populism, all components of Ur-Fascism. The voice of Trump's supporters became the *true* voice of the American people, and all of his supporters were *true* Americans. Everyone who supported Trump became a hero and an *Übermensch*. Liberals, people of color, and the LGBTQ community became the enemy and *Untermenschen*. This discourse propelled Trump to victory, and Trump existed to create the second era of Redemption, rolling back all the progress of Reconstruction and abolition to create a third authoritarian Founding era.

As Trump rose to the top of the GOP and eventually the White House, many Americans watched in disbelief and were astonished by Trump's impoverished vocabulary. His tweets were filled with grammatical errors and his word choices were on par with a middle school student's, yet the simplicity and underdeveloped nature of his language increased his appeal with the "average Joe" American. They believed that he was just like them except rich, and this made them want to believe in Trump, because if they believed in him they could believe that they could become rich too. Trump was a millionaire with juvenile syntax who shot to fame because of his ability to manipulate the press and his unceasing desire for attention on television. Trump's language and craven desire for media attention reminded me of the final tenet of Ur-Fascism—"All the Nazi or Fascist schoolbooks made use of an impoverished vocabulary, and an elementary syntax, in order to limit the instruments for complex and critical reasoning"—and how an impoverished vocabulary was a core aspect of Newspeak in George Orwell's *1984*. Trump's inability to have complex thoughts while also being rich is what made him attractive to so many Americans.

—

The first three Wednesdays of 2021 showed that America might finally be ready to break the American Cycle and continue Reconstruction. On Wednesday, January 6, Trump supporters stormed the U.S. Capitol to stop the certification of the Electoral College votes. Their attempted coup d'état did not succeed, and a week later on Wednesday, January 13, Trump became the first president in American history to be impeached twice. With a week left in Trump's presidency, Republican senator Mitch McConnell, who was the Senate majority leader at the time, successfully delayed the Senate hearing for Trump's impeachment until after Biden was sworn in. The po-

tential prosecution as a result of Trump's impeachment would now be the responsibility of the new Democrat-controlled Senate. (The Republicans want
power, but not the responsibility that comes with freedom.) On Wednesday,
January 20, Biden became the forty-sixth president of the United States, and
our country, and the world, finally saw the potential for a continuation of
Obama's Reconstruction and an end of Trump's Redemption.

During his campaign, Biden stated how the white supremacist attack
in Charlottesville, Virginia, in 2017 inspired him to run for president.
Charlottesville is a quiet college town and the home of the University of
Virginia, which was founded by Thomas Jefferson in 1819, but in August
2017, American neo-Nazis, Confederate sympathizers, and the alt-right
descended upon the city to protest the removal of a statue of Confederate
general Robert E. Lee that had stood in the city since 1924. As ethnocidal
Americans terrorized the residents of Charlottesville to defend the *mauvaise
foi* and propagated the Lost Cause narrative of the treasonous Confederate,
they also chanted "Jews will not replace us." President Trump responded
by claiming that there were "very fine people on both sides," and directed
the blame for the chaos toward the Americans who stood up against Ur-
Fascism. Just as during America's first Redemption, the cultural narrative
disseminated by ethnocidal Americans attempted to demonize and ridicule the Americans who fought against racism and bigotry. Following the
white supremacist attack, I wrote a column proclaiming that Charlottesville proved that America had entered the second iteration of American
Redemption.

During Trump's campaign and into his presidency, his "Make America
Great Again" movement professed the American ideology of Redemption,
and I wondered if America had the capacity to sustain or bring back Reconstruction. Had we merely continued the American Cycle, and were we
now destined for an era committed to dismantling Reconstruction so that

America could commence another Founding Era (or Jim Crow)? During Trump's presidency I was anything but an optimist, yet Biden's presidential campaign gave me hope. The fact that he decided to run for president in response to a grotesque manifestation of American Redemption emboldened my faith in his campaign.

To the chagrin of most of my friends I supported Biden very early in his campaign. Most of the people I know did not believe that Biden was progressive enough, so instead they supported senators Bernie Sanders, Elizabeth Warren, or Kamala Harris. Honestly, I did not disagree with most of their complaints about Biden, but I saw his campaign as a potentially revolutionary endeavor that preceded policy and politics, and spoke to the cultural change America required to successfully attempt to continue Obama's Reconstruction. Biden's presidential campaign was revolutionary because he was a white man campaigning for the highest office in the land based on his friendship with a Black man.

Biden became a U.S. senator in 1973, at the age of thirty, and had continuously worked in the federal government until Obama's presidency ended in 2017. He has always had the experience to be a good president, but what put him over the top was his friendship with Obama. Biden ran for the presidency as a continuation of Obama's legacy, and as his campaign unfurled I wanted to see if his unprecedented campaign strategy could work. Would Black voters support Biden as they did Obama, or would they support Black candidates senators Kamala Harris or Cory Booker instead? Would he be able to appeal to progressives who supported Warren or Sanders? Could he successfully campaign as the front-runner and avoid a gaffe that could derail his campaign? Would Biden ever attempt to distinguish himself from Obama, falsely take credit for Obama's achievements, or talk negatively about the former president? Would he throw Obama under the bus as his campaign got more stressful and desperate? Biden's campaign held many questions, but I wanted to see if a white man could successfully become president based on sustaining, nurturing, and defending his close friendship with America's first Black president.

Following lackluster results at the Iowa caucuses and the New Hampshire primary, Biden's campaign appeared dead in the water, but his victory in the South Carolina primary propelled him to the White House. South Carolina is the first primary whose voters are primarily people of color, and as America has become more diverse and equitable, its political significance has grown. In 1860, nearly 60 percent of South Carolina's population was enslaved, and in 1861, the state launched the Civil War, but now South Carolina's Black voters are selecting the United States' presidents. Obama's success in South Carolina in 2008 solidified his delegate lead over Hillary Clinton. In 2008, Black voters chose to vote for the upstart Black candidate instead of the carpetbagger candidate and her scalawag husband. This dynamic echoed Reconstruction, but in 2020, Biden did not fit within these existing classifications held over from the 1860s. Biden is from Delaware, which has straddled the border between the North and the South for the entirety of its existence, and in 2020 his narrative of authentic friendships across America's racial divide resonated with the Black voters in South Carolina. Biden is neither Black, a carpetbagger, a scalawag, nor a Northern progressive, so despite working in government for half a century, he actually breaks the mold. Following his victory in the South Carolina primary, Biden effectively monopolized the Black vote, and his support among people of color propelled him to the White House.

Throughout his campaign he never proclaimed to be better than Obama or minimized Obama's accomplishments. In fact, Biden would frequently correct people and remind them that he was Obama's sidekick, and that he hopes to be as successful of a president as Obama. Prior to the Civil Rights Movement of the 1960s, it had always been impossible for Black and white

Americans, especially in positions of power, to forge a friendship akin to the familial bond that the Obamas and Bidens share. It has taken half a century of sustained racial progress and the dismantling of Jim Crow for this iteration of dynastic, pre-racial friendship to shape the trajectory of American life. The Obamas and Bidens have a familial, cultural bond and it should be no surprise that Barack and Joe often refer to each other as "brother." This is what reconstructing America at a cultural level looks like, and I hope that this cultural shift can reconstruct America's democracy and help us transcend our ethnocidal limitations.

Throughout his campaign, Biden always spoke about it as a mission to save the soul of America. Biden's rhetoric echoed the narrative of the ethnocidee and the white Americans who formed a brotherhood with people of color to dismantle ethnocide. The ethnocidee has always focused on cultivating their own souls as well as America's. During his inauguration speech, Biden recounted the words Abraham Lincoln said after signing the Emancipation Proclamation, "If my name ever goes down into history it will be for this act and my whole soul is in it." We must cultivate *Geist* to combat *Geistmord*, and if America is ever to reconstruct itself into an equitable and just society, white Americans must also be able to speak this language.

The highlight of Biden's inauguration was twenty-two-year-old poet Amanda Gorman's reading of her poem "The Hill We Climb." As a young Black woman, she follows in the footsteps of Maya Angelou, who recited the poem "On the Pulse of Morning" at Bill Clinton's inauguration in 1993, and she carried the weight, spirit, and culture of her ancestors on this day. Prior to all of her performances, Gorman recites the mantra, "I am the daughter of Black writers. We are descended from freedom fighters who broke through chains and changed the world. They call me."

As Trump left the White House with a whimper and elected to break from tradition by refusing to attend Biden's inauguration, America was able to clearly see an equitable, diverse culture beyond the clutches of Trump and America's ethnocidal, Ur-Fascist way of life. It is only fitting that the most discussed and inspirational passage of Gorman's poem was inspired by the Capitol insurrection that Trump orchestrated.

> We have seen a force that would shatter our nation rather than share it,
> Would destroy our country if it meant delaying democracy.
> And this effort very nearly succeeded.
> But while democracy can be periodically delayed,
> It can never be permanently defeated.
> In this truth, in this faith we trust.

American fascism is different from its European counterparts because ours emerges from America's foundational ethnocidal culture. American fascism could be called Trumpism, MAGA, segregationists, Jim Crow, and many other manifestations of America's ethnocidal culture that combine political power with domestic terrorism to oppress the ethnocidee. Europe's fascist movements also use the mask of an authentic political party to give the guise of legitimacy as they infiltrate a nation's government and oppress their own people. The Republican Party's decision to acquit Trump in his second impeachment trial for sending a mob to attack the Capitol and terrorize Republican and Democrat politicians shows their commitment to sustaining America's Ur-Fascist norm under the guise of legitimate governance. The Republican Party's appeasement of Trump after he terrorized them equates to a dystopian commitment to ethnocide that prioritizes essence, *mauvaise foi*, the master-slave dialectic, and *Geistmord* ahead of existence. If we aspire to break the American Cycle, we must also be aware of the dangerous lengths the ethnocider will go to sustain it.

To break the American Cycle and our dependence on fascist language, we must create a culture and language for liberation and existence, and this language and culture primarily come from the ethnocidee. America's language has long been one of erasure and obfuscation, and I was able to clearly see the American Cycle by focusing on the lives of the Americans our ethnocidal society exploited and attempted to erase. These people must speak the truth because parasitically living off of exploitation is not an option for them. Forming good-faith relationships is the foundation of their culture, and these relationships can transcend racial division. The ethnocidee must speak with clarity and not obfuscation, and throughout American history their poetry, oratory, and wisdom has inspired Americans to elevate beyond our ethnocidal norms. Giving the ethnocidee a voice reveals the true American narrative and the potential to break the American Cycle.

10

THE NARRATIVE
OF THE
ETHNOCIDEE

> The North won the Civil War, but the South won the
> narrative war. We have to do better at creating a narra-
> tive that pushes us into a new place.
>
> BRYAN STEVENSON

After graduating from the Medill School of Journalism at Northwestern University in 2011, I found myself alone in my apartment in Chicago. All of my friends and classmates had already graduated and left the city, but I still had a month left on my lease and I needed to figure out my next step. During my last quarter at Medill I had worked in London, but that internship didn't turn into a full-time job as I'd hoped it would. I returned to Chicago without a job and with no attachments—and I loved every second of it.

There were no classes to attend, no people to see, and no one to tell me what to do. I examined and thought about what I needed to do and why each and every day, from the quotidian to the more profound. What time should I wake up or go to bed? What tasks are essential for each day? Where would I like to be by the end of the month and how do I intend to get there? Should I stay in Chicago or move to New York City, Washington, D.C., Atlanta, or someplace else? This was the most untethered I had ever felt. Before this, my life had always been attached to a job, school, or familial pressures, but in Chicago—during this single month—I had distanced myself from all of these anchors. Without any social obligations pulling me in one direction or another, I started to think about my life in a new way, and a yearning to learn more about my family history became my new focus.

As I sat alone in my apartment, it dawned on me how my perceived limitations and possibilities had been largely shaped by my environment. The actions that I believed were possible or impossible had roots in my awareness of my surroundings. For example, I knew that I did not want to live in the suburbs, but I knew this because I had always lived in the suburbs and never enjoyed it. The suburbs always felt like an environment where people aspired to do nothing and remain comfortable, and everything looked the same. I remember driving around Marietta as a high schooler and being constantly disappointed with what I saw. There is no geographical reason for Marietta to exist. It is not on a waterway or in a valley; it is merely a stop on the railroad built to transport goods produced by slave labor. This city could look like absolutely anything, yet everything looks the same. It exists as an overprocessed absence of culture. I desperately wanted to leave so that my imagination would not get trapped within and devoured by the *letzter Menschen* aesthetic of my hometown. Wanting to leave was the reaction—and this was simple—but determining where I wanted to go and why was far more complicated.

I knew I needed to do something more than just the opposite of what I did not want. I struggled to find a cultural reference point that was not reactionary. I needed to find some proactive reference points, and if I could not find them in the present, I knew I needed to look to the past.

When I called my mother and asked about our family's history, she recommended that I reach out to my uncle Artie, her younger brother. Unbeknownst to me, Artie had for years been doing extensive research on our family history, and he had traced many of our family lines back to our first documented Black ancestor. It is incredibly difficult to find documentation of Black Americans prior to emancipation, because unless they were free persons of color, the only documentation of their existence was most likely a bill of sale. Unless a white American sold an enslaved Black person to another white American, there is hardly any documented evidence that one's Black ancestor even existed.

Artie traced the Mack branch of our family tree back to the 1850s, to our enslaved ancestor Charlotte Stevenson. She was owned by the Stevenson family in Florence, South Carolina, and when Mary Stevenson married George Washington Byrd, she came with her. Charlotte had a son with Mr. Byrd. Charlotte was only a quarter Black, and her octoroon son was so light that he passed as white. Mary already had a son named Redden with Mr. Byrd, and after Charlotte died a couple years after childbirth, Mary chose to raise my light-skinned ancestor as her own son. Just before my ancestor's birth, Mr. Byrd died while fighting for the Confederacy in the Civil War. For the first fifteen years of my ancestor's life, he believed that he was a white person, and that Mary was his biological mother. Today, we know him as Doc "D.J." Mack, but as a white man his name was James Byrd, a descendant of the celebrated Byrd family that colonized the Virginias and Carolinas. My family is not sure why Mary chose to raise James as her own child, but we speculate that Charlotte might have been her half sister: the offspring of her father and an enslaved woman. If this is true, James was both Mary's nephew and her son's half brother.

When James was about fifteen the secret of his birth was revealed, and now he ceased to be considered a white man, and had to live as a Black man. He was no longer a Byrd, and had to rename himself. We do not know why he chose the surname Mack. By all accounts, D.J. (Doctor James) traversed a whirlwind of emotions as he came to terms with his Blackness, and I often wonder how radically his perspective changed as his world was flipped upside down. Most significantly, I wonder if D.J. was racist when he thought he was white. We have no documented evidence that D.J. had racist beliefs, but as the white son of a slave owner who died fighting for the Confederacy, it is not far-fetched to believe that my Black ancestor might have hated and dehumanized Black people when he thought he was white.

D.J. eventually married Harriet "Hattie Gee" McCants, a dark-skinned Black woman, and they had thirteen children together. Their daughter Beulah, my great-grandmother, was born in 1899 and lived to be 101. In many ways, Beulah was the family matriarch in Charleston, and she played a major role in my mother's life. Whenever my family would visit Charleston we would always visit Beulah, yet at no point did anyone talk about the fascinating story of D. J. Mack. I'd never heard this story until I was nearly thirty years old.

After learning about D.J., I called my mother to see what she'd known about this story, but she had not even heard it. To my knowledge, none of my mother's siblings had heard the story of D. J. Mack until Artie began his research. Artie only learned about D.J.'s story after uncovering a letter written by Evelyn Castelow—one of D.J.'s daughters and Artie's grandaunt—that detailed her father's life. The letter is less than a thousand words, and Evelyn wrote it only two years prior to her death in 1956. It seems obvious that D.J.'s whiteness was a secret that my family hoped to keep and a past they wished would be forgotten, and without my uncle and Evelyn's letter, a significant part of my family history would have been lost to history. The story of D. J. Mack made me wonder about the other stories my family had concealed and if most of these stories consisted of traumas inflicted by white Americans.

D.J.'s identity and essence were stripped away from him, and the white essence that he was raised with potentially taught him to hate the Black essence he would be forced to identify with and would define his family in perpetuity. Acknowledging or celebrating a white essence that he could no longer claim would undermine his new identity as a Black man, and unsurprisingly he married a Black woman whose complexion made it impossible for his children to have an ambiguous identity or essence. The new identity that D.J. forged, the identity that was passed down for generations, included the erasure of the human stain that was our white past. This erasure was not due to an ethnocidal cultural commitment to destroy the culture of the other, but an acknowledgment of the fact that a white essence is a zero-sum identity that can only be claimed by those who can pass the one-drop rule. For D.J., apart from the pseudo-maternal relationship he kept with Mary Byrd, his whiteness amounted to a nothingness that would only hinder the new life he was forced to create. This was a whiteness he could neither claim nor use to his benefit. Whiteness might have been part of our culture at one point, but it could no longer be, and based on the hatred toward Black people that white culture instilled, it was also not a culture we should ever embrace.

I began talking to Artie more regularly to learn about the rich family history that I had never been taught, and I also started talking to my family about their childhoods. My parents, aunts, and uncles would usually talk about the "good times," and they rarely mentioned the hardships of growing up in the South during the Civil Rights Era. For years, I had wondered why my father never spoke about his experiences during the 1960s. He had never been forthcoming, and I discovered that the reason for his silence is both logical and traumatic. My father grew up in Prattville, Alabama, and was in middle school during pivotal moments of the struggle. He saw plenty of Black men who were bigger and older than him coming home beaten up, with broken bones, and he knew that he needed to stay away. He doubted his ability to physically withstand inevitable beatings.

I can see why a Black man would not want to relive and share that trauma with his own children. I could see how different his experiences might have been if he had been bigger or even just a little older; the likelihood of his being seriously hurt would have been much greater. Likewise, if he had been in elementary school, his parents might have instead sheltered him inside the house, only allowing him out into the world once desegregation was being implemented. Both of my parents lived in the middle, and I can now see how their experiences during this time have shaped their lives and mine. There was an obvious desire on both of my parents' parts not to relive the moments of trauma they witnessed, to shelter us from these stories so that we would not be instilled with a hatred toward white people as we grew up in an increasingly integrated America.

My uncle Vernon is two years older than my mother, and his experiences combatting segregation are markedly different than my parents', but like my parents he also sheltered others from the trauma he experienced in America. When we visit Charleston, we normally stay at Vernon's house, and during one family gathering my parents' generation reminisced about the terror that dominated their youth. The growth of the Black Lives Matter movement, and the increased awareness of the brutality inflicted upon people of color, made my elders more comfortable opening up about their own generational trauma. Yet despite the terror that consumed us today, the consensus remained that we should consider ourselves lucky compared to the horrors faced by their generation.

During this conversation, my uncle Vernon shared with us a story that he had never shared before. As the oldest of my mother's three siblings, he set the example and earned a full scholarship to Tuskegee College in Alabama. His siblings followed his lead and earned full scholarships to college, too. During Vernon's freshman year at Tuskegee, his class went on a field trip, and eventually the bus needed to stop for gas in rural Alabama. Upon leaving the sanctuary of their bus, which was not divided between "Whites" and "Colored," these Black students had entered into a hellscape created by white essence. Many of the students needed to use the restroom, but Alabama was still segregated at the time, and this gas station did not have a "Colored" restroom. For the women, this meant that they would just have to "hold it" until a "Colored" restroom could be found. For the boys, it was customary to walk to the backside of the building and relieve yourself. As the bus finished fueling and the students boarded the bus, my uncle and his classmates heard a gunshot and a white man yell, "These niggers need to learn some manners!" A white man had shot his classmate in the head for the "crime" of urinating behind a gas station. As everyone frantically boarded the bus, they knew that there was nothing they could do. No court in Alabama would convict this man of murder. If they confronted him, he would probably kill them too. The crying students wanted to know what they had done wrong because it was customary across the South for boys to urinate around back if there was not a "Colored" restroom. Their teacher had to tell them that it was different in Alabama, and that both girls and boys had to "hold it." To this day, my uncle wonders what happened to his classmate's body.

The murder of my uncle's classmate happened early in his college life, and he had never been away from home before. He wanted to return to Charleston, but he also feared what would happen if he returned. Everyone was so proud of him for getting a scholarship, and he might look like a failure if he came back. He also had three younger siblings who looked up to him, who wanted to go to college, and if he told them about the terror of Alabama, they may decide against getting an education and might never have the chance to leave Charleston's housing projects. My uncle decided to stay, never told this story, and instead gave his siblings as much information as he could to help them get an education and get out of Alabama alive. This story had remained buried within him for over forty years. Every generation of Black Americans has concealed these types of stories. We do not want to relive the trauma of the past and we hope that in shielding the next generation they may be able to create a more peaceful and equitable future.

When I began the next chapter of my life in Washington, D.C., I took with me those family histories I had learned during that month in Chicago, and I made sure to continue to learn even more. As a Black person in America, I was amazed at the incredible amount of effort it took to learn about my own history. Accurate Black history did not exist in conventional American textbooks, and when broaching the topic of the past within your own family, you knew that you may be unearthing a traumatic experience. I thought that I had a good understanding of my own history, but after talking with my uncle, I realized that I had known almost nothing. As I continued to learn, I recalled a phrase my uncle Artie had told me, "You can't know where you're going without knowing where you're from."

—

In 2015, I began contributing opinion columns to *The Daily Beast*, and in August of that year I penned the Trump piece about fascism that propelled me on the journey to create and eventually find the word *ethnocide*. I did not see his rhetoric as merely racist language, but as a continuation of America's ethnocidal society. I saw his words within a historical context, and my increasing awareness of my family history led me to this perspective. When I heard Trump speak I did not think of the race riots of the 1990s or the Civil Rights Movement of the 1960s. Instead, I thought about the 1860s, and the application of a 150-year analysis rather than one of thirty or sixty years radically changed my perspective. Everything became clearer and decidedly grimmer, but this is expected when the rhetoric of 2016 most parallels the experiences of your Black ancestors during the Civil War.

When Trump spoke, I did not think about the experiences of D. J. Mack. During the 1860s, D.J. was still James, and his life most likely bore almost no resemblance to that of a Black American. When Trump spoke, I thought about the Hills family line of my tree, who had lived as free persons of color in Charleston since the early 1800s.

John Hill II was born around 1790 in Kershaw, South Carolina, in the foothills of the Appalachian Mountains. (In future generations, our surname would change from Hill to Hills.) He was a mulatto, and we believe that his father was a white man named John Hill who also lived in Kershaw. Around 1809 my ancestor married Fannie Mitchell, and soon thereafter John, Fannie, and their newborn son, Nathaniel, moved to Charleston to live among the vibrant community of free persons of color that was being created on the outskirts of town. John and Fannie had two more children—Bass, born in 1813, and Jane, born in 1815—and ever since, the Hill family has had strong roots in Charleston.

Nathaniel, my grandmother Althea Hills Holmes's great-great-grandfather, grew to become a minister in Charleston, and like his father and mother, he stayed in Charleston during the Civil War. For decades, FPCs were able to live as subjugated but "free" people in Charleston. So long as they did not foment rebellion and try to change Charleston's ethnocidal status quo, they could live within a social class that was above enslavement, though the prospect of enslavement or death was never far away.

In 1822, Denmark Vesey, a formerly enslaved man who won his freedom in a slave lottery, organized one of the largest slave rebellions in American history, but on the eve of the assault the secret of the planned rebellion was revealed. Vesey had planned on killing slave owners in the city of Charleston and surrounding plantations, liberating enslaved people, and setting sail for Haiti. By some accounts, thousands of slaves and FPCs would have launched the revolt, and Vesey had been planning and organizing the rebellion for years.

Many French slave owners sought refuge in the port city of Charleston when they fled Haiti during the Haitian Revolution, and the narrative of a liberated island of African people had permeated throughout the Black community. Free and enslaved Blacks in Charleston knew about Haitian freedom, and they wanted not only to replicate that freedom in America, but to assist Haitians in their continued fight for freedom. The growing language of freedom spreading throughout the Black community in Charleston enraged the ethnocidal white community, and the Haitian Revolution further galvanized their commitment to suppressing Black freedom. Prior to the Haitian Revolution, the essence-driven stupidity of these white ethnociders made them believe that Black people were incapable of winning their freedom, or that they enjoyed a life of subjugation, but now they could clearly see that a successful rebellion was a legitimate possibility.

On June 22, 1822, after learning of the planned rebellion, white Charlestonians sent the militia to capture Vesey and other freedom fighters. Vesey was an important figure in Charleston's FPC community and was one of the founders of an African Methodist Episcopal (AME) church in Charleston. The AME was the first fully independent Black denomination in the United States. Previously, Black Americans who worshipped in white-dominated churches were forced to practice a religion of subjugation where they were relegated to the back of the church or the basement, or were forced to practice their faith at the odd hours when whites were not around. Even when Black Americans organized their own churches, white churches attempted to exert control and authority. The creation of the AME Church in 1816 gave Black Americans total control over how and when they could worship. The AME Church was first founded in Pennsylvania, New Jersey, Delaware, and Maryland, but by 1818 it had spread to Charleston. For decades, FPCs had worshipped in white churches in Charleston, but when a white congregation in 1818 built a garage for their hearse atop a Black cemetery, the outraged FPC community realized that they needed to form their own church. Nearly two thousand FPCs left their white churches and created their own AME church in Charleston. Vesey's church would grow to become Emanuel "Mother Emanuel" AME Church. Emanuel today remains a pillar of the Black community in Charleston, and on June 17, 2015, the racist white terrorist Dylann Roof entered the church and killed nine church members during a Bible study class.

After being captured, Vesey and five enslaved men were sentenced to death after a farcical show trial whose outcome was known before it started. On July 2, 1822, Vesey and the five enslaved men were hanged in the town square. Soon thereafter twenty-nine more men were executed and hanged, and other suspects, including Vesey's son Sandy, were deported from the United States. Following the executions, a white mob burned the AME church to the ground, and from 1822 until after the Civil War, the church sustained itself by meeting in secret. Only after the Civil War did it officially become the Emanuel AME we know today.

The rumored date for Vesey's rebellion was July 14, which the French refer to as Bastille Day. His planned rebellion was inspired by the French Revolution, the Haitian Revolution, and the fight for religious freedom among Black Christians in America. None of these narratives for freedom could coexist in the South, and Vesey was killed to sustain white ethnocide. Roof's terrorism in 2015 is not dissimilar from the terrorism of 1822, and

Trump's rhetoric is a continuation of America's oppressive, ethnocidal norm. When Trump spoke about deporting immigrants and people of color, and demanding that people show their papers, I thought about the deportations of Vesey's freedom fighters, and I specifically thought about my ancestor Nathaniel Edward Hills, the son of Rev. Nathaniel Hill, and his trials and tribulations during the Civil War.

—

The Civil War started on April 12, 1861, when the Confederate Army fired upon Union troops stationed at Fort Sumter, an island fort off the coast of Charleston. Following South Carolina's declaration of secession on December 20, 1860, the state's militia and government authorities had demanded that the U.S. Army abandon its facilities in Charleston Harbor. Six days later, due to increased tension between the U.S. Army and South Carolina's militia, the military secretly relocated to Fort Sumter. On April 12, after food and supplies had already run low, Confederate soldiers (the Confederate Army was created in February 1861) began bombarding Fort Sumter with artillery fire. By the next day, April 13, the Union troops at Fort Sumter surrendered because they had run out of supplies, exhausted their ammunition, and could not withstand the shelling. All in all, the Southern state with the highest percentage of enslaved people responded to the election of Abraham Lincoln by attempting to starve and kill the Americans that could potentially give these Black Americans rights. It represented an expulsion of civility and a celebration of barbarity.

In many ways, Fort Sumter symbolizes the narrative battle America has always engaged in with white supremacy. White Americans start a conflict and elevate an uncivil way of life, but then attempt to win the narrative war to disguise their incivility. They work to depict their immorality as moral victories and their moronic losers as heroic martyrs who should be lionized and remembered. Fort Sumter was a sad show of force, but it inspired a society of racists to wage terror against humanity so they could continue their inhumane way of life. The best way to counter the inhumanity of the ethnocidal South, and the ethnocider, is to learn as much as you can about the humanity of the oppressed people of the South.

In Charleston, FPCs were supposed to carry papers proving their freedom, but after decades of being registered on the census as an FPC, it was common for many to leave home without such documentation. Also, there were many pathways to becoming an FPC. You could be a mulatto like John Hill II, who moved to Charleston by his own free will around the founding of this nation. You could be an old slave no longer physically capable of engaging in the backbreaking labor of harvesting rice, and whose slave owner has decided that killing you would be more of a hassle than simply letting you go free. You could be like Denmark Vesey and win your freedom via lottery. You could be a slave who escaped to the Sea Islands off the coast of Charleston and now lives as a free person on the almost exclusively Black islands. As such, FPC and enslaved communities were both distinct and interwoven. It was also common for an FPC to save up their money to buy the freedom of a family member or friend. In America's immoral society the notion of "freedom" still came with ownership. When an FPC bought the "freedom" of an enslaved Black person, they actually bought the right to own that person. The acts of transferring ownership and granting freedom were two completely different things. Within the FPC community it was common for a free Black man to technically own some of his friends and family members. Charleston cared more about ensuring that the Black community, both free and enslaved, knew their place and did not foment rebellion, but all of this changed during the years leading up to the Civil War.

As tensions grew following *Dred Scott*, white Charlestonians soon started demanding that FPCs always have their papers on their person. If FPCs were found to not have proper documentation, they were assumed to be runaway slaves. Additionally, the fact that it was illegal to educate Black people in the South meant that not all FPCs were literate. Most FPCs learned how to read either by leaving the South to obtain education in the North, or were secretly taught how to read and write by other FPCs. Educating Blacks had long been illegal in the South, and even when FPCs had proper documentation, white militias felt empowered to discredit its legitimacy. If an FPC could not read and articulate exactly what their papers said, ethnocidal white Southerners would claim the documentation was fraudulent, declare that this free person was instead a runaway slave, and arrest them. This dynamic is a corruption of language that America still suffers from today.

Within ethnocide, words cease to have any meaning. If a Black person speaks the truth—"These papers prove my freedom"—a white Southerner has the power to declare that the words have an alternate meaning that suits their purpose. Words no longer have a denotation and instead only have a connotation that is determined by the whims of ethnocidal white oppressors. As with the master-slave dialectic, there is no longer a discourse for finding truth, and only one for sustaining the power of the master.

Without the potential for truth, laws and governmental structures have no legitimacy, and corruption and untruths are the foundation of society. Trump's corruption of language extends from professing facts as "fake news" to his surrogates' constant "spinning" to proclaim that his words are not in fact what the denotation states, but are instead the connotations that his sycophants proclaim. Trump, his words, and his supporters are the progeny of the ethnocidal philosophy and culture of the South and American colonialism. Additionally, standards of Southern "policing" still hold true today. Law enforcement in the South never existed to protect everyone, but instead to sustain white ethnocidal society by terrorizing the other and denying the other of their freedoms such that the ethnocider may profit from their bodies. In 2015, Trump's rhetoric reminded me of the terror that befell my ancestors, and in 2020, the murder of George Floyd and the chants of defunding the police made America's centuries-long dystopian norm all the more apparent.

When doublethink becomes the norm, we live in a society where people do not know how to think. There is no dialectic for finding truth, only one for crushing souls, and thoughts become meaningless. *Geistmord* becomes the norm; soulless language the only means of communication. The thoughtless Pozzos own the "thinking hat" and profess the authenticity of their bad faith. A pathetic battle at Fort Sumter committed to starving and killing Americans who fight for freedom becomes a heroic battle that launches a war, a region of America known for slavery becomes celebrated for its hospitality, and Confederate traitors become national heroes. None of us should be surprised that George Orwell's inspiration for *1984* stemmed from his experiences as an officer in the Indian Imperial Police in Burma. He wrote about a dystopia in which he lived and was paid to perpetuate. The dystopian methods British colonizers used to oppress and divide Indian people are a trademark of colonization, and these methods have clearly shaped the United States too. Mahatma Gandhi's nonviolent resistance movement, Satyagraha, which means "holding on to truth" or "truth force" in Sanskrit, both defeated British colonialism in India and inspired Martin Luther King Jr.'s philosophy of nonviolence in the United States. In a soul-crushing society that actively destroys the truth, "holding on to truth" can be a revolutionary act.

As Charleston denied my ancestors freedom of movement by demanding that they show their papers, South Carolina also made it illegal for Black people to leave the state. If Confederates were about to launch a war to continue slavery, Southerners were definitely not going to allow Black people, free or enslaved, to leave easily. As a result, smuggling FPCs out of the state became a lucrative business that forced many FPCs to sell almost all their belongings for a one-way ticket out. Due to the growing terror, Nathaniel Edward and his brother John decided that they had to leave the state. Between August 1860 and April 1861, the Hills brothers found themselves on a ship headed to Haiti. Their parents stayed in the city and hoped to weather the storm of the Civil War. Nathaniel Edward and John set sail to freedom to the very place Vesey dreamed of taking our people forty years earlier.

After arriving in Haiti, Nathaniel Edward and John stayed for about a year and a half. We are unsure of how long they had originally planned on staying in Haiti, but it is certain that Haiti afforded them more freedom than America. Not only did Haiti provide more freedom, but the journey gave them a safer passage to freedom. Successfully traveling from Charleston to the North by land would have been nearly impossible with the threat of being caught and forced into slavery. The Atlantic Ocean provided them with a security that was impossible to find in America.

While in Haiti, Nathaniel Edward and John had been following the progress of the Civil War, and when news of the Emancipation Proclamation arrived, they determined they could return home. Soon thereafter, Nathaniel Edward and John sailed to the United States, but not to Charleston. In the spring of 1863, the brothers arrived in New York City, and in April of that year they enlisted in the Union Army. After the war, Nathaniel Edward moved to Brooklyn and started a family. John, as the oldest son, returned to Charleston to look after their parents, Nathaniel and Rose, and work alongside his father in their carpentry business. Nathaniel Sr. and Rose had stayed in Charleston throughout the war, and they needed help rebuilding their business. By the mid-1870s, Nathaniel Edward had returned to Charleston with his family, and I am one of his descendants.

My ancestors were freedom fighters, and they were only some of the many freedom fighters within the Black community. Our culture has been defined by the persistent fight for freedom, but America prefers to not tell these stories. And it certainly does not want these stories to define America, instead stigmatizing and demonizing the struggle. Black freedom fighters are cast as disruptors of the peace—terrorists. Likewise, non-white immigrants who come to America for freedom—just like the freedom my ancestors hoped to find in Haiti—are labeled "illegal," forced to show their papers, held in inhumane detention centers, and have their families ripped apart via government policies. Then-candidate Trump's demonizing and dehumanizing rhetoric toward Latinos and communities of color made me think about the Hills family and their generational struggle for freedom as free persons of color. They had a life of "freedom" without freedom. Through an Orwellian lens you could say that Big Brother—America's white ethnocidal culture—professed the narrative of FREEDOM IS SUBJUGATION. America tolerated people of color so long as they "knew their place," and American *mauvaise foi* promised a freedom to people of color that it never intended to allow.

The presidency of Barack Obama was a manifestation of Black people no longer "knowing their place," and rather quickly the Black experience in America started becoming our new cultural narrative. President Obama soon became the most respected man in America, and accordingly, ethnocidal Republicans sought to cripple his presidency and challenge his legitimacy to even hold office in the hope of preventing a shift in the American narrative. Trump's rise represented the continued response of white ethnocidal culture; a white *poshlyi* landowner who challenged Obama's legitimacy was the ideal ethnocidal rebuttal. Under Obama, America appeared capable of *Aufhebung* and transcending the limitations of ethnocide, but America's authoritarian status quo refused to go down without a fight.

As a Black American I felt and understood this regressive American trajectory. In 2008, my grandfather Arthur Leon Holmes was a staunch Hillary Clinton supporter despite being a big fan of Obama. He did not believe that white America would allow a Black person to become president. Supporting Obama, in his mind, equated to wasting his vote, and unnecessarily getting his hopes up before they inevitably came crashing down. My grandfather fought in World War II and the Korean War, and he lived through all of the assassinations and terror of the Civil Rights Era of the 1960s, so his understanding of how America could crush Black dreams was founded on lived experiences. When we spoke during the 2008 primaries, I knew that I could not fault his logic, but I hoped he would be proven wrong. After Obama won the Democratic presidential nomination, my grandfather became a staunch Obama supporter, and he lived to see Obama become president, which had been literally beyond his wildest imagination. Throughout Obama's presidency there was a rarely articulated yet constantly felt concern within the Black community that white America would find a way to take him away. America's *letzter Menschen* would inevitably try to destroy our *Übermensch*, and we feared that they may succeed.

By applying a longer perspective to the American narrative, encompassing centuries and not decades, and focusing on the lives of Black and not white Americans, I found a new language for articulating the history and trajectory of America. The language countered America's usual narrative of progress, and provided words for what I had always seen but struggled to say—namely the systematic, generational terror inflicted upon my people. By focusing on Black life, I could see the American Cycle. White ethnocidal America wants no one to see the American Cycle.

—

The narrative and culture of the ethnocidee is a paradox, because despite being the true narrative of their society, it is still the narrative of a dystopian society. One can take pride in articulating the narrative of a nightmare, but the end goal must be rectifying the nightmare. Eloquently proclaiming a nightmarish existence does not remedy the problem, and the Gullah Geechee song "Kum Ba Yah" demonstrates how, within an ethnocidal society, the ethnocider is ill-equipped to even understand the truth-filled language of the ethnocidee.

Gullah Geechee people hail from the coasts of South Carolina and Georgia, and stretching into the northern coasts of Florida and the southern coasts of North Carolina. My Charlestonian family is all Gullah. I am Gullah. Gullah people descend from African people who were brought over by the slave trade, but upon arriving in Charleston or Savannah, were able to escape bondage and find refuge on the many small, hard-to-access islands off the coast. On the Sea Islands Gullah people could retain many of their African customs and mix many disparate African traditions into a new cultural tapestry in the Americas. Many Gullah people also escaped to the mainland and formed vibrant communities of free people. Gullah people had a freedom that few Blacks in America could ever cultivate. There are countless stories of escaped slaves being captured on the shore and weeping as they gazed into the ocean, realizing there was no escaping American terror. Gullah people saw islands in the distance and swam to freedom. Because they were able to keep more of their African roots, Gullah people commonly speak with a Caribbean-sounding cadence. People have always thought my mother is Jamaican, and she pronounces my name as "Bah-rhett" and not the Anglicized "Bear-ett." However, the freedom of the Sea Islands did not shield Gullah people from ethnocidal terror, and this perpetual threat created "Kum Ba Yah."

In Gullah English, *kum ba yah* means "come by here," and the song implored God to "come by here" to help rescue Gullah people from ethnocidal terror. However, upon hearing this Gullah spiritual, white people did not understand its meaning, enchanted instead by the cadence. "Kum Ba Yah" became "Kumbaya," and the white-dominated meaning of the song came to symbolize peace and harmony. The radical shift in meaning shows how far removed from reality an essence-based, ethnocidal culture can indoctrinate the ethnocider. Eventually, white Americans even encouraged Black Americans to sing the white rendition of "Kumbaya." Think about the normalized insanity of this scenario. The ethnocidee is now being encouraged to sing a stolen manifestation of their own culture as a sign of progress and equality. "Kumbaya" does not represent a malicious theft, but it does show how the narrative of the ethnocider has a greater connection to dominance than truth, and this destroys the legitimacy of their narratives.

The narrative and the culture of the ethnocidee is grounded in truth. Their existence is not founded upon dominance and the extraction of another's culture. They must create a sustainable culture, though the ever-present danger isn't posed by the North Sea as in *polderen*; the danger comes from white ethnociders who live in fear of non-white people existing as anything more than subjugated bodies. White ethnociders may burn our towns and churches to the ground, poison our water in Flint, Michigan, and let the levees break in New Orleans, but we survive. The threat to our existence does not come from nature. It comes from a culture of people who have made terrorism an integral part of their nature. Terror is their essence. American police and militias in the South were created to capture and terrorize runaway slaves, American courts sentence Black Americans to death for fighting for their freedom, and today American police and white vigilantes kill Black people for exercising their freedoms. The Black Lives Matter movement is an act of rebellion and revolution akin to Denmark Vesey's and countless other slave rebellions. It is an act of liberation against ethnocidal oppression, and the ethnocider risks their life to suppress these rebellions because their way of life cannot exist without oppression.

The white ethnocider uses lethal force to sustain their ethnocidal way of life because their concept of existence has nothing to do with existence and everything to do with essence. Black, or non-white, existence within a space that they believe they own creates an essentialist crisis because white essence is a zero-sum identity. You cannot be partially white and still white. You may be able to pass as white, but passing as white means that you are not white. The one-drop rule created by ethnocidal white colonizers and the founders of the United States of America meant that anything non-European on a continent that is not Europe was a threat to their essence. Black people demanding equality is a profound threat to white essence.

My ancestor D. J. Mack was no longer white nor even partially white once the secret of his Black mother was revealed. James Byrd passed as white, but was never white. D. J. Mack rebirthed a Black lineage that might have disappeared via James Byrd following generations of white men raping and impregnating Black women. Obama became America's first Black president and not our first mixed-race president. His was not a narrative of a harmonious mixing of Black and white people, but instead of the equitable rising of Black people and the erasure of whiteness. The erasure of whiteness was not due to an intentional act of terror akin to the ethnocider, but merely the inevitable, natural outcome of human existence preceding white essence. Because white essence is based on preventing *Aufhebung*, his existence transcended his whiteness, and by transcending whiteness by having Black blood, he is emancipated from an untranscendent white identity. The identity that white people in America created for themselves means that they will be perpetually at war with existence. The only way white essence could prevail in the perpetual war with existence that white people have created for themselves would be by defeating existence. The destruction of everything is *omnicide*. They aspire to be the literal Last Men, *letzter Menschen*, before we all fall into the oblivion they have created. It is a cultural suicide mission.

For the ethnocidee, the capacity to survive and create culture despite the persistent threat of ethnocidal terror creates a resilient, dynamic, and beautiful culture; but it must not be forgotten that this culture is born from tragedy. Ethnociders have created a culture built upon profiting from the destruction of culture, and the cultural icons of American society come from the ethnocidee and not the ethnocider. Both Barack and Michelle Obama remain cultural icons celebrated around the world. Martin Luther King Jr. and Malcolm X remain iconic American figures. When we discuss sports and entertainment, Black Americans are also in the pantheon of American culture. Michael Jordan remains the most famous athlete in the world. In 2020, the entire world mourned the death of Kobe Bryant. Beyoncé is arguably the biggest pop star in the world, and hip-hop remains one of America's greatest cultural exports. Chadwick Boseman's death, too, reverberated around the world.

The paradox of the ethnocidee's celebrated cultural icons centers on the fact that their lofty status is commonly depicted as a sign of equality and opportunity within America's ethnocidal society, when in fact it is the opposite. The culture of non-white people in America is used to fill the soulless cultural void that ethnocide creates, and normally cultural appropriation helps fill the void. "Kumbaya" helps the ethnocider feel peaceful and harmonious as they fall into the abyss. When total appropriation and erasure are not possible, Black Americans become these iconic figures, yet once they reach the top they are pressured to profess the "beauty" of American life and refrain from telling their cultural stories. Colin Kaepernick takes a knee during the national anthem to raise awareness of police brutality and systemic racism, and the NFL forces him out of the league. LeBron James speaks about Black Lives Matter, and Laura Ingraham and other ethno-cidal Americans tell him to "shut up and dribble." Muhammad Ali refuses to fight in the "white man's war" in Vietnam, and he is sentenced to jail. America's Black cultural icons fill America's cultural void, but once they are celebrated, they are incentivized to remain silent or propagate white society's ethnocidal narrative, and punished when they speak the truth. To retain their wealth and livelihood, they are encouraged to tell lies, become a lie, and live in bad faith. They are incentivized to consume culture, and as the ethnocidee this means that they are prone to devouring themselves. This devouring is different than the ethnocider's destruction because the ethnocider has already destroyed their own soul, and they slowly die as they destroy the world around them. It is the *poshlyi* turning to alcohol and becoming depressed once they have to work because the deaths of their serfs means they no longer know how to "live." The ethnocidee, however, cultivates his individual and collective soul. He rises to the top by having an existence filled with *Geist*, but then he destroys his own soul in order to curry favor with the soulless, *poshlyi* ethnocider. The end goal of ethnocide, despite the ethnocider's myopia, is the destruction of the ethnocider and the ethnocidee as the ethnocider wages a perpetual war against existence. As the ethnocidee, the goal must be to always reach America's cultural pantheon, continue to tell the true story of your people, and then profess a new American narrative that exists beyond the shackles of ethnocidal op-pression. They must embrace, defend, and fight for existence.

Articulating the post-ethnocidal narrative is the most difficult obsta-cle, because America only knows ethnocide. How do you articulate the necessity of a world that Americans have never lived and struggle to even imagine? If you have only known an abusive relationship, it may be easy to articulate the need for the abuse to stop, but it is much harder to imagine, create, and sustain a relationship without abuse. One has to emancipate oneself from abuse, and this applies to both the abuser and the abused, yet the onus normally falls upon the abused to instigate change. This is the dilemma of the ethnocidee. In addition to creating a culture that they can be proud of within ethnocide, there is also a greater need to create a culture that can exist beyond ethnocide. The journey toward a post-ethnocidal existence has always been shaped by the lives and identity of African Diaspora people. Through understanding the American Cycle, it becomes clear how America's brief eras of Reconstruction play a decisive role in cultivating a post-ethnocidal society.

—

The Civil War began with the threat of Black emancipation once the abolitionist Republican Party controlled the White House, and the Civil War and Reconstruction commenced emancipation. Reconstruction aspired to create an equitable society, and equality is post-ethnocidal. However, as the American Cycle shows, America enjoys the idea of equality, but has never had the stomach to implement it once it becomes obvious that equality would dismantle white dominance. America's reluctance to fulfill its promise of equality does not erase the desire of the ethnocidee to forge a new culture, identity, and essence beyond the shackles of ethnocide, and a key component of this emancipatory shift are the new names that the ethnocidees call themselves.

Under ethnocide, the identity of the ethnocidee is no longer self-determined but becomes an identity forced upon them. The identity that the ethnocider creates has no attachment to place, and instead denotes their lower station within a dystopian ethnocidal world. There is no place called Nigger, Negro, Coon, Colored, or Black; but ethnociders forced these identities upon African people in the Americas. Under ethnocide, the ethnociders actively work to prevent the ethnocidee from having the capacity to self-identify. Therefore, one of the first emancipatory acts of the ethnocidee is the act of naming oneself.

Prior to emancipation most Black Americans had last names that came from a slave owner. FPCs might have had last names that did not derive from a slave owner, but no Black Americans were able to keep African names. Within my own family, we know that D. J. Mack's mother was named Charlotte, but we have less certainty about her last name. She was owned by the Stevenson family and traveled with Mary Stevenson to live with George Washington Byrd, so we list her last name as Stevenson. We know that she might have never been given a last name and that it is unjust to identify her with the family who owned her, but as of now it is only an adequate placeholder. Maybe it would be better if we gave her a new last name, and maybe it makes more sense to leave it blank to demonstrate the inhumanity of American society. We do not know the correct solution, but we do know that her son was neither a Stevenson nor a Byrd. By being ex-pelled from the white community, D.J. was forced to emancipate himself, and in doing so, he gave himself and future generations a new last name.

D. J. Mack created his new familial identity after the fall of Recon-struction, but the identity and last names of many other Black Americans radically changed during the Civil War and throughout Reconstruction. Emancipation meant that Black Americans were no longer tethered to the identity of their white oppressors, and during this era the last names "Free-man" and "Freedman" started popping up all across the South. Freedom became the new identity of countless Black Americans. The identity of Black people in America has always been a quest to free themselves from ethnocidal oppression in both action and identity. The linguistic progres-sion from *nigger* to *negro* to *colored* to *African American* to *Black* displays a generational endeavor of African Diaspora people to identify with language that has less and less connection to ethnocide, and a greater connection to Black freedom and equality.

This linguistic progression manifests in numerous ways within the Black community. Members of the Nation of Islam and other American Islamic practices often emancipate themselves from their American names: taking on Islamic names or replacing their last name with an X. Black families give their children African, "African-sounding," and foreign-sounding names to forge this connection to the freer cultures that exist beyond America. American society has spent a long time ridiculing Black Americans for these "ethnic" names, and studies show that people with Black-sounding names are less likely to get job interviews. In an ethnocidal society, anything perceived as Black, or from the ethnocidee, becomes devalued so that the ethnocider can profit off of its exploitation. Barack Obama is an American with an African-sounding name who many Americans did not believe should be able to get the job he desired because of his Black essence. His name signaled an emancipation from ethnocidal identifiers, and the fact that he was raised by a white mother showed the possibility of white people both emancipating themselves from ethnocide and cultivating a white essence compatible with equality, while also cultivating Black existence. This cultural progression toward equality was only made possible following the *Loving v. Virginia* decision in 1967 that overturned the ban on interracial marriage in America. Obama's presidency heralded a profound societal and cultural shift toward existence and away from essence that America had not experienced since Reconstruction. The second era of Reconstruction gave more and more Black Americans and other ethnocidees the confidence to tell their stories and take their existence to new horizons.

In 2008, I canvassed for Obama during the South Carolina primary, and in Georgia I volunteered for his campaign. After his victory, I felt a greater desire to do more with my life, so I left home and went to journalism school at Northwestern University in Evanston, Illinois. I visited his house in Chicago. When I finished school, I moved to Washington, D.C. When I had finished undergrad six years earlier, I had no interest in our nation's capital, but it was now a completely different city. I had friends there, and it seemed like the perfect environment to start a journalism career with a focus on politics. I found a place to live not far from Howard University, and whenever I had a particularly bad day at work I would walk by the White House to raise my spirits. Without anyone giving a command or making a declaration, my life became more proactive and less reactive.

As I left home and worked to create a new path for myself, I needed to learn the stories of my ancestors to give me strength, comfort, and guidance. I spent more time speaking to my parents about their childhoods and the traumas inflicted upon them by an ethnocidal white America. More and more Black Americans felt comfortable talking about the abuses we suffered in the present because we knew that America's Black president would listen to our stories. When I would visit my parents in Marietta, photos of the First Family adorned our house and were positioned as if they were part of our own family. Having a "family member" in the White House made us more confident to speak our truth and chart an existence beyond ethnocide. The Black Lives Matter movement, starting from the murder of Trayvon Martin to the murder of George Floyd and the other unjust deaths that will occur between the finishing of this book and its publication, emerged because the Black community knew that the most powerful man in America not only would listen to our cries but understood our anguish. After Obama left office, the movement had to readjust to a Trump presidency that wanted to silence our voice, but we knew we needed to continue to speak and make people see American ethnocide so that the next president would listen. After Dylann Roof killed Reverend Clementa Pinckney, Cynthia Marie Graham Hurd, Susie Jackson, Ethel Lee Lance, Depayne Middleton-Doctor,

Tywanza Sanders, Daniel L. Simmons, Sharonda Coleman-Singleton, and Myra Thompson at Mother Emanuel AME Church, Obama paid his respects and sang "Amazing Grace" from the pulpit. He was part of our family, understood our trauma, and knew the tragic, resilient, and beautiful traditions we have created to cope with the inevitability of white ethnocidal terror.

The terror that befalls Black people today is the same as countless days before, except now our cultural authority allows us to tell our narrative. Our tragic story is the true story of America. The American language of freedom and emancipation originates from the ethnocidee. Our existence in America has always been about liberating ourselves from ethnocidal oppression.

11

BETTER THAN UTOPIA

When I found I had crossed that line, I looked at my hands to see if I was the same person. There was such a glory over everything.

HARRIET TUBMAN

After finishing undergrad and deciding not to pursue a career in political science, I took an unexpected professional trajectory and started working in film production. I took a camera along when I studied abroad in France during my senior year, and I decided to try to make a film. I enjoyed the undertaking, and the French department at my school enjoyed my finished film, so I decided to try my hand at film production after graduation. I had no clear goal during my foray into film, but I instantly took to the process of filmmaking. During film production a small society of talented, creative, and hardworking people comes together. Making a film consumes your entire life. You work a minimum of twelve hours a day, five days a week. You eat breakfast, lunch, and sometimes dinner on the set. While you are working on set everything you do matters, and the outside world is temporarily put on hold. You are only there because you provide a skill essential to the completion of the film; therefore, you need to be able to consistently perform that skill. There is a lot of pressure, but it is a helpful pressure.

Everything is meticulously planned, but reality means that rarely does the plan unfurl exactly as detailed. Sometimes it takes longer than we expect to get the shot that we need, and this impacts the course of an entire day. Sometimes the weather forecast is wrong, and it rains on a day that was predicted to be sunny and the schedule is filled with exterior shots. Now the production crew must completely readjust the shooting schedule. On film sets I learned about the necessity of planning in order to achieve your goals, but also the importance of being able to make new plans when life requires change. An inability to adapt and change when confronted by existence would quickly ruin a movie.

All of us were there because we wanted to make a great film. Obviously, it was also our job and we needed the money, and plenty of the projects that I worked on were not masterpieces. Working on a boring commercial, television show, music video, or film was normal, but these projects were tinged with disappointment. Nobody had this job because it was just a job. We had our jobs because we wanted to be a part of creating art and beauty, and we existed as a mini-society for this explicit purpose. On set I loved hearing the director of photography say, "Fly out this wall," and then some grips would expeditiously arrive and completely remove a wall. Film sets are filled with phrases that are entirely normal and casual within this environment, but would be outrageous at a job where the same level of creativity and boldness is not embraced.

On one of the films that I worked on, an extra—a person hired to stand in the background of a shot—turned out to be a girl with whom I went to elementary school. I was on set buzzing around to prepare for the next shot, and she called out my name. Turns out she was married and with a couple of kids, and this was the first time she had ever been an extra. The job was a nice break from parenting, and she loved being an extra. During one of our conversations on set she told me how my mother's art classes during elementary school had sparked her interest in art, and that she still draws and paints when she gets a chance. The creativity that my mother inspired might have helped lead her to the film set where I was working nearly two decades later. In the good place that a film set aspired to be, not only did the environment need to be creative, but it also needed to be welcoming even to the passengers who would only be there for part of the ride. Their role in the process might be small, but it was still essential. Also, the stories, friendships, and creativity that the experience on a set could cultivate would last far beyond the finite process of making a movie.

I also enjoyed how the production office disappeared at the end of film production. For months, this office existed to answer almost all of my questions and distribute my paychecks. But suddenly the phone number no longer worked, the office was vacant, and the world that you were a part of had officially ended. I could now do whatever I wanted and had no obligation to be anywhere except to swing by my parents' house in the Atlanta suburbs about once a week. One world had ended and now I had to create a new world. Sometimes after a project ended, I would immediately try to find the next production in town, and other times I would take a month or so off from working. For a couple of years, I even signed up to be a substitute teacher to ensure I had at least something to do between jobs. If I had done a good job on the last project and kept in touch with the people on the film, another opportunity would eventually show up, and when it did I would jump back into a society specifically created to make something beautiful.

The normalized creativity and effort that existed on film sets snapped me out of the bland norms of typical American life. I needed an escape from ethnocide, and film provided that for a while, but obviously it was not a complete escape. There were jobs where they tried to not pay me, and far too many productions relied too heavily on unpaid interns. I primarily worked in film in Atlanta, and whenever we had productions in the more rural parts of the state I could see how ethnocide had shaped the landscape of the entire region.

During one commercial shoot in Monticello, Georgia—pronounced "mont-i-sell-o" and not the same Italian pronunciation as Thomas Jefferson's slaveholding plantation "mont-i-chell-o"—I noticed railroad tracks bisecting the town. We were shooting on the side of the tracks where all the white people lived. There was a small city center with a general store and shops. The public high school was also on this side of town. Everything you needed was on this side of the tracks. The other side looked more run-down, there was no reason to venture over there, and this is where the Black people lived. I had this job far before I knew the word *ethnocide*, but as I looked at this town I saw its manifestation. I did not receive any racist abuse in the white part of town, and everyone I interacted with was nice and polite, but everyone was polite within a framework of systemic division that should never be considered normal. The town was "united" by a dividing line, and it was created with the intent to normalize and perpetuate systemic division. In America, we use the phrase "the wrong side of the tracks" to refer to the "bad people" who live there, but we never talk about how these "bad people" are just Black or other people of color, and not bad at all. We do not talk about how America intentionally imported these "bad people" and then defined them as bad because they have always been unwilling to accept a life as oppressed people. The "bad" that emanates from "the wrong side of the tracks" is a Black existence that challenges ethnocide.

After this job, I thought about how ethnocide—though I didn't know its name—did not simply manifest in our human interactions, but how it shaped the entire social structure of the South. Cities were built around dividing lines, and these cities were the remnants of old plantations. The South lagged behind the North in industrialization because there was very little desire to build machines when the South had already created a society committed to turning Black people into machines. The South does not have large industrial port cities like the North, because human beings were a primary import and large warehouses were not needed to store people for months as you would with grains and other commodities. You get them off the boat as quickly as possible, make them look as healthy as they can be so that you can get top dollar, and then you send them into the divided, ethnocidal landscape to continue the process of dehumanization. This atrocity required only a small market with a stage to present the human merchandise. Over time, once the slave trade ended, this market was repurposed into something more palatable and less overtly dystopian. Even after Congress abolished the importation of slaves to America in 1807, the domestic slave trade remained until the end of the Civil War, and America had already built towns and infrastructure committed to sustaining ethnocidal division. My experience working in film inclined me to begin to imagine what a good place that exceeded my dystopian American norm could look like, and the importance of this exploration grew in significance as I examined ethnocide in America.

—

In 1516—twenty-four years after Christopher Columbus landed in what is now called the Bahamas—Sir Thomas More, a celebrated British statesman, philosopher, and Catholic theologian, published a satirical novel in Latin titled *De optimo reipublicae statu, deque nova insula Utopia* (Of a Republic's Best State, and the New Island of Utopia). Today, we simply refer to More's book as *Utopia*, and after its publication, Europe began dreaming about the good places they could erect in the New World.

The structure of the book is fairly straightforward and consists of a long conversation between More—he wrote himself into his novel—and a fictional adventurer named Raphael Hythlodaeus who had sailed to South America with Amerigo Vespucci. Colonization is at the heart of the novel, and the fictional republic of Utopia is essentially a colony unattached to Europe. Throughout the novel Hythlodaeus describes the social structure of Utopia to More. More is positioned as the listener in his own novel, and this structure allows him to not be personally attached to any of Hythlodaeus's controversial ideas. For example, in the fictional republic of Utopia, priests are allowed to marry, euthanasia is permissible by the state, divorce is allowed, and the many religions in Utopia are tolerated and live peacefully together. As an influential Catholic, More could have been excommunicated if he had openly expressed a belief in allowing priests to marry. More was a devout Catholic, but decided to not pursue monastic life and the priesthood in order to marry. (In 2000, Pope John Paul II declared More the patron saint of statesmen and politicians.) Additionally, his stance on religious tolerance runs counter to his criticism of Protestantism as it spread across Europe. In 1517, Martin Luther wrote his *Ninety-five Theses* and the Protestant Reformation was born. Utopia also provided a robust welfare state with free health care, and people have questioned if More held Communist beliefs. Marx would not invent Communism for another three hundred years, so it would be more accurate to say that More understood the importance of a social safety net and so did Marx. To this day, people still question if More held the beliefs expressed by Hythlodaeus. However, with regard to ethnocide, the most significant aspects of the book are the exclusion and forced assimilation of Indigenous people in Utopian society, the normalization of slavery (every household had two slaves), and the language More created and used throughout the book.

Despite being first published in Latin in 1516, *Utopia* was not published in English until 1551—sixteen years after More's death. It's a book written in Latin, structured to obfuscate the author's intent, and heavily reliant on the author's Greek-based neologisms—but this does not even begin to address the complexities of translation. More, once a trusted advisor of King Henry VIII, was executed for treason in 1535 for refusing to support the annulment of Henry's marriage to Catherine of Aragon and Henry's role as the supreme leader of the newly created Protestant Church of England. One could argue that More was killed for his objections to divorce and religious tolerance, so why would he profess that a utopian republic would have both? Because he was executed before the book was translated into English, More was never able to express his true opinion to the English-speaking world.

Additionally, More's new Greek words often meant the opposite of what a reader might think. For example, Hythlodaeus's last name roughly translates as "dispenser of nonsense." In English translations, the character is commonly known as Raphael Nonsenso. The man who tells the fictional More and authentic Europe about Utopia exists to spew nonsense. There is a river in Utopia called *Anydrus*, meaning "no water," and the unofficial title for a mayor and the class of intelligentsia in Utopia is *Ademus*, meaning "no people." However, the biggest example of this linguistic nonsense, which some people interpret as wit, is the title of the book. *Utopia* means "nonexistent good place," and this runs entirely counter to the idyllic, perfect, or good place that most people believe it means.

More fabricated the word *utopia* by combining the Greek prefixes *eu-*, meaning "good," and *ou-*, meaning "not," with the Greek word *topos* or *topia*, meaning "place." More dropped the *e* from *eu-* and the *o* from *ou-* and added the remaining *u-* to create *utopia*, meaning "not good place" or "nonexistent good place." Some scholars shorten the meaning to "no place," but I disagree with this translation for two reasons. If More wanted the word to simply mean "no place" he would have used the prefix *a-*, meaning "not" or "no," and named it *Atopia* just as he did with *Anydrus* and *Ademus*. More obviously wanted to coin a pun from the Greek word *eutopia*, meaning "good place," since the words can sound almost identical. In Greek, *eu* is commonly pronounced as *ev*, but in English this pronunciation is ignored, as we can see with countless English words, such as euphoria or euthanasia. (Euthanasia means "good death.") More's novel gave Europeans the language of a "nonexistent good place," and a continent became emboldened to colonize the planet in order to make "good places" that normalized slavery and the marginalization of Indigenous people.

Unsurprisingly, the word More used to describe the name of the society governed by the Indigenous people left no room for misinterpretation. Also, More describes the Indigenous people as "a pack of ignorant savages" and they were defeated in battle by Utopos, who then named his new republic after himself and transformed his colonized land into "what is now, perhaps, the most civilized nation in the world." More called the Indigenous people's society, which preceded Utopia, Sansculottia, meaning "society of people without underwear/breeches/pants." He did not need to conceal his disdain for non-European people, yet I find Sansculottia to be one of his more ironic terms, because in late eighteenth-century France the common people and lower class were called the *sans-culottes*. At first, it was a derogatory term, but soon it became a rallying cry as the *sans-culottes* helped topple the French monarchy, end the ancien régime, and fight in the French Revolutionary Wars.

It seems as though More's wit and obfuscation has resulted in the westernized world arguably not having a word for the "good place" we would like to live in. For five hundred years, Europeans have proclaimed that *utopia* means "good place"—and produced more utopian fiction and philosophy—when it means the opposite. Ironically, the popularity of utopian fiction and ideas resulted in the need for a word to describe a "bad place." In 1818, English philosopher Jeremy Bentham coined *cacotopia*, and in 1868 his pupil English philosopher John Stuart Mill coined *dystopia* from the Greek prefix *dys-*, meaning "bad." Dystopian fiction has been a staple of modern literature, and much of it exists to articulate how many of the systems and structures that we are led to believe are good are in fact bad. George Orwell's work may be the perfect crystallization of this bizarre linguistic circle that only leads us to bad places.

—

George Orwell's first novel, *Burmese Days*, published in 1934, depicts the bleak reality of colonial Burma under British rule, and in *Finding George Orwell in Burma*, writer Emma Larkin—a pseudonym—describes how Orwell's experience as a member of the Indian Imperial Police in Burma influenced much of his work. The authoritarian practices used by British troops in India not only formed the foundations for the dystopia depicted in *1984*, but are being used by Myanmar's military junta, who still control the nation today despite the Burmese people pushing for democratic reforms. (In 1989, the nation changed its name from Burma to Myanmar.) In 2008, Myanmar created a new constitution to foster "discipline-flourishing democracy." In 2015, pro-democracy activist Aung San Suu Kyi became the de facto head of state of Myanmar. In November 2020, her party, the National League for Democracy, won Myanmar's parliamentary elections in a landslide, but Myanmar's military refused to accept the results. In February 2021, the military staged a coup d'état and retook control of the country, and Aung San Suu Kyi was detained by the military and placed under house arrest. Following the coup, protests erupted across the nation. Thousands of people have fled the country, and within the first two months of the coup, nearly five hundred people have been killed by the military and thousands of protesters arrested. The growth of democracy in Burma weakened the military's control of the truth, so to sustain their dystopian control of the "truth" they have used violence and terror to end democracy.

The inspiration for 2 + 2 = 5 in *1984* derived in arguably equal measure from the British forces who controlled the "truth" and used this power to manipulate the Burmese people, and from the authoritarian regimes rising up in Europe. This ownership of the truth and the requisite surveillance state, which the British primed the soil for, are still used in Burma today. Larkin must conceal her identity in order to travel within Burma and report the truth of what transpires within the country. She is a character within a real-life dystopian novel trying to share the struggles of an oppressed people with the world.

Orwell's first nonfiction book, *Down and Out in Paris and London*, published in 1933, describes his struggles surviving off low-wage jobs in Paris and London. His next nonfiction book, *The Road to Wigan Pier*, details the inhumanity and alienation of industrial life in England, and his last nonfiction book, *Homage to Catalonia*, describes Orwell's trials and tribulations fighting in the Spanish Civil War. Orwell was shot in the neck and nearly died during the war. *Animal Farm* and *1984* were his last two books, and they are repositories of a lifetime of knowledge and experience about the destruction Europe inflicted upon itself and the rest of the world. Orwell's dystopian fiction was inspired by dystopian fact, and the exploration, examination, and awareness of societal and human regression became the core theme of dystopian literature.

In the afterword of the Signet Classics edition of *1984*, Erich Fromm, who was associated with the Frankfurt School, articulated the primary question posed in dystopian literature as "Can human nature be changed in such a way that man will forget his longing for freedom, for dignity, for integrity, for love—that is to say, can man forget that he is human?" What makes Orwell's work so powerful and relevant is that he articulates how human nature can be changed by corrupting systems and language. If a government or invading British army demands ownership of the truth, then it no longer matters if the truth is actually true or false. The truth is only what the authorities say it is, and this commences the process of changing human nature. If the truth no longer needs to be true, then the government or any authoritarian force can proclaim that FREEDOM = SLAVERY, DIGNITY = VULGARITY, INTEGRITY = HYPOCRISY, and LOVE = HATE. The person being bombarded with propaganda has not forgotten their "longing for freedom, for dignity, for integrity, for love"; it is just that they believe that they will achieve these goals via perpetuating slavery, vulgarity, hypocrisy, and hate. They will engage in bad actions fully convinced that they are doing good. Bad faith has become good faith. They believe in the goodness of bad faith.

American politicians, especially Republicans, continually obfuscate and avoid answering questions, and they thumb their noses at people who aspire to ascertain the truth. By invoking the idea of "gotcha" questions, these bad-faith obfuscators openly acknowledge that they do not want to be caught telling the truth. Instead, they try to precede the question by ridiculing even the notion of asking them questions that could reveal the truth. However, even if the question gets asked, they are equally skilled at dodging it. The three Supreme Court confirmation hearings during Trump's presidency have all been a farce. Despite days of questioning, the intent of the nominees was to conceal their true beliefs because the truth could undermine their nomination prospects. Obfuscation has been an overt strategy for conservative judges during Supreme Court nominations ever since the failure of Robert Bork's nomination in 1987. They know that their true beliefs would be scorned by the American public, so it is best to hide their beliefs in order to obtain a lifetime appointment to the court and force unpopular beliefs upon the American people. By lying, concealing, and obfuscating, they get to exercise their truth.

The United States, and especially the South, remains filled with "good" people who perpetuate bad actions. The white people of the South who live in a small town defined by a dividing line between white and Black probably believe that they are "good" people as they passively or actively sustain America's ethnocidal norms. The white Georgians who left Atlanta in droves in the 1960s and 1970s as Black people moved into the city probably consider themselves to be "good" people too. My hometown was built around the white flight of this era.

This inversion of the truth as depicted in *1984* always brings me back to the word *utopia*. The true meaning of the word has been overlooked for five hundred years, yet this obfuscation or suppression of the truth was not implemented by an authoritarian regime. Rather, it appears as though Europe was so enchanted by colonization and the potential to build a perfect society outside of the continent that they collectively overlooked the fact that utopia means "*nonexistent* good place." They believed that they had the opportunity to create the perfect society that they were incapable of building inside Europe, and in their exuberance, language, meaning, and truth were cast aside. America, in many ways, was an attempt at utopia, and it either succeeded or failed depending on how you define the word. As they sailed around the world, Europeans may have succeeded in creating "nonexistent good places" in their quest to build utopias.

—

As we examine the dystopian, utopian, nonexistent good place that is ethnocidal America, we must examine what ideas or systems inclined Europeans to forgo their humanity. Colonization and the transatlantic slave trade, as previously discussed, represent Europeans prioritizing their essence ahead of the existence of non-Europeans, but that alone does not commence colonization, genocide, and ethnocide. A false sense of supremacy did not create this inhumanity, but the desire to obtain wealth by dehumanizing other people did. Colonization became a corporate venture that condoned and encouraged the killing of Indigenous people, forcefully removing them from their land, and enslaving African people in order to cultivate that land for the profit of white people. Since America's first permanent British settlement in Jamestown, Virginia, in 1607, established by the Virginia Company of London, colonial civilization has always been a business venture prioritizing white and European wealth ahead of existence.

The ethnocide and genocide that has long been normalized in the United States presents a profound and troubling question: Can white society and even white people exist without money? The ethnocidal transatlantic slave trade destroyed the culture of African people to make their bodies into dehumanized machines that exist to generate profit for white Americans. White ethnocidal slave owners could even expedite the production of new machines by raping and impregnating Black women. As my ancestor D. J. Mack shows, the child of a white man and Black woman would not be white. George Washington Byrd impregnated his slave Charlotte before the end of slavery, so did he believe that he was creating a son or an object to dehumanize? Regardless of George's intent, his generational wealth would not pass down to D.J. due to his African blood, and D.J. was required to live on the "other side of the tracks" and create an existence shaped around the inescapable oppression and exploitation of the South. White existence in America is inextricably interwoven with the accumulation of wealth, and our society condones the act of acquiring this wealth at the expense of others.

Whenever I ask people if white people can exist without money, I get basically two responses. Some people say, "No. White people cannot exist without money," and then I follow up by asking them if Black people can exist without money, and without fail they say, "Of course, Black people have basically existed without money for almost the entirety of their lives in America." Those who believe that white people can exist without money point to poor white people, but this rebuttal falls apart rather quickly.

Many white Americans certainly live below the poverty line, but these impoverished white Americans rarely believe that uniting with impoverished Black people to form unions, pool their money together, or live off the grid is the pathway out of poverty and into stability. More often, they align with rich white Americans as their source for economic stability. They sympathize with wealthy white Americans to sustain their white essence and to hopefully provide a pathway out of poverty. Donald Trump's most devoted supporters are uneducated poor white Americans. They believed that Trump could bring back American jobs from countries and people who are not white. They believed that he could negotiate a deal or provide tax breaks or subsidies to ensure that they kept their job regardless of whether their job benefits society. Conservative Americans still pour billions of dollars into outdated industries such as coal mining that destroy our environment, because poor white voters depend on these jobs. The heartbeat of their downtrodden towns remains large industrial factories, and if the factory closes the town has no reason to exist. They are the low-paid employees of the master, and their way of life sustains the master-slave dialectic instead of transcending it.

Many of these jobs are incredibly dangerous and bad for your health, so these white Americans sacrifice their well-being in order to sustain their white essence. The pollution emitted from these factories harms not only the workers but also the entire town. People in these communities often have higher rates of cancer and shortened life expectancies. Many of these Americans also disliked the universal health care offered by a Black man through the Affordable Care Act, and have yearned for Trump to end the

ACA and replace it with a better form of health care given to them by a rich white American. I believe most of the people in these small industrial towns do not perceive their social and economic dynamics explicitly across racial lines, but their way of life is tethered to having access to the wealth that whiteness provides while living in a white-dominated society. They actively engage in alienating, destructive jobs and dismiss the aid of powerful Black Americans, placing their faith in the idea that the wealth of a rich white person may trickle down.

Many of these communities actively push back against people of color working in these factories and "taking their jobs." Racial abuse is common in these work environments, as they attempt to intimidate people of color into quitting. Throughout parts of the South, the presence of multiple factories within the same or neighboring towns for decades had created an abundance of work and a de facto social safety net. If you were fired from one factory, you could simply go to another. The job application in these areas was comically called a "mirror test," but this mirror exam had nothing to do with race. If the interviewer hypothetically put a mirror under an applicant's nose and could find the impression of breath on the mirror, then you were hired. No skill or education required, merely the existence of rich white men who owned factories to support your way of life. The existence of non-white people competing for their jobs either domestically or internationally provided an essentialist crisis and the prospect of a whiteness without money. A whiteness without money could result in having to equitably commingle with non-white people, and interracial coupling would result in the end of their whiteness, so even poor whites depend on the money that can sustain the perpetual division necessary to sustain their essence.

If a community of color had a similar predicament where the primary industry of the town may disappear due to globalization or not keeping up with technological advancements in their industry, America's ethnocidal culture would not even consider subsidizing this industry in order to save Black jobs. The United States would talk about how these people instead should stop being lazy and asking for handouts. A lack of education or a failure to adapt in a competitive industry would be blamed for the factory's closure and the resulting unemployment. If the people of this community turned to drugs and alcohol to deal with the ensuing depression, the United States would address this problem by criminalizing their actions and claim to solve the problem by mass incarceration with many people being sent to private prisons where their incarceration generates revenue. When the same scenario occurs within a white community, it is discussed as a national health crisis that needs to be addressed with treatments for drug abuse and addiction. The solution for white America costs money, and the solution for Black America generates money for white America at the Black person's expense.

The United States' ethnocidal society exists to extract the culture and soul of the ethnocidee in order to generate the money required to sustain white essence, and this extends even to the essence of poor white people. Money in America primarily exists to sustain division. Growing inequality is inevitable in a society where the majority of the population struggles to buy necessities, while a minority has more money than they know what to do with and still aspires to acquire more due to the value of elevating their social status. Unregulated capitalism encourages businesses to fight to stay alive at the expense of humanity—exploiting and underpaying workers.

Despite the inherently exploitative nature of American capitalism, white Americans often consider obtaining a job as their pathway to freedom and salvation. They hope that the alienating labor bestowed upon them by a white business owner or politician will allow them to obtain the income necessary to sustain their whiteness. They wantonly subjugate themselves before the white plantation elite, politicians, and business owners in a desperate attempt to sustain their white essence. This is why they adore Trump. He echoes the rhetoric of the Redeemers, believes everyone is his subject, and demands they exist to do his bidding. There is no loyalty or trust in this relationship or dialectic: just power and subjugation.

This way of life is inherently authoritarian à la the master-slave dialectic, and it also adheres to Adorno's F-Scale—used to identify fascists—because authoritarian aggression and submission are foundational to sustaining white essence in America. The white Americans without the wealth to fund the perpetual division to sustain their white essence submit to the wealthy authoritarian and do his bidding with the hope that he can fund their white essence. If Trump tells them to attack the Capitol, they will do so because their essence matters more to them than their existence. It should come as no surprise that in February 2021 at the Conservative Political Action Conference (CPAC), the largest and most influential gathering of American conservatives in the world, Trump's supporters created a gaudy, culture-less, gold statue of their *poshlyi* president to deify and show fealty to their leader. Trump's *mauvaise foi* does not matter to his die-hard supporters because they already live to be his subjects.

America's chattel slavery system was created not only to generate wealth for white Americans, but to provide them with the essential services of life. Money was no longer a tool white people used to obtain necessary goods and services when bartering failed, but a social status obtained by white Americans by denying non-white people necessary goods and services. Enslaved people cooked food, cleaned house, and helped raise children, in addition to generating revenue. This dynamic still exists today despite the end of slavery. During the COVID-19 pandemic of 2020, America's "essential workers" were primarily people of color, surviving off a low wage that made it incredibly hard to acquire enough money to use their capital to generate more capital, and their labor primarily provided services that were essential to the lives of white Americans. This iteration of capitalism with oppression and exploitation as foundational tenets meant that capital flowed through society without an emphasis on providing people with necessary goods and services. Destroying the existence of the other provided the necessities of life, and capital existed primarily to generate status. Ethnocide extended this status beyond an economic caste system and determined one's essence. Within this exploitative ethnocidal society, money no longer exists for its primary purpose but is instead a tool for sustaining and widening inequality, across both economic and racial divisions.

A capitalist society that understood the problems of exploitation and cultural destruction would not bemoan taxation to the extent many Americans do today. Perhaps people would understand the absurdity of arguing against giving a portion of your money to the government so that it can transform money into capital that can provide people with essential goods and services. The debate would not be about whether taxes are good or bad, but instead about the specific services that people need and the amount the government needs in taxes to provide those services.

America has a vulgar relationship with money more akin to the *poshlyi* landowners in *Dead Souls* than a dignified society. Our government is built upon the bad faith of ethnocide, and people rightly believe that it cannot be trusted. Why give your money to an untrustworthy institution that will unequally distribute services? Our ethnocidal culture has created a democratic government based on denying rights and services to the ethnocidee under the guise of equality. White essence in America is dependent on the accumulation of wealth, so distributing the wealth of white Americans through taxation to provide essential services to all Americans regardless of race poses an essentialist crisis to those with a white essence. They perceive taxation as being forced to give away part of their essence, which they interpret as their existence, to the people who exist in America in order for white

America to profit off the destruction of their culture. How can they destroy the culture of the ethnocidee if they redistribute some of the money gained from the destruction back to the ethnocidee?

This dislike of taxation even extends after death. Since they must pass on all of their wealth to their children, many white Americans, even poor white Americans, bemoan the "death tax" as an immoral postmortem murder that will kill their ethnocidal culture for generations. This postmortem disdain for taxation makes sense for an ethnocidal culture defined by the acquisition of wealth. If they cannot give their children all of their wealth, then they rarely have anything else to give. Their wealth is their culture.

Americans are encouraged to obtain their capital at the expense of other people while also having no expectation of a social safety net provided by the government. This ethnocidal norm harms all Americans regardless of their essence.

—

When I worked in film, every now and then there would be a moment on set that I could only describe as surreal. Fleeting moments would feel like a dream. It could be an exceptional piece of acting, an incredible conversation, or simply the wonder upon someone's face as they experienced being on set for the first time. A surreal experience is supposed to be an elevated sense of reality akin to living a dream, and the attraction of filmmaking largely derives from its capacity to create the surreal. I have always applied this positive understanding of the meaning of *surreal* because this is its intended meaning, but throughout Trump's presidency I have consistently heard *surreal* being used to describe a deplorable action of the president that beggars belief. I think about this application of *surreal* in relation to our understanding of *utopia*. With the former, we are changing a word created to describe something positive into a word to describe something negative. With the latter, we converted a bad idea into not only a good idea, but a perfect, idyllic aspiration. To me this seems like a linguistic and psychological regression at home in an Orwellian dystopia, so we can ill afford to continue in this manner.

In 1924, during the interwar years between World Wars I and II, French writer and poet André Breton published the first *Manifeste du surréalisme* and articulated that the aspiration of surrealism was to "resolve the previously contradictory conditions of dream and reality into an absolute reality, a super-reality." The term "super-reality" in French is *surréalité*, which in English is "surreality." Also, *sur* in French can be translated as "super," "above," or "over," similarly to how *Übermensch* in German can be translated as "superman," "above-man," or "overman." The impetus of surrealism was to provide an artistic, literary, and philosophical counter to the excessive rational thought and bourgeois values that they believe led to World War I. Via a Marxist perspective, the bourgeoisie used their capital to create more capital at the expense of the proletariat, who barely had enough capital to buy necessities despite being forced to work in the alienating and dystopian factories that both Marx and Orwell wrote about. Surrealism was created by Europeans to elevate them out of the chaos of their own creation, so it bothers me to hear *surreal* being used by Americans to describe the chaos of our own creation.

As dystopian literature points out, the majority of the people within the society do not perceive their environment as dystopian. There may be a Winston Smith in *1984*, and it is unclear if he prevails in the end, but his neighbors and other characters who are merely trying to survive do not believe they live in a dystopian world. When I think about the ethnocidal foundation of the United States, I cannot help but think about the championing of meaningless consumption and the normalcy of describing human beings as consumers. People are not seen as creators or cultivators that contribute to the world. Instead, they primarily exist to consume, and in this condoned regression into consumption we also diminish our language and thoughts.

When I articulate this bleak perspective of American society, people respond by saying that I have to admit that America is filled with good people, and I have never understood this rebuttal. Every society on the planet has people who aspire to do good in the world, but the existence of good people in a particular place does not mean that said place is also a good place. The response is a defense of an American essence of goodness that both ignores and replaces our understanding of reality. If a good Black man is thrown in jail for marijuana possession and meets another good person in prison who was wrongfully convicted, does the presence of these two good people now mean that prison is a good place? If two slaves fall in love on a plantation in Georgia in the 1800s, does that mean that the antebellum South is a good place? The presence of good people does not make a good place, and it is tragically dystopian to proclaim that one's society is a good place when one's culture's word for "good place" actually means "nonexistent good place."

As more and more Americans wake up to the realization that they live in a bad place, I refuse to describe the shock of confronting a living nightmare as surreal. Instead, I say *sousreal*, exchanging the French word for "under." If the United States aspires to be a good place, we must confront the realization that we have made the previously contradictory conditions of a nightmare into an under-reality, a beneath-reality, and made it our societal norm. We must transcend, move beyond, and be better than utopia if we are to ever live in a good society.

12

CULTIVATING EMPATHY

How the facts of American history have in the last half century been falsified because the nation was ashamed. The South was ashamed because it fought to perpetuate human slavery. The North was ashamed because it had to call in the black men to save the Union, abolish slavery and establish democracy.

W. E. B. DU BOIS,
Black Reconstruction in America 1860–1880

In the late summer of 2017, a coworker and I met for drinks at a bar, where we vented our frustrations with our employer—a small journalism start-up aspiring to find common ground across our political divide—and, ultimately, with the state of the nation. The white supremacist march in Charlottesville, Virginia, had happened earlier that summer, and I wrote a column for *The Daily Beast* describing how that protest and Trump's response showed that America had truly commenced the second iteration of American Redemption. The idea of the American Cycle intrigued my colleague, and she wanted to know how I as a Black American perceived the radical changes that had occurred following Trump's victory.

For many Americans—particularly white Americans—Charlottesville seemed like a new low, but for me it was just more of the same. Throughout Trump's campaign, his presidency up until that point, and certainly in the years to come, Trump frequently said and did things that white America considered a nadir for American political culture. With each new low, they hoped and expected that the inherent goodness of the American people would force some kind of change. Their confidence in America's goodness seemed to make people believe that if they passively let the United States' system of checks and balances run its course, our society would correct itself. But when white Americans' inaction inevitably did not lead to positive outcomes, they had no idea what to do next. It seemed like my white friend's frustration, and the frustration of others like her, derived from a belief in American Exceptionalism, and they desperately needed the lie to be true. I had completely different frustrations, and our society's reliance on this bad-faith narrative was my biggest annoyance.

During most of our conversation I articulated why nothing about America's present chaos surprised me, and I also spoke about how I believed it was absurd to expect Black Americans to like America or to think America was "good." Sure, America is our "home," but not because we had a choice in the matter. We had been brought here for the explicit purpose of fueling the white American Dream while receiving next to nothing of that dream. This is the *sousreal* nature of American ethnocide. But we are promised that perhaps one day we could—this equates to telling the exploited that they should embrace their exploitative society because one day they may have the opportunity to become the exploiter. There's the suggestion that the exploiters have created a pathway out of exploitation. In the past, this false promise was called *uplift suasion*. American bad faith can never provide salvation.

As the ethnocidee, I already knew I had a good culture, which had persevered despite the terror of the ethnocider. I never saw any benefit of aspiring to become the ethnocider, and I understood that succumbing to this false promise would only expedite the ethnocidal devouring of my culture and my soul.

As I articulated my frustrations, which as a white person she could not have, I casually made a statement that completely shifted our discourse. I said something like "Being white is rough. I wouldn't wish whiteness on my worst enemy." The majority of the difficulties of being Black in America do not come from within the Black community. The problems that imperil us primarily come from the ethnocider within ethnocide, and far too often the perversity of American life encourages the Black community to take responsibility for and not blame the oppressors for their oppression. By "taking responsibility," Black people will allegedly find their freedom, but all this does is sustain the irresponsible power of the master-slave dialectic. I have never taken responsibility in this manner, just as I did not internalize nor "take responsibility" for the racist abuse I received as a child. I never felt that I had done anything wrong to make white Americans not like me. I was not responsible for their racism. Their insanity would not shape how I saw myself, but the systemic normalization of their racism did influence how I understood American life and white culture.

I told my friend that though I certainly encounter race-based obstacles in America that impact my income and my safety, these problems have nothing to do with me as a person. I might earn less money, and the cops might find some arbitrary reason for ending my life, but the culture of the ethnocidee makes it easier for me to be a good person. I got to be raised

within a culture that did not prioritize exploitation, a culture in which
achieving success at the expense of others was not normalized. When the
holidays came around, I never had anxiety about interacting with a relative
whose core beliefs were utterly repugnant and racist, yet this concern has
become ubiquitous to much of white America. I do not have the awkward
conversations that many white millennials have with their baby boomer parents about creating a less prosperous society for their children. My parents
are baby boomers too, but they are not responsible for America's systemic
inequalities. Instead, they are part of a Black generation who benefited from
the new educational opportunities afforded to the Black community as we
fought for freedom from ethnocide during the Civil Rights Movement. The
ethnocidal white man's burden consists of emancipating themselves from
their own culture in order to become the good person they mistakenly already thought they were, and I would not wish this dilemma on anyone.

This explanation resonated with my friend. She understood that I simply
meant that white ethnocidal culture made it much harder for white Americans to become the good people they aspire to be. The values of the previous
generation far too often are not values the next generation aspires to continue, so who or what is there to teach them how to become good people?
Within American ethnocide there is hardly any emphasis on oral storytell-
ing or transferring wisdom to the next generation, but there has long been
an emphasis on transferring wealth to descendants. I did not know this at
the time, but this friend of mine is a descendant of a notorious and wealthy
slave owner from Charleston, South Carolina. Her ancestor owned a large
plantation on one of the Sea Islands. These islands provided freedom for
many Blacks in Charleston, but it was not solely a vibrant archipelago of
liberation. Ethnocidal white Americans still aspired to conquer and own
these lands. Even today, American ethnocide works to take away the land
of Gullah people on the Sea Islands. My friend and I were two Americans

whose ancestral home was Charleston, but when I looked at the stories of my terrorized and oppressed ancestors, I found freedom and inspiration. When she did the same, she found shame, and the financial largesse of her familial shame helped provide her family with economic stability for generations.

A couple years later when I learned about her ancestry, I was reminded of the Byrd family in America and the Reimann family in Germany. In the 1940s, *The Secret Diary of William Byrd of Westover, 1709–1712* was first published and Americans got an unfiltered peek into the daily events of one of America's most influential colonizers. Byrd helped establish the colony of Virginia and is considered the founder of Richmond, the capital of the state. He is one of Virginia's most celebrated figures and the Byrd family has remained influential and involved in the politics of the South.

William's descendants Harry Byrd Sr. and his son Harry Byrd Jr. were both U.S. senators from Virginia in the 1900s who were influential in American conservative politics. Harry Sr. created the powerful "Byrd Machine" that controlled Virginia politics, and he vocally opposed the Supreme Court's decision to desegregate schools in *Brown v. Board of Education*. He oversaw the creation of the Southern Manifesto opposing *Brown* and called for "massive resistance" that included defunding public schools that integrated. As part of the manifesto, whites in the South took their children out of public schools, and instead created new private schools that were partially funded by public dollars. When he left the Senate in 1965, his son took his seat and continued the Byrd family's support of segregation. As a senator, Byrd supported legislation to reinstate the citizenship of Confederate general Robert E. Lee and to enhance America's economic ties with the white supremacist government of Rhodesia (now Zimbabwe). In 1982, the year of my birth, Byrd Jr. still publicly defended his family's opposition to desegregation and the Southern Manifesto of "massive resistance" they created. D. J. Mack's white father is supposed to be a distant relative of William Byrd II, author of *The Secret Diary of William Byrd of Westover, 1709–1712.*

In Byrd's diary we get a glimpse into a patriarch of this powerful American family. He talks about affairs of state, his travels, his religious practices, his philandering, and also his treatment of his slaves. Below is a collection of diary passages from 1709.

Friday, June 10, 1709 - I rose at 5 o'clock but could not read anything because of Captain Keeling, but I played at billiards with him and won half a crown of him and the Doctor. George B-th brought home my boy eugene. I ate milk for breakfast, but neglected to say my prayers, for which God forgive me. The Captain and I had some discourse about the philosopher's stone which he is following with great diligence. He stayed to dinner. I ate mutton for dinner. In the afternoon he went away. I read some Greek in Homer. In the evening I took a walk about the plantation. eugene was whipped for running away and had the bit put on him. I said my prayers and had good health, good thoughts, and good humor, thanks be to God Almighty.

December 1, 1709 - I rose at 4 o'clock and read two chapters in Hebrew and some Greek in Cassius. I said my prayers and ate milk for breakfast. I danced my dance. eugene was whipped again for pissing in the bed and Jenny for concealing it.

December 3, 1709 - I rose at 5 o'clock and read two chapters in Hebrew and some Greek in Cassius. I said my prayers and ate milk for breakfast. I danced my dance. eugene pissed abed again for which I made him drink a pint of piss. I settled some accounts and read some news. About 12 o'clock I went to court where I found little good company.

The majority of Byrd's secret diary does not consist of whipping his slaves and/or forcing them to drink urine, but the casual manner in which he describes these atrocities as perfunctory occurrences that are part and parcel of everyday life indicates a profound lack of empathy that is foundational to American society. Byrd possesses the thinking hat, and his thoughts justify the normalization of a vulgar, amoral lifestyle concealed in a façade of dignity and civility. Byrd does not empathize with Eugene because he does not even consider Eugene to be a human.

The nonchalant inhumanity described in Byrd's diary may have been the societal norm at the time, but the question of the present must focus on how we choose to relate to these figures of the past. Far too often America ignores or dismisses these daily atrocities as vestiges of the past without condemnation, and this negligence and passivity allows his descendants to be unabashed segregationists with the power to influence American society at a national level hundreds of years later. America neither distances ourselves from Byrd's culture nor cultivates a cultural narrative encouraging us to empathize with the enslaved.

Byrd, without skipping a beat, read the Bible, read Greek, danced his dance, said his prayers, and then committed an act of terror against a Black child—and all before noon. He accumulated a pint of urine and forced a Black child to drink it so that he could terrorize him for wetting the bed. Byrd may have even thought he was doing something good as Eugene drank the pints of urine, and that Eugene was lucky, or *Lucky*, to live among colonial America's white plantation elite. According to Byrd, when Eugene ran away it was not because he wanted to escape a life of terror, but for "no reason but because he had not done anything yesterday." In Byrd's eyes, the lazy slave forced his master's hand, the responsibility of the terror fell upon the slave. Byrd's secret diary is the master-slave dialectic in print, and the sustained power of the Byrd family without any atonement for the past shows how America still embraces this dialectic.

The Reimann family is the second-richest family in Germany. Their multibillion-dollar fortune comes from their massive consumer goods conglomerate JAB Holding, which owns Krispy Kreme Doughnuts, Dr Pepper, Panera Bread, and Calvin Klein perfume. Albert Reimann Sr. and his son Albert Reimann Jr. ran the company in the 1930s and 1940s, and they were enthusiastic Hitler supporters and anti-Semites. During the Nazi era, the Reimanns used forced laborers, primarily Russian civilians and French prisoners of war, in their industrial factories and homes. Women laborers were forced to stand naked and at attention in their factory barracks, and if they refused, they were subjected to sexual abuse. Workers in their factories and their homes were regularly beaten. Following the collapse of the Nazi regime, Albert Sr. and Jr. never spoke about the atrocities they committed, and these crimes were not uncovered until the younger generation of the Reimann family hired an investigator in the 2000s to research any connections to the Nazi Party in their family's past.

After releasing their findings, the family denounced their previous patriarchs and committed to giving over $10 million to charity. The work of this generation of the Reimann family demonstrates the necessity of atoning for the past in order to make a better future, and this level of atonement remains largely beyond the scope of most Americans. Our society still scoffs at the ideas of reparations and restructuring exploitive systems that disproportionately harm communities of color—such as the police. It's almost unheard of for an American family to voluntarily conduct an investigation into the extent of their slave-owning past and then provide compensation for their familial atrocity. I have no expectation of the Byrd family engaging in a similar audit. Acknowledging the past and claiming responsibility for the past's horrors goes completely against America's master-slave dialectic.

Moreover, American society would need to do more than merely atone for a cultural aberration that lasted less than two decades. It would require an atonement for the nation itself, the colonization that preceded it, and the multigenerational cover-up and bad faith that has aspired to normalize atrocities and terror for centuries. Power and irresponsibility remain the fuel to justify and make banal America's culture of destruction. If America never claims responsibility for the destruction it continues to sow, then it's easy to pretend that it has never occurred. This charade becomes impossible to sustain when the ethnocidee remembers their history and culture and speaks their truth.

Whenever I think about this conversation with my friend who is descended from slave owners, I am reminded of the importance of empathy, and how empathy manifested in a distinctly non-American manner during this dialectic. One might expect the Black person to hope that the white person can empathize with our struggles in America, but this dialectic places far too much responsibility for America's inequality on the ethnocidee. It is a step in the right direction to hope that a white American can feel the heartache of a Black parent who worries about their child's life and fears that the police, instead of protecting that child, pose a legitimate threat. However, recognizing that a Black American's *angest*—fear, dread, and angst—derives primarily from structures white America has created remains far more important than empathizing with the struggle of the ethnocidee. By only hoping that white people can empathize with the struggles of people of color, we allow white America to emotionally distance themselves from the systemically oppressive structures that their ethnocidal culture has created. This iteration of empathy, which was not the empathy expressed in my conversation, never adequately addresses the severity of American ethnocide. The empathy expressed in this conversation derives from the ethnocidee empathizing with the ethnocider's progeny, who aspires to create an equitable culture and emancipate themselves from a shameful past, but does not know how to do so despite having all the power, wealth, and opportunity that America can provide.

—

In October 2017, I was fired from the journalism job that my friend and I had been complaining about over drinks. She called me up and had to fire me. Management had given her no choice, and they had grown tired of my editorial decisions leaning too far to the left. The small start-up that I worked for wanted to remain moderate, unbiased, and appeal to both the left and the right. My decisions appealed more to the left, and the final straw was my coverage of the Las Vegas shooting massacre.

My employer claimed to believe that if everyday Americans could have their voices heard within the editorial structures of American news, then a moderate, less-divided narrative would emerge. They believed that the division within American news derived from traditional news sources unfairly putting their finger on the scales and tilting it to either the left or the right. As someone who helped edit content, reviewed user comments, and influenced the direction of the publication, it became clear that the end goal of having a user-influenced publication that stayed moderate was a naive fantasy. Conservative users were in the minority on the website and the logic behind their opinions was far too often so absurd or offensive that we would only be enabling insanity by allowing these views to influence editorial decisions. For example, *The Daily Beast* completely removed commenting from their website around 2016 because of an abundance of racist comments. My family members were constantly concerned for my well-being because of the far too often vitriolic and threatening comments in response to my columns. I knew firsthand how the comments and viewpoints of the right not only prevented any semblance of moderation but could quickly devolve a news publication into a cesspool of hate.

I was fired because I did not select an equal distribution of pro- and anti-gun-rights reader comments for a newsletter on the Las Vegas shooting massacre. Stephen Paddock, a sixty-four-year-old white male from Mesquite, Nevada, fired a thousand rounds of ammunition into the Route 91 Harvest country music festival, killing sixty people and injuring 411. The majority of our readers were outraged by the shooting and supported an increase in gun regulation, so on this day our content appeared "biased" and anti-gun. This editorial decision confirmed to the higher-ups that I had horrible editorial judgment. People were furious with me, and they found it inconceivable that I could not understand the importance of appearing unbiased for such a significant story. The credibility of their brand depended on their unbiased, moderate opinions organically emerging from the voices of their users. If their users skewed toward a clearly left- or right-leaning opinion, the editorial team should then tilt the scales toward moderation. According to their editorial standards, the voices of the murderers and their enablers were just as important as the murdered and those who wanted to stop the senseless killing. They believed that if only we could get the terrorists and terrorized in a room together to share their opinions, we could find some common ground. They did not understand that you cannot find a moderate or acceptable amount of terrorism, but too many Americans need to believe in this possibility. They need to believe that common ground can be found, because the existence of commonality will "prove" that the terrorism never existed. Common ground absolves white Americans of the hereditary sin of ethnocide. The publication existed as a lie that the white Americans who ran it needed to be true, and as a Black man I am not nearly as good at sustaining these white lies.

When my friend fired me, I was pretty upset, but not because I enjoyed that job. I had just moved into a new place in Washington, D.C., and I needed this income to pay rent. After realizing that I now needed to get creative to avoid an eviction, I felt sad for my former employers and my friend who still had to work there. My former employers genuinely believed that they were doing something good, and when things truly mattered they felt that the right thing to do was to empower those who support murderers. This was how they chose to combat the widening divisions exacerbated by Trump. Their American morality depended on excluding the perspective of the ethnocidee; my presence proved the dangerous absurdity of their "morality." For them to have "equality," they needed to perpetuate inequality.

My people have been terrorized by ethnocidal white Americans for generations, so the common ground that they seek I know as a dangerous fantasy. When white Americans find common ground among themselves, they often create systemically oppressive structures, and America's two Founding eras demonstrate this dynamic. The white progressives and moderates who I worked with did not espouse beliefs that celebrated ethnocide, but they did believe that their ideas only had legitimacy if they could find common ground with ethnocidal Americans. Vladimir and Estragon believed that they needed to find common ground with Pozzo, and that equality and fairness could exist by silencing Lucky. This dynamic impairs the ethnocidee from creating equitable change with white Americans who profess a desire to change America for the better. Their supposedly progressive or equitable ideals can only exist alongside systemic oppression, and this impediment derives from an absence of white culture.

—

How exactly does ethnocide fit within American politics? Are Republicans ethnociders? Are all white Americans ethnociders? And does being an ethnocider mean that you are knowingly committing ethnocide, or does it extend to those who are unaware of their ethnocidal actions? The answer to these questions is both complicated and straightforward, and it also explains why white progressives can also impede American progress.

The answer derives from the same Existentialist pillar: existence precedes essence. America prioritizes essence ahead of existence, and this complicates our understanding of ethnocide. Far too often Americans place government and politics ahead of existence and culture.

Considering that ethnocide has long been an unexplored concept in America, I cannot say that anyone is intentionally engaging in ethnocide. However, countless Americans are intentionally engaging in actions that perpetuate ethnocide and are overtly ethnocidal. These people are racists who dehumanize the ethnocidee, and more often than not they align with the conservative faction of American politics. Since they have not been intentionally engaging in ethnocide because they have not been aware of the concept, they may be described as an ethnocider. But once they learn about the word and then intentionally implement ethnocide, it would be fair to label them as an *ethnocidaire*, akin to the perpetrator of genocide, a genocidaire. Despite their ignorance of ethnocide, American conservatives unite around an ethnocidal culture and sustain it via bad faith. They either lie to others about their divisive and exploitative intent, lie to themselves, or both. Their commitment to their ethnocidal culture shapes their politics and American government. American progressives do not have the same dynamic.

Progressives and conservatives derive from the same cesspool of ethnocide, but progressives aspire to liberate themselves from ethnocide. Yet the tragedy of this quest is that within white American society, ethnocidal culture is all they can find. Some white Americans try to connect with a non-white culture to exist beyond their ethnocidal roots, but their white essence built upon *mauvaise foi* makes it difficult to create these bonds. At some point, they may engage in cultural appropriation and undermine the trust they have worked to build. Some go to the extreme lengths of Rachel Dolezal and Jessica Krug and attempt to covertly live as Black Americans, or the foreign culture they are attempting to claim as their own. However, most progressives do not genuinely look for culture from the ethnocidee. They frantically search for culture within their white ethnocidal society and rarely find it. They may instead embrace their pre-American culture, become apathetic, or find the closest cultural approximation. For many Americans, their cultural substitute becomes American democracy, which is not a culture, but an essence or identity. The democratic principles of equality provide them with a nonexploitative narrative that they can connect to as they distance themselves from ethnocide. The principles of democracy help foster the equality for which many Americans yearn, but democracy is not a culture. Democracy derives from culture; a people's culture shapes how they structure their democracy. The Dutch's *polderen* culture helps shape their democracy. America's ethnocidal culture determines how America structures our democracy, and this is why our democracy is systemically exploitative and divisive.

The Americans who use democracy as a substitute for culture believe in a governmental system that both exists without the culture that created it and is also the culture that creates and sustains itself. Governments, and especially democracies, exist to serve the people of a society, but America has never had a united people or culture. America's ethnocidal society created perpetual division, and ethnociders created a democratic system based on serving themselves and exploiting the ethnocidee. By embracing America's democracy as if it were one's culture, Americans embrace exploitation when they believe they are championing equality.

The celebrated moments of American democracy that these progressive Americans embrace almost always derive from the liberating actions of the ethnocidee. The abolitionist movement, the end of slavery, the Reconstruction Amendments, the Civil Rights Movement of the 1960s, the end of segregation, and the presidency of Barack Obama all derive from the culture of the ethnocidee. Abraham Lincoln is considered America's greatest president because he abolished slavery. He may have signed the Emancipation Proclamation, but the yearning to be free and culture of liberation derived from the culture of the ethnocidee and preceded Lincoln's noble statesmanship. Even the democracy that many white Americans embrace as their culture does not derive from the efforts of white Americans.

As a Black man, I believe in America's democracy as a way to obtain liberty, but it is not my culture. I have always been amazed at how Americans elevate our democracy above existence and struggle to comprehend how life could continue without it. For my community, much of American democracy has been denied to us, so we know existence without it and we strive to cultivate ideas to improve our democracy that exist beyond the imagination of our ethnocidal society.

Prior to learning the language of ethnocide and Existentialism, I spent much of my time thinking about America's relationship with democracy, and studying French in college proved invaluable. Here was a nation who inspired America's democracy, yet their path to their current democratic state could not be more different. As an undergrad, I was surprised to learn that France has had multiple governments and constitutions since the French Revolution—yet it remained France. France remained culturally French even as they experimented with various forms of government. This was not a peaceful process, and France has long had conflicts among the various cultures within the country, but when their government collapsed, they still had a culture to fall back on that could empower them to make

another government and try again. America, however, is the inverse, and
we view our democracy as some sort of ideal because we have had the same
system of government since the 1700s. But our government exists primarily
to exist, not to serve the people. Our government only really comes to life
when forced into action by the ethnocidee. It exists to serve as a façade of
legitimacy for our unequal ethnocidal norms. If our government collapsed,
countless Americans would not know how to live because they equate our
government to their existence and culture, and the proponents of ethnocide
would gladly construct an authoritarian government in its place. By treat-
ing our democracy as their culture, progressives far too often expect our
democracy to create progress and equality. By overlooking the importance
of culture, they far too often exclude the ethnocidee from the work of im-
proving our democracy.

The dynamics of this ill-fated employment make me think about the
difficulty of living a good life when you are indoctrinated into destroying
your own culture. Ethnocide destroys the ethnocider and the ethnocidee,
but since the ethnocidee must create culture, they have a more tangible escape route. Ethnociders exist in a culture of self-harm. Their end goal is not
to find purpose in their meaningless toil, but to find a way to stop condemn-
ing themselves while also taking responsibility for the harm they have inflicted on themselves and others. Their quest against condemnation brings
us back to America's bizarre relationship with empathy and the importance
of reimagining empathy in order to cultivate equality and a non-ethnocidal
culture.

The word *empathy* did not exist in the English language at the founding
of the United States. It didn't emerge until the twentieth century. We live in
a nation that celebrates humanistic, democratic ideals, but it does so without any empathy. As Trump demonized and divided any class of Americans that he considered to be other, conservative politicians nonchalantly

shrugged and proclaimed that he lacked the "empathy gene." Trump's lack of empathy echoed the divisive eras of the past, those epochs of American life that also existed without empathy. A lack of empathy fuels ethnocide, cultivating empathy combats ethnocide, and to understand America's absence of empathy we must examine its introduction to our country.

—

In 1873, German philosopher Robert Vischer published his doctoral thesis on aesthetics, and his paper is the first time that the word *Einfühlung*, or "empathy" in English, appeared in print. The direct translation of *Einfühlung* is "in-feeling" or "feeling-into" and in Vischer's thesis he discussed the act of "feeling-into" inanimate objects such as a work of art. *Einfühlung* had already existed as part of spoken language, and one could "feel-into" another person or an object, but finally putting the word in print allowed for the analysis, understanding, and usage of *Einfühlung* to grow exponentially. German philosopher Theodor Lipps expanded upon Vischer's work, and in 1909 British American psychologist Edward Titchener translated the German *Einfühlung* into the English word "empathy." In the English-speaking world, we have been able to be empathetic for only a little over a century.

It's jarring to imagine living in a society absent of empathy, and English speakers often attempt to substitute sympathy for empathy. *Sympathy*, which translates as "feeling together," has existed in the English language for hundreds of years. While sympathy does show a capacity to share feelings with another, it should never be considered the same as empathy. British philosophers David Hume and Adam Smith made sympathy an integral part of their work. Smith is considered the father of economics and capitalism, yet seventeen years before the publication of *The Wealth of Nations* in 1776, he published *The Theory of Moral Sentiments*, which spoke extensively about the importance of sympathy. Smith defined *sympathy* as "fellow-feeling" and considered the ability to feel with one's fellow man as both an integral component of creating the moral foundation of a society and in one's self-interest. Yet he also examined the limitations of sympathy between people who are not fellows. According to Smith, sympathy was essentially a mental or emotional projection of how one person perceives the experiences of another person. The accuracy of these projections depends on how similar the lives are between those who aspire to sympathize and the subject of their sympathy. For example, a poor person would struggle to sympathize with a rich person because their lives are so different, and Smith warned against the poor sympathizing with the rich because a poor person's need for money would incline them to emotionally project a goodness upon a rich person that may not exist. Despite a rich person obtaining wealth from a system that makes another person poor, the poor person may want to see the rich person as a good individual because they aspire to become rich one day. The inaccuracy and misguided foundations of this iteration of sympathy could be detrimental to the poor and therefore not in one's self-interest.

As the colonizers and the founders of the United States created an ethnocidal chattel slavery system in the Americas to fuel global capitalism, there was almost no desire for white Americans to "feel together" with the enslaved. In fact, the way of life of white Americans, and the wealth of the nation they created depended on being unable to sympathize with Black people. The desire to keep white existence separate from non-white life made the prospect of "fellow-feeling" an impossibility. Despite sympathy being a precursor to capitalism, it had no place in America, and empathy would not arrive on this side of the Atlantic for over a century.

Due to our ethnocidal division, the United States' iteration of sympathy became bifurcated, and the ethnocider would sympathize with the ethnocider, and the ethnocidee would sympathize with the ethnocidee. However, the ethnocider would also encourage the ethnocidee to sympathize with the ethnocider; if the oppressed form an emotional connection with the oppressor and do not rebel against their oppression, it becomes much easier for that oppression to continue. Additionally, the less the oppressed rebel against their oppression, the easier it is for oppressors to justify their behavior, to consider their actions as something other than oppressive. The absence of rebellion makes it easier to propagate the false narrative that the enslaved enjoy their enslavement.

This dynamic between the ethnocider and the ethnocidee creates a *mauvaise foi* ruse that blurs the distinction between sympathy and empathy in America. The oppressed are encouraged to embrace their oppression so that they can become part of the ethnocider's community. The ethnocidee is lured into submission by the prospect of sympathy. Only if they accept their place can they receive the sympathy of the ethnocider and the chance to feel together. This corrupt bargain presents the possibility of equality while maintaining that equality remains an impossibility. *Uplift suasion* is also an example of this bad-faith narrative. America promises the togetherness of sympathy—if only one works hard enough—but our ethnocidal culture sustains the divisions that make authentic sympathy an impossibility. Eugene is encouraged to believe that if he worked hard enough and stopped wetting the bed he may get the sympathy of Byrd, and Byrd needs Eugene to believe that the false freedom of his sympathy is more attainable than fighting for or escaping to a freedom beyond ethnocide.

Because the ethnocidee both hopes that a humanity still resides within the ethnocider and is enticed to search for the sympathy of the ethnocider in order to find a semblance of freedom, they encourage themselves to trust the ethnocider and hope that the ethnocider's bad faith could become good faith. The unceasing inhumanity of the ethnocider presents a life of un-ending terror for the ethnocidee, and finding the humanity of your abuser provides a potential escape from that terror. The opportunity for a shared humanity between the abuser and abused means that the abuser may be willing to stop their inhuman actions. However, this search for humanity poses a profound risk. Embracing the humanity of an oppressor can incline the oppressor to see their inhuman acts as human. The ethnocidee's search for a shared emotional connection can tragically be perceived by the ethno-cider as an absolution of their sins, encouraging them to continue oppress-ing others.

For example, during the Civil War and Reconstruction, many slave owners were astonished that their newly liberated slaves proceeded to loot and destroy the property of the slave owner. These ethnociders believed that they had been good masters and had treated their slaves well. On their property white people were the minority, so the slave owners reasoned that if the enslaved had hated their enslavement, they would have risen up and killed the slave owners much earlier. Their "logic" completely ignores the numerous slave rebellions in the South, the existence of the Underground Railroad, and the fact that the United States' slaveholding states were struc-tured to perpetually police the enslaved and deny them any semblance of freedom. Slave owners had created a belief system that could only be proven incorrect upon their untimely death; therefore, they became a populace in-capable of learning. If only death, or a grave proximity to death, can incline an entire society to learn something new and empathize with another, that's a bleak, nihilistic, dystopian environment. This is the society cultivated in the American South and propagated throughout America. This is also the essence-driven devotion to Donald Trump that Republican congressmen displayed after they acquitted Trump during his second impeachment trial. They demonstrated a total inability to empathize with their fellow congressmen, and when confronted with the threat of death, they still refused to learn.

Even today segments of white America remain astonished when people of color want to destroy white property. During the Black Lives Matter movement when some protestors destroyed and vandalized buildings, many white Americans struggled to understand that these institutional structures equated to an extension of systemic oppression and not financial freedom for many of the protestors. A plantation and ethnocidal capitalism meant financial freedom to the slave owner too, and these oppressors were astonished that the oppressed wanted to destroy the structures that oppressed them. Unsurprisingly, America has continued to profess the need to protect property with lethal force, and this condoned violence means that this destructive cycle will continue just as it has for hundreds of years.

In America, empathy has long been an impossibility, and sympathy has been a false promise given to the oppressed in order to absolve the ethnocider of their sins. Therefore, as more descendants of ethnocidal Americans aspire to liberate themselves from ethnocide, we now must cultivate a new understanding and application of sympathy and empathy. I did not realize it at the time, but my relatively brief employment at the start-up equated to this cultural shift. When I spoke with my friend, I had no desire to sympathize with her struggles as a white American. We could not feel together as if we were part of the same culture, and her ancestor, and mine, helped ensure this division that has lasted for centuries. I did not pursue the false promise of attempting to sympathize with her, but I did empathize with her. I felt into her struggle, and in doing so, I could see our distinct struggles more clearly. Her struggle was what Kierkegaard would describe as "hereditary sin." The United States often speaks of the "original sin" of slavery, invoking the biblical origin story of how sin was brought into the world when Eve ate the forbidden fruit from the tree of knowledge of good and evil. But the problem with original sin is that the responsibility falls entirely on Adam and Eve. Their descendants are merely condemned to suffer from their original sin for eternity. The acceptance of original sin leads to an acceptance of the inevitability of sin, and even the belief that we are all born sinners. In this passive acceptance of original sin, self-flagellation and the hopes of divine intervention are considered actions. Kierkegaard in *Begrebet Angest* wrote about hereditary sin as a sin that is passed down from generation to generation. Therefore, it is also possible to liberate yourself from hereditary sin by actively learning how to pass down another practice to the next generation. My friend and other white Americans carry the hereditary sin of ethnocide, and they have never been instructed on how to escape. The idea of America's original sin also gives them a comforting, yet hypocritical justification for not needing to escape sin, while never being held responsible. They are disincentivized to find a solution for their problems due to the language that they speak.

I do not speak their language, and because of this I could empathize with her hereditary struggle against the sins of her ancestors. I could now articulate an emotional connection not guided by absolving the sins of white America, but instead acknowledging those sins and recognizing how troubling it must be to come from the culture of the ethnocider. The emotional relationship became grounded in the recognition that ethnocide harms all of us, and encouraging the responsible parties to take responsibility for the crimes of their predecessors. *Erinnerungskultur* and atoning for the sins of your ancestors as the Reimann family did with their Nazi-supporting predecessors is essential to America's growth and the cultivation of empathy. Otherwise, the unwillingness to combat ethnocide once you know it exists makes one an ethnocidaire, and it is impossible to find common ground with someone whose life revolves around perpetuating bad faith.

Once America, by cultivating empathy and eventually sympathy, creates an equitably shared culture that does not exist to normalize and continue the atrocities of ethnocide, the United States will be even closer to becoming a truly free and equitable society.

13

EMANCIPATION AND CREATING CULTURE

I don't paint dreams or nightmares, I paint my own reality.

FRIDA KAHLO

Around the same time that I began the linguistic and philosophical journey to find the word *ethnocide* and describe the destruction inherent to American society, I embarked on a parallel journey to create culture and, to my surprise, I found the impetus for both explorations via America's Latino community. When Trump demonized Mexicans as rapists and promised to deport all undocumented immigrants, I was reminded of the rhetoric that has been used against my people for centuries, specifically the treatment of my ancestors in Charleston during the Civil War. My awareness of the past shaped my present, and I understood that Trump's rhetoric was not a unique manifestation. Recognizing the overlapping oppression and demonization that Black and

Latino communities experience in America propelled my quest to find the word to describe this American oppression that extends beyond race.

Later that year, my journey to create culture began when I attended a Día de los Muertos (Day of the Dead) party with my Mexican American girlfriend and found myself the quiet Black American who couldn't speak Spanish, trying to understand and absorb the impact of this tradition. This was my first experience with Día de los Muertos, and I wanted to learn and remain humble without appearing awkward. This was not my culture, and I wanted to know more before actively participating. As I looked at the altar the hostess had made for her ancestors, I wondered if a similar tradition would benefit my own community. It reminded me of the many altars created for Trayvon Martin, Michael Brown, Eric Garner, and the tragic faces of the Black Lives Matter movement. By the start of 2016 the importance of creating a cross-cultural ancestor remembrance tradition had become a passion of mine alongside the quest to name ethnocide. I thought about it all the time, but I did not know how to implement such a project.

Trump's victory in 2016 forced me to put my ideas into action. My Latino friends cried on election night. A man who rose to power by demonizing their community had just become the president. The equitable America that they believed in—for which Black Americans have fought for centuries—was disappearing as a modern-day Redeemer ascended to the White House.

When I called my parents on election night, my mom cried too, saying that the progress of the 1960s and Obama's presidency were being dismantled. It reminded me of the last time that my mother and my sister had visited Washington, D.C., when she cried at the Martin Luther King Jr. Memorial. I had been to the memorial countless times by then, and its emotional impact on me had waned. At the moment I was more focused on hanging out with my sister. My mother, on the other hand, wanted to peacefully take it all in. She wanted to read and absorb every quote and feel the spirit of a monumental cultural icon who was assassinated by a *letzter Mensch*. Her adult children's laughter disrupted her serenity, and she looked us in the eyes with tears streaming down her face and said that we did not understand how she was feeling. We did not understand what it meant that America had killed and assaulted all of the cultural icons who cared about Black people. John F. Kennedy was assassinated on November 22, 1963, and then five years later Martin Luther King Jr. was murdered on April 4, 1968. Two months later Robert F. Kennedy was assassinated on June 6, 1968. Three of the biggest icons who had promised equitable, cultural change at a national level had all been murdered in less than five years. These were my parents' formative years, and they are happy that their children did not have to suffer the same terror, but they also demand that we respect the sanctity of the space where we remember our departed. In the 1960s, my mother never imagined that America would create a place of remembrance for a Black leader that our white-dominated society terrorized and killed. Fifty years later she wanted her children to not only give her the space to peacefully remember, but to join in the remembrance with her. The tears of my friends and family on election night increased my conviction that cross-cultural remembrance was truly necessary.

In 2017, when I first began talking to people about a cross-cultural Day of the Dead, they questioned the possibility of sharing culture without cultural appropriation. Day of the Dead, as Día de los Muertos has become more well-known in America, has been increasingly consumed and commodified by America's ethnocidal culture. This sacred celebration has far too often been used as an excuse for non-Mexicans to have meaningless parties and get drunk, and large American corporations are creating sterilized imitations of Day of the Dead and marketing them to Mexican Americans. The spirit of the practice is being extracted, and this is not dissimilar to Disney's extraction of Germanic culture via their mass-produced interpretations of the Brothers Grimm. However, the Mexican community still has their culture, and they have no need to embrace the mass-produced replica. A replica of culture is the only kind of culture that ethnocide can create, and our ethnocidal society consumes this cultural replica instead of cultivating culture. People questioned whether a Black man could be successfully un-American and avoid consuming and commodifying Mexican culture regardless of my intent.

I understood this criticism and never took it personally, but it does speak to how the normalization and anticipation of ethnocide shapes our thoughts. America is a society built upon cultural appropriation. Colonizers took the land of Indigenous people, and our societal narrative has long proclaimed the benefit of this theft due to the wealth that it provides to white people. Taking culture, regardless of whether it is your own or someone else's, and altering it for others' consumption for profit has long been the cultural ethos of our ethnocidal society. People in America do not consume the culture of another because they are knowingly evil, but because they believe they are doing something good. People understood that I aspired to do something good, but they worried that it would manifest into an American interpretation of "good." In 2017, I was only at the beginning of cultivating the language to explain my vision and shift people's thoughts, and I struggled to answer these questions.

Some in the Black community questioned why I wanted to embrace a Mexican tradition and not a Black one. They believed that by elevating another culture I was dismissing my own, and this is also a by-product of ethnocide. Within ethnocide, lies, an absence of trust, and division are the norm. We are expected to be unable to work equitably with another group, and are forced to always put our own group first. Black Americans have a multitude of remembrance traditions, but we do not have a practice that is universal within our community on a scale comparable to Day of the Dead. Some Black Americans thought one of these practices within our community should be expanded nationally instead, but I was aiming for a cross-cultural celebration. The idea of using Day of the Dead as a foundation for elevating Black culture made people question if my goal was actually to consume Día de los Muertos, make it Black, and appropriate Mexican culture. Again, my impediment was linguistic because we only had the language of normalized destruction, and we could neither articulate nor imagine a reality where creation became the norm. We linguistically believe that *aufheben* means "to abolish" instead of "to transcend." This inability to communicate meant that people felt comfortable believing that I was a Black man who wanted to both disrespect Black culture and consume Mexican culture.

—

On October 1, 2017, my cousin Arthur Leon "Ardee" Holmes III passed away in his sleep at the age of twenty-eight. The day after Ardee's passing, I was fired from the journalism start-up. Later that week, I left D.C. to attend Ardee's funeral in Youngstown, Ohio, and I received another reminder of the importance of ancestor remembrance traditions in my community.

Ardee was young. His death was unexpected, and I could see how my brilliant uncle Artie—who has done extensive research into our family history—struggled with the prospect of how to keep his son's memory alive. Though we were cousins, I did not grow up around Ardee. His family lived in Ohio, and they rarely made it down South. During family get-togethers in Charleston, Marietta, and other parts of the South, Artie's family rarely came. Life and work kept them too busy. At the service, as my family and Ardee's friends shared stories, I had very little to contribute. To keep his son's memory alive, my uncle decided to create a college scholarship in his name, but I could tell that beyond distributing money in Ardee's name we all struggled to find a ritual to keep his memory alive. Ethnocide had destroyed much of our culture, and money had become the method for remembering people.

In the days after the funeral, I would call my uncle to check in on him, and despite handling this situation with much dignity and strength, there was an obstacle in the grieving process that he was struggling to physically and emotionally surmount. Ardee had his own apartment in Youngstown, but he still went back to his childhood home nearly every day. His bedroom was still filled with decades of Ardee's possessions, and my uncle could not figure out what to do with all of Ardee's things. He did not know if it made sense to keep everything or throw everything away, and he had no idea what needed to stay and what needed to go. And what would he do with the things he chose to keep? Should Ardee's bedroom stay frozen in time for eternity? These are difficult and profound questions, and America had not given him the tools to confidently answer, despite his Ivy League education. When I heard my uncle's struggle, I thought about Día de los Muertos and the importance of creating altars for remembering the dead. I imagined how an ancestor remembrance tradition that extends into the Black community could provide my uncle with guidance and comfort during this struggle. Maybe if the plan was to create an altar for Ardee, he might feel more comfortable saving some items for the altar and discarding others without feeling as though he were discarding his son who had passed away. The importance of ancestor remembrance had become less of a theoretical endeavor and now had shifted to something that I knew could help my family.

—

In late 2017, I knew that I did not have the words to succinctly describe my vision, but around the beginning of 2018, I had settled on *ethnocide* as the word for describing America's systemic cultural destruction. This was an empowering and uplifting moment for me, but when I would talk about ethnocide with others it seemed to make many people feel helpless, sad, and disempowered. America has conversations about race, inequality, police reform, voting rights, women's rights, etc., and we are encouraged to believe that solving one of these siloed issues will be the watershed moment that creates unprecedented change. Ethnocide shows that America's problems are more all-consuming than these individual issues, and it became easy for people to perceive the problem of ethnocide as being too big to solve. They felt condemned to be punished by and unknowingly perpetuate ethnocide, and to alleviate their despair they wanted a specific action that they could do to counter ethnocide. I understood that what they really needed was a word that could focus their thoughts toward creating and not destroying culture. Soon thereafter I began using *ethnogenesis* and *cultural naissance* as interchangeable terms to describe the process of creating or giving birth to culture, and I realized that my Day of the Dead project represented an attempt at creating culture and countering ethnocide.

Día de los Muertos is a Mexican tradition started by the Indigenous Nahua people of the region, and the origins of the tradition go back three thousand years. Originally, these ancestor remembrance rituals occurred in August, but now they are held from October 31 to November 2. The influence of Spanish conquistadors and their practice of All Souls Day and All Saints Day, which have pre-Catholic pagan origins, moved the celebration to correlate with the Catholic calendar. During Día de los Muertos, people erect altars to remember their ancestors. An ancestor can be a family member, but also friends, cultural icons, and even pets who have passed away. It is perfectly okay to erect an altar with items to remember a great-grandparent, a beloved childhood pet, those who have died of COVID-19, Kobe Bryant, John Lewis, George Floyd, Chadwick Boseman, and a friend who died. All of these disparate people can harmoniously come together in an altar. No altars look the same, and they can be of any size. Your altar can be inside your house, and it can also be a large public altar that the community can share.

By embracing Day of the Dead across cultures, America would not only provide a platform for Black and Latino cultures, but also for Indigenous cultures to share and remember their history. This tradition provides a framework for expanding ancestor remembrance traditions to many other American communities. However, it was not my role to tell other American groups that they needed to celebrate this practice. I must instead create a foundation for collaboration and give others the opportunity to participate. I must search for the language to articulate this idea so that it resonates within my Black community.

The altars for Día de los Muertos first reminded me of the altars my community had made for the tragic faces of the Black Lives Matter movement as we worked to keep the memories of Trayvon Martin, Michael Brown, and Eric Garner alive, but Día de los Muertos also had a profound difference from the BLM remembrance practices. With BLM the discourse and actions were in response to terror, and I wondered if being reactionary provided an adequate template for liberation and progress. If we always make altars after a white person unjustly kills a Black person, our attempts at liberation are dependent on an act of terror. If terror must provide the impetus to strengthen and remember our culture, are we strengthening ourselves so that we can withstand terror or are we strengthening ourselves so that we can liberate ourselves from terror? It seemed to me that our altars were predicated on withstanding inevitable terror, and I wanted to work toward being proactive and preempting terror. The fact that Day of the Dead already has fixed days on the calendar provided a proactive opportunity to create a safe space to remember and celebrate Black life and cope with our generational trauma. By gathering people together for Day of the Dead, we create a community where people can talk about the emotional trauma of loss. This communal support helps people cope with this trauma, but it also strengthens our communal bonds and encourages us to remember our own history.

This is not to say that we should not react to injustice, but that a proactive celebration—completely independent from the actions of ethnocidal white America—adds a vital layer to our struggle for freedom from ethnocide. A foundational pillar of ethnocide has been the fracturing of African communities and preventing Black people from having the space to peacefully gather. If Black people in the 1800s were allowed to gather, they would not only have been able to sustain and share their African cultural traditions, but they could also have banded together and attempted to liberate themselves from slavery and ethnocide. Gullah culture is the result of Black Americans being able to gather, and unsurprisingly, as Black Charlestonians obtained more agency, Denmark Vesey organized what would have been the largest slave rebellion in American history. The simple act of proactively gathering has always been a revolutionary act for Black people in America.

Ancestor remembrance traditions challenge America's ahistorical status quo. The history of the terrorized is erased and the history of the terrorists becomes whatever the terrorists proclaim it to be regardless of whether it is true or false. Including ancestor remembrance traditions as part of the narrative of the ethnocidee demands that the ethnocidee must remember their history and hold on to their truth. Their culture, steeped in their history, proactively challenges the ahistorical propagated narrative that an ethnocidal society needs to survive. By remembering the past, the ethnocidee proactively challenges a dystopian present and cultivates the space to make a more equitable future.

Day of the Dead is also significant as a potentially transformational

American practice as it occurs right before our national elections. Enslavement, terrorism perpetrated by the Ku Klux Klan, voter suppression, Jim Crow, and felon disenfranchisement are just some of the methods America has used to present itself as an authentic democracy while systematically preventing people from voting. America's democracy becomes democratic when the ethnocidee participates, and encouraging Black Americans to remember our history and the many cultural icons who have fought and died for our voting rights might boost voter turnout among communities of color. By taking the time to remember the past, we could reshape America's democracy.

—

Ethnogenesis and *cultural naissance* both mean the "birth of culture," but both terms are necessary so that we remind ourselves that we are not engaging in a rebirth. Even though we are remembering the past and working to continue cultural practices that ethnocide has sought to destroy, we are doing so with the knowledge that the past cultures will mix and evolve with the present to give birth to something new. Ethnogenesis is not a renaissance, and this is important to note because colonization and the United States is an attempt at a European renaissance outside of Europe. The desire to create a rebirth of Europe outside of Europe meant that the existence of non-European people posed an essentialist threat to European colonizers who did not hesitate to destroy existence to sustain their white essence. This foundation of cultural destruction, or cultural appropriation, is why Americans struggle to imagine how to create culture without destroying the other. Ethnogenesis without cultural naissance could easily be interpreted as a confrontational and destructive cultural renaissance, so we need *naissance*, meaning "birth" in French, to linguistically and psychologically remind us that we are creating something new and not merely bringing back something old.

A cross-cultural Day of the Dead seeks to create a cultural naissance through creating entirely new types of altars while being guided by the wisdom of the past. The altars that my partner and I make in our house are a cultural first for our families. My family had never celebrated this tradition, and embarking on this practice was ethnogenesis. At first my parents needed some convincing, and the animated Pixar film *Coco* helped them understand that this was not a weird, morbid practice. They understood that it was a celebration of life, and in 2018, I returned home to Marietta to help my parents celebrate Day of the Dead.

Since my family had never participated in the practice, I decided that our altar should be simple: consisting almost exclusively of photos that we would place on the mantel of our fireplace. My parents are not Mexican and we did not have any similar cultural practices, so I believed that the most authentic expression of our cultural naissance would be to start from scratch. We gathered photos and mementos of our loved ones who had passed away, and we stood in front of our fireplace and told stories about them to help keep their spirit and memory alive. At first my mother and a neighbor were the main participants in the celebration, and my father stood off to the side or watched television in another room. I did not pressure anyone to participate. If you did not participate this year maybe you would next year, the year after that, or ten years down the road. Committing myself to an annual, proactive celebration removed the stress, anxiety, and urgency that comes with a finite celebration. I wanted to give birth to something new for my family and others, and the infinite possibilities gave people the opportunity to participate at their own pace.

Eventually, my father emerged from my parents' bedroom, and he asked me if I had put the bills of sale on the altar. I had not, so my father went down to the basement, removed them from the bookshelf they have called home for over two decades, and placed them on the mantel alongside our other departed ancestors.

My father's family hails from Prattville, Alabama, and the story that I have always been told is that my ancestor was one of the first enslaved Black Americans Daniel Pratt took to Alabama from Georgia when he created his eponymous town. As the descendant of a "founder" of Prattville, my father has always wanted to sustain a connection to the city and ensure that we remember our history. When I was a child I remember my dad's excitement when one of his family members found the bills of sale for our ancestors. Soon thereafter my father drove the three hours from Marietta to Prattville and brought them home. Ever since, the bills of sale of Charles and Eliza, plus Eliza's two young girls, have lived in our house.

> Received of Daniel Pratt seven hundred dollars for a Negro mulatto boy named Charles, which boy I warrant sound and healthy and a slave for life – the title to which boy I warrant against all claims said boy is about thirteen years old this 30th day of March 1843.
>
> > -Samuel Griswold

> Received of Mr. Daniel Pratt eighteen hundred dollars in full payment for a Negro girl Eliza, age 19 and her two children, little girls, coming 4 and 2 years old, which I warrant sound in body and mind and in titles, Slaves for Life.
>
> > -Amos Smith Sr.
> > March 2nd, 1859

Annually remembering the first documented ancestor from the paternal side of my family by reciting their bill of sale is a harsh reminder of the barbarity of the American South, but my family has refused to succumb to the inhumanity of our society and allow our ancestors to be forgotten. We know these bills of sale are not the souls of our ancestors, but by saying their names and remembering our past we help to keep their spirit and *Geist* alive.

The altar in my parents' house in Marietta and mine in Washington, D.C., look nothing alike, since mine also includes Mexican imagery, yet as we collectively create our own altars, we are embarking on a new iteration of cultural naissance. Additionally, the fact that the altars in my house are equal parts Black and Mexican American adds another layer to the cultural naissance. We cherish the connection to the past, but are well aware that we are creating something new. The creation of culture does not consist solely of new practices or rituals, but it requires new names, and again America's Latino community proved an invaluable guide.

—

One day I was talking with a Mexican friend of mine about culture, race, and identity and how they vary between Mexican, Mexican American, and Black communities, and at some point she said, "We're all Mestizo." The "we" she referred to included Mexicans and Mexican Americans. I'd heard the word *mestizo* countless times, but I understood it differently when she said it because I was actively differentiating between culture and race, and focusing on the core meanings of words. Previously, I *believed* that I understood what *mestizo* meant, but I had never thought about or examined the word. In this conversation, a light bulb went off and I realized that *mestizo* represented a new and distinct culture created in the Americas.

Mestizo essentially means "mixed" and refers to the culture of people in Mexico who are a mixture of Indigenous and Spanish. The origin story of Mestizo people in Mexico derives from Spanish conquistador Hernán Cortés and an Indigenous Nahua woman. Her Indigenous name is unknown, but she was christened Marina by the Spanish. Indigenous people modified the name for their Nahua language to Malintzin, and she is commonly referred to as La Malinche. She was one of the slaves given to Cortés in 1519, and she gave birth to Cortés's first son, Martín Cortés el Mestizo, in 1523. Their child, according to legend, is the first Mestizo person in the Americas. A new culture of people was born, and this is also ethnogenesis.

A Mexican person would probably never say that their culture is exclusively Spanish or Indigenous, as their Mestizo culture is shaped by both. The acknowledgment of the brutality of colonization and its destruction of much of Indigenous culture is integral. Cortés is not considered a hero, and in 2019—five hundred years after Cortés's arrival—one of his descendants returned to Mexico to apologize for the brutality his family inflicted on Indigenous people. For a very long time, the perception of La Malinche was negative, as many Mexicans viewed her as a traitor who sided with the Spanish and betrayed her own people. Recently, this narrative has shifted as our awareness of power dynamics has grown. As a slave and translator for Cortés, La Malinche had extraordinarily little power in this relationship, and the birth of Martín was less a cultural betrayal than another manifestation of colonial oppression. Mestizo culture provides an enlightening perspective of ethnogenesis in the Americas because it demonstrates that a culture can have an unsavory origin story with parents who are loathed by the culture they birthed, yet the people are not defined by this original evil. Their cultural naissance allows a people to liberate themselves from the hereditary sin of their forefathers.

It must be noted that Mestizo culture is not devoid of tension, conflict, and controversy. Mexico's Afro-Mexican community has been marginalized and ignored for centuries. Indigenous people remain stigmatized and marginalized in Mexico, despite the embrace of Indigenous culture within the Mestizo identity. Mexican author Octavio Paz in *The Labyrinth of Solitude* describes how Mexican culture has been influenced by the initial violation of La Malinche by Cortés. In his chapter "The Sons of La Malinche," he describes a cultural dynamic where you are either violated à la Malinche or you are the violator à la Cortés. This founding relationship, devoid of trust, creates an environment where people are reluctant to be vulnerable and must always exude strength. The machismo culture that still influences Mexican society supposedly derives from this violation. I believe that there are obvious parallels between machismo culture and America's toxic masculinity, embracing of guns, and our normalization of white male domination. Both of these cultural impediments derive from colonization—when you are in a foreign land and consider the existence of non-European people as an essentialist threat, the entirety of your environment outside your immediate control will be a perpetual threat. A constant war against existence becomes the status quo. Trust can no longer exist within this dynamic, and strength becomes the most important virtue. In the untrustworthy world created by colonization, we exist within a constant battle between being violated or becoming the violator. There are numerous imperfections with Mestizo culture, but it is profound that a cultural identity of mixed people with a distinct cultural name exists in Mexico and not in the United States.

Additionally, the distinction between Mestizo being a culture or a race is often blurry. This confusion stems from the dangerous facility of moving between existence- and essence-based perspectives. The Germans have already shown the dangers of misrepresenting existence as essence, and in the Americas essence precedes existence. We are encouraged to make this dangerous misrepresentation so that a particular essence can engage in meaningless and destructive battles for supremacy because the various iterations of ethnocide in the Americas are driven by normalizing and perpetuating this destructive status quo. However, even if you are not engaging in an existence vs. essence conversation, it remains true that the mixing of Spanish and Indigenous people has created a new culture and "race" of people. If we are to apply modern conceptions of race, the mixing of two races of people would certainly result in a new race. Unlike the United States, which adopted the one-drop rule to create a clear racial division between Black and white, Mexico, Latin America, and other places colonized by the Spanish engaged in a far more complex iteration of racial division. These nations created elaborate charts with numerous racial classifications based on one's mixing of European, Indigenous, and African ancestry, yet these charts were destined to expand and become more complicated as people inevitably mixed more and more. As these racial charts grew, the classifications and identities became increasingly absurd and useless. The inevitability of mixing made notions of race increasingly meaningless. Mestizo people are a "race" of people that are so mixed that their "race" has become one of being mixed. This concept of race is the absence of race and the existence of culture, a new culture. We are merely encouraged to articulate and perceive it as a race because ethnocide inclines us to interpret everything as an absence of culture.

I had known the word *mestizo* before this conversation with my friend, but in this moment I understood the word differently. Mexicans had a national identifier, Mexican, and also a cultural identifier, Mestizo. The United States does not have a cultural identity. We have racial identities and attempt to use "American" as a cultural identity, but this is insufficient since American culture is primarily associated with white essence and the ethnocidal destruction of culture. This is why asking non-white Americans where they are *from* is so problematic. This question seeks to deny their American identity that—as it is for all of us—is an absurd mixture of nationalism and a white-dominated culture that non-white people can never obtain despite being told that it is attainable with hard work. "American" is a national identity that projects the lie of being a cultural identity. In the absence of a cultural identity, American people yearn for the lie to be the truth.

Mexicans, and other Latinos, do not have this same dilemma, because they are accustomed to having cultural identities in addition to their national identities. This dynamic makes them more well versed in ethnogenesis, and this culture extends to Latino immigrants in the United States. Mexican immigrants to the United States actively create new cultures as they exist as Mexican people outside of Mexico. Mexican Americans in Southern California and Texas created Chicano and Tejano culture, respectively. These cultures have strong Mexican influences, but they do not exist within the nation of Mexico. Puerto Ricans also culturally identify as Boricua, and the word derives from the Indigenous Taíno people's name for the island: Borikén. If you look again at Latin America, you will find that many Latino people have a cultural name that precedes their national identity.

Within the United States, our Latino community is a compilation of numerous cultures with distinct cultural names, yet since America prioritizes essence ahead of existence, we try to redefine them as a cultureless, monolithic race of people. The cultural diversity of America's Latino community can frustrate pundits who seek to predict how they will behave during elections. Not only is there significant cultural diversity, but the fact that Latinos come in all complexions means that they also have different racial classifications in America. Despite many American Latinos being able to pass as white, Latinos still suffer ethnocidal oppression because the existence of their culture challenges the dominance of white essence. In America, Latinos are considered a race of people not because they are a specific "race," but because their non-white culture means that they must come together to fight against ethnocidal oppression.

—

By looking at Latino culture through the lens of culture and not race, it became easier for me to differentiate between the culture and race of my Blackness, and to articulate the ethnogenesis that is inherent to Black existence in America. By using the Existentialist formula of existence precedes essence, it becomes obvious that culture also precedes race. Instead of aspiring to be post-racial or anti-racist, we need to be pre-racial. Race is merely an essence, but culture is what people create to exist and survive. As the ethnocidee, Black Americans must always create new culture to survive. In Tulsa, Oklahoma, our vibrant culture was burned to the ground by white Americans, and we made a new culture from the rubble. We create culture and then the ethnocider appropriates or destroys that culture, and we must create culture again. The new cultures that we create allow us to survive within an ethnocidal society, but the goal must be to create a new culture that liberates us from ethnocide so that we can survive beyond the terror. Making an altar in response to ethnocidal terror helps us survive within ethnocide, but proactively making an altar that is not in response to terror can help us defeat ethnocide. Black American ethnogenesis has been both a survival mechanism for the ethnocidee and the parasitic sustenance of the ethnocider that sustains ethnocidal oppression. Our culture of ethnogenesis must evolve to liberate and emancipate us from ethnocide.

Gullah culture is an example of an American ethnogenesis that was able to exist primarily as an emancipatory culture due to having greater liberation from the ethnocider than many of the other Black cultures on the American mainland. This distance allowed it to exist with a decreased threat of ethnocidal destruction, and the Gullah culture retained much of its African cultural predecessors. The presence of strong African cultures within Gullah culture does not make it an African culture, but instead a cultural naissance heavily influenced by African cultures and America's ethnocidal oppression. By recognizing the cultures of my Latino friends, it became easier for me to identify the unique ethnogenesis within my own community. By acknowledging the distinct cultural name of Gullah people, it became easier to articulate the perpetual struggle for self-identity that the ethnocidee always confronts within ethnocide.

From the beginning of the transatlantic slave trade, ethnocidal Europeans worked to destroy African culture by destroying the cultural identity of African people. Stripping Africans of their cultural attire, shaving their heads, destroying families and communities, chattel slavery, and preventing Africans from speaking their language or practicing their religion were some of the methods of cultural destruction. Preventing Africans from self-identifying and forcing upon them dehumanizing European identifiers was another tool of destruction whose ramifications are still felt today. The names that America, and the world, uses to describe Black Americans are for the most part names that ethnocidal oppressors have forced upon us, and our culture also exists to free ourselves from these dehumanizing, oppressive identities. Whenever Black people earn more agency and freedom within America's ethnocidal society, we work to give ourselves names with more freedom from ethnocide. The progression from *nigger* to *Black* most succinctly articulates the continued struggle for emancipation from ethnocide relating to our own identity.

Nigger is not a name that enslaved Africans decided to call themselves. It is a name defined by perpetual dehumanization and cultural destruction. As America's Black community obtained more authority, *nigger, negro,* and *colored* became unacceptable terms for identifying Black people. Not until the late 1980s, when Black Americans began identifying as *African American*, did we have an en masse cultural identifier that came from within our own community. From 1619 to 1988, America's ethnocidal society prevented Black Americans from self-identifying. Over the last thirty years, our community has made progress in regard to solidifying the name of our collective identity, but there is still much more work to be done.

African American liberated us from being *colored* or *negro*, but that title does not accurately identify our community. Yes, we come from the African Diaspora, but ethnocide has destroyed much of our African culture. *African American* also plays into America's false narrative of being a nation of immigrants where *African American* sounds similar to *Greek American*, *Italian American*, and *Irish American*. American immigrants bring their culture to America, so in their name their culture precedes America. Black Americans had their culture forcefully removed from them. By creating an identifier that implies an African culture and immigration narrative that does not exist, *African American*—despite being liberating and empowering—does not accurately describe the culture of Black people. *African American* is a step in the right direction, but cannot be the end goal.

While I have never embraced *African American*, I understand the purpose it serves. Despite its imperfections, it was a necessary step. However, there are few linguistic options to choose from to articulate your identity if you do not embrace *African American*. *Colored* and *negro* are not viable options, despite "Negro" still being listed as an option for Black identity on the U.S. Census until 2013. (The 2020 U.S. Census is the first census without "Negro" on it since the term first appeared on the census in 1900.) For most of my life a lowercased *black* and the fraternal usage of *nigga* were the only options besides *African American*, and both of these choices are representative of the cultural destruction of ethnocide.

Nigga became a term of endearment within certain segments of the Black community because America's centuries-long commitment to ethnocide eradicated the non-dehumanizing cultural language that preceded the racist language of ethnocide. When Black Americans liberated themselves from being called *niggers*, they collectively confronted the bleak reality that their previous language had been destroyed. Due to this linguistic void, our strategy became using our enhanced cultural power within America to redefine *nigger* to empower the Black community and shield us from the dehumanizing usage by white Americans. White Americans could no longer say the word. Even if a white American was trusted within the Black community, he still could not say "nigga," because his use of the word would now open up the Pandora's box of allowing other white Americans to say "nigga." America would rapidly regress into normalizing dehumanizing language toward Black Americans and all progress would be lost. *Nigga* is also a linguistic progression, but it can only foster an intra-racial and not an interracial dialectic. It does not transcend and only survives within ethnocide.

The differing application of *nigga*, *nigger*, and South Africa's *kaffir* demonstrate an interesting juxtaposition that highlights the severity of American ethnocide. In South Africa, the white Afrikaners who created apartheid called Indigenous Africans *kaffirs*, and it is considered their equivalent to *nigger*. However, when apartheid fell, South Africa's African-controlled government banned the usage of *kaffir* with their *crimen injuria* law. South Africa's *crimen injuria* law makes "unlawfully, intentionally, and seriously impairing the dignity of another" a crime, and saying *kaffir* has become an actionable offense. There was no desire to redefine *kaffir* to put a positive spin on it because African people had still retained a plethora of cultural identifiers. They remained on their land, still spoke their languages, and could demand that racist white colonizers refer to them by their existing names of Zulu, Xhosa, and Sotho. Black Americans do not have this luxury, so we must redefine negative language into positive language or create new positive language as a replacement. America's ethnocidal society uses the mask of dignity to conceal our vulgarity, and we struggle to create laws to protect people's dignity—especially the dignity of the ethnocidee.

A lowercased *black* bears the stamp of ethnocide because it is a color-based identifier absent of culture. Until recently, according to the Associated Press Stylebook, *black* was interchangeable with *African American*, but also should not be capitalized like "the proper names of nationalities, peoples, races, tribes, etc.: *Arab, Arabic, African, American, Caucasian, Cherokee . . .*" Within America's ethnocidal discourse, *black* was another cultureless mass of people defined by their color. The lowercasing of *white* also falls within this discourse, and America's championing of our immigration narrative facilitates America's absence of culture because people feel empowered to claim the culture they had prior to their arrival in America as their defining culture. Upon arriving in America, those who can become white actively destroy their culture and existence, and replace it with a white race and essence, and when they feel the need to attach themselves to culture and existence, they claim the European culture they left behind. The elevation of our immigration narrative allows our ethnocidal society to keep an emotional connection to culture while destroying culture. Encouraging Black Americans to define themselves within the false narrative of American immigration allows the narrative of the ethnocider to remain dominant. However, as the Black community tried with *African American*, attempting to define ourselves within ethnocide does not work, and as our agency grows we continue to redefine America's oppressive racial identifiers into empowering cultural identities. The call to capitalize *Black* speaks to this progression.

My culture was never just a color even if America aspired to reduce us to that decultured status. Having editors constantly "fix" my grammar by lowercasing the identity of my own people has been a consistent source of frustration. Having them justify this reduction by citing the lowercasing of *white* is infuriating. Why does Black have to be tethered to white? Why does white America's desire to define themselves via an absence of culture mean that the rest of us cannot have or be a culture? It should come as no surprise that when Black Americans obtained more agency in America, we began to call for the need to capitalize *Black*, and, in so doing, further distance our culture and identity from white ethnocide. To further liberate ourselves from ethnocide, we infused our culture into a decultured language, and while this is also progress, just like *African American* was in the 1980s, the next step must be a liberation from ethnocidal language.

—

A Latino friend recently told me about the history of the word *Chicano*. This is another word that I had heard countless times and *believed* that I knew what it meant, but I did not know nearly enough. The word organically emerged from Southern California's Mexican immigrant community, and its etymology derives from removing the *Me* from *Mexicano* to create *Xicano*, which then evolved into *Chicano*. Chicano people were Mexican people living outside of present-day Mexico and within a culture that Frida Kahlo called "Gringolandia," so part of their Mexican culture and identity had been severed and their new American culture and identity needed to articulate this reality. After our conversation, the concept of creating an American cultural identity that articulates the destruction of culture became an obsession of mine, and I committed myself to attempting to coin this word. *Freecano* is my attempt.

    Freecano starts with the word *African*. To symbolize ethnocide's destruction of culture and our removal from Africa, I severed the *A* from *African* and was left with *Frican*. Upon surviving the apocalyptic, dehumanizing ethnocidal journey across the Atlantic Ocean, *Frican* people were now forced to live within an ethnocidal world. The continued destruction of their African culture and humanity became the status quo. The capacity to collectively gather as Frican people could have resulted in the sustaining of African cultures and the organizing of uprisings as they fought for their freedom. Due to ethnocide, Frican people could not primarily unite around their shared African cultures, but they could instead unite around a new culture, a cultural naissance, of liberating themselves from ethnocidal oppression. Freedom became the unifying cultural bond, and to symbolize this foundational cultural pillar of African Diaspora people, *Frican* becomes *Freecan*.

Following the Emancipation Proclamation, when newly freed Black Americans had the opportunity to untether themselves from the oppressive surnames of ethnocidal slave owners, many Black Americans chose Freeman or Freedman as their new surnames. The language of freedom has been in Black American names since America allowed us to name ourselves beginning in the 1860s. This is a cultural reality that we know, but have been unable to truly *know* because of our decultured ethnocidal discourse. America celebrates Abraham Lincoln because he helped liberate enslaved Black Americans, but America also tries to normalize, excuse, and find common ground with abhorrent Confederates to conceal the shame that the Civil War exposed. The dynamic of overlooking Black liberation, celebrating white liberators, and excusing white oppressors still manifests today.

Freecan could have been the term that I settled on to articulate the cultural identity of people of the African Diaspora in the Americas, but since its linguistic origins are entirely English, it excluded the other Black people of the Americas who experienced Spanish, Portuguese, and French ethnocide. In an attempt to be more inclusive, I added an *o*, forming *Freecano* to include Spanish and Portuguese speakers. *Freecana*, *Freecanx*, and

Freecane are equivalent alternatives. French speakers may prefer *Freecain* or *Freecaine*, or another variation.

Expanding the word to acknowledge other languages invites the examination of the politics and power dynamics of gendered words. I intend no hierarchy within any of these terms. *Freecano* occurred to me first because of my own identity as a Black man rather than any notion of masculine supremacy. The complexity of gendered words does not derive from the terms we use as individuals, but the words we use as a collective. What do we call a group of men, women, and people whose gender identities lie outside the binary? Avoiding gendered terms entirely might be the most equitable solution, and we could say *Freecanx* or *Freecane*, but the growing popularity of the *e* instead of the *x* within Spanish-speaking communities demonstrates that even this discussion has not been settled yet. Perhaps we should instead forgo the suffixes entirely and say *Freecans*.

There is room to expand the conversation about *Freecano*, to see if it resonates with people, and to discover equitable ways to answer lingering questions. By the start of 2020, I was already cultivating the ethnogenesis structures and identities I believed America needed to adequately combat ethnocide, and coincidentally I began testing these ideas during a tumultuous year.

—

In early 2020, I started talking to people about Freecano and collaborating with artists. We erected a transportable town square where we could have life-affirming conversations with the support of artists, and the vast majority of the people I interacted with loved the word. Prior to the COVID-19 outbreak in March, I had been trying to have conversations about Freecano with any Black person I bumped into. I did not filter people based on age or education. I just wanted to know what a nearly random selection of the Black community thought. These conversations were surreal, and by the time they ended, many people liked the idea of identifying as Freecano. Within a five-to-ten-minute conversation, people left with a new way to self-identify. People loved how the word sounded, how it told our cultural story, and how it reframed the conversation of American freedom with an enhanced emphasis on Black culture.

The positive responses I received from the Black community were heartwarming, and I felt proud that my community might appreciate my work. Since that time in elementary school when I understood the madness of American racism and responded by trying neither to obtain the approval of white Americans nor to exist within the comfort of a predominantly Black environment, there has always been a subtle distance between myself and my community. Growing up, many of my Black classmates thought I was a Black American who wanted to be white because I played soccer and took advanced classes. Once they got to know me, they knew that I had no aspirations to be white, but I also did not aspire to do typically Black things either. I functioned as a Black man in America who existed apart from yet within the Black and white communities. To this day, many Americans seem to assume that there is something foreign about me. For years and years, I struggled to find the language to articulate my vision within my own community, and this void created a division and distance. In 2020, Freecano helped fill that linguistic void.

Eventually, my conversations about Freecano extended beyond the Black community, and now a new dynamic emerged due to the conversation prioritizing culture ahead of race. People who were not from the African Diaspora or "racially" Black wanted to know if they could also be Freecano. The Asian and white Americans I spoke with acknowledged that their cultural experience with ethnocide did not mirror that of Black Americans, but they too wanted a cultural identifier that could emancipate them from ethnocide. They too wanted to culturally identify with freedom, and not oppression with a mask of freedom. This was unexpected, and I did not have an answer, but I did know that they could not culturally appropriate Freecano. These non-Black Americans could not claim Freecano culture before the Black community had the opportunity to accept or reject it. By being aware of ethnocide and intentionally claiming the culture intended for another community as their own, they would be engaging in ethnocide. They would have become an ethnocidaire. Maybe if the Black community embraces Freecano, the culture may evolve beyond the divisive limitations of America's one-drop rule, and America can cultivate a shared culture not dependent on the color of our skin. Maybe there could be "Asian Freecano" or "white Freecano," or maybe white Americans could cultivate a cultural identifier that emancipates themselves from ethnocide without claiming democracy as their culture. Maybe the as-yet-to-be-created cultural identifier for white Americans who combat ethnocide could be the first step of linguistic and psychological emancipation for the white community, and in the years to come a new word could emerge that merges this new identifier with Freecano. I could not answer yes or no to this question, but I was encouraged by the question. Americans were thinking about *aufheben*.

It's obvious that the conversation over Freecano has only just begun, and that shifting the conversation from racial to cultural identifiers creates transformational opportunities for change. People outside the Black community who previously would have labeled themselves as allies for racial justice and equity had now instigated a conversation about how they could become a part of our culture. Creating cultural bonds that precede race transcends the limitations of American ethnocide.

—

By the end of the summer of 2020, my organization, The Sustainable Culture Lab (SCL) had shifted its programming focus from primarily raising awareness of ethnocide and discussing Freecano to our cross-cultural ancestor remembrance celebration. I had been talking to people about this idea for years, and it was abundantly clear that I needed art to further the conversation. People struggled to believe in the possibility of creating a cross-cultural practice without cultural appropriation. Nothing that I could say would convince people, so now we had to show people. And to show people, we had to enlist artists.

Linguistically, the language or tone of our event could sound neither as if we were claiming Día de los Muertos as our own nor that we were oblivious of the tradition. We had to be a part of it and also apart from it, while giving people the opportunity to experience the celebration and realize that it was not a threat and that there was a pathway to participation. Artists provided that emotional pathway, so for the festival we commissioned a diverse array of artists to create altars that spoke of their culture. There were no instructions to follow.

Because Day of the Dead is among the most well-known ancestor remembrance practices in America, there is a subtle pressure to replicate this practice to remember your ancestors, and this inclination has always bewildered me. Mexican altars look how they do because of the environment in Mexico. The flowers, food, colors, and materials that adorn a Día de los Muertos altar look the way they do because they derive from the culture that exists in that specific place. If you do not exist in that specific place, your altar should look different than a Mexican altar and be representative of the place in which you live. Due to America's ethnocidal culture prioritizing essence and ideas ahead of culture, existence, and place, Americans struggle to recognize the importance of an attachment to place. Our essence-driven perspective inclines people to think that it makes more sense to extract and mimic the culture of Mexican people, so that Americans can have a cultural foundation to talk about their own ancestors. To liberate people from this destructive perspective, I needed artists to manifest ancestor remembrance altars that were untethered from Día de los Muertos and were instead attached to their community.

In the middle of October, I received photographs of the first altar. It was a pyramid shape composed of a series of rusted tin cans stacked on top of books that spoke to Haitian liberation. I immediately shared these photos with my Mexican American partner, and despite appreciating the aesthetic of the piece, she did not understand it. None of the features of this altar appeared to align with what she was accustomed to. She needed more information about what the books and the cans meant to fully appreciate the altar, but her hesitation was all the approval that I needed.

For the altars to be a manifestation of cultural naissance, they could not be a rebirth of a Mexican tradition, but instead the birth of a new tradition that was inspired by Mexican and other ancestor remembrance practices. The fact that a Mexican American did not understand the meaning behind the altar of this Haitian American artist meant that we were on the right track for creating ethnogenesis and freeing ourselves from cultural appropriation. To create new culture and combat ethnocide, we needed to practice cultural appreciation.

The subsequent altars of each artist followed the same trajectory. None of them looked the same. Some were public altars that encouraged participation. One altar was performative and remembered the more than two hundred thousand Americans who had died of COVID-19 by October 2020. Another altar was not a physical altar at all, but a short film dedicated to the remembrance of the artist's father and twin brother who had recently passed away. In addition to creating altars, two young artists also performed spoken word describing the meaning of their altars. Our artists were Black, Asian, Latino, and Middle Eastern, and by proactively sharing our distinct cultural stories and histories together, we created a new cultural space. Not only was this space welcoming for the artists and the organizers of the event, but the participants in our online event also felt empowered to make altars too.

The vision for this cross-cultural celebration was always to encourage Americans to create an empowering shared culture, but within an ethnocidal society where division and appropriation are far too often perceived as unity and sharing, there will always be a significant concern that the practice becomes corrupted by ethnocide once we attempt to scale it. During our festival, I was heartened by the feedback I received from our attendees and the photos of the altars they erected in their homes. My white friends confidently made altars without attempting to appropriate anyone's culture. If that meant they had no cultural items that they could add to their altar and instead their altar was simply a candle alongside photos of loved ones, they knew that their altar still had meaning and spoke to their soul. Ethnocide has destroyed much of our culture regardless of our race. Acknowledging the importance of starting from scratch and building new culture also helps us combat ethnocide.

Our relatively small festival was a success, and in the years to come we plan on growing this festival each year, but as we grow we anticipate that ethnocidal Americans will attempt to corrupt, appropriate, and destroy this celebration. Accurately remembering your ancestors and the past is foundational to existence, and it poses an essentialist threat to America's white essence–dominated ethnocidal society. As the celebration grows, segments of white America will inevitably create altars to profess the "greatness" of segregationists, Confederates, slave owners, and American colonizers who forced Black children to drink urine. Their altars will not be about remembering the past, but for propagating a narrative to sustain their destructive dominance. As people of color gather publicly and privately and erect altars to remember a true American narrative that counters our normalized propaganda, segments of America will try to desecrate, vandalize, and destroy these altars. The peaceful gathering of people of color has always equated to the end of their ethnocidal way of life, and they will gladly resort to violence to shatter the peace.

There is an inevitability to this violence, but the profound cultural power of Día de los Muertos and ancestor remembrance traditions means that as the terror increases so does the importance of the celebration. Día de los Muertos has been around for three thousand years, and it survived colonization because of a culture's need to remember their past and the people who shaped that past. As more people are killed, the necessity of remembering their lives and history increases. With each victim of police brutality and systemic racism who becomes a new face in the Black Lives Matter movement, the importance of ancestor remembrance grows. If an altar dedicated to BLM is destroyed by a white supremacist, then we are now incentivized to remember that attack each and every year. America will struggle to repeat the physical and historical erasure of a Black community by ethnocidal white Americans as in the Tulsa massacre. Instead, we will remember these attacks every year with our altars, and soon after we will vote in our national elections. When a *letzter Mensch* kills an American icon fighting to combat ethnocide and cultivate ethnogenesis, we will have a proactive ethnogenesis practice for remembering that person and coping with our generational trauma.

The practice of ethnogenesis has only just begun in America, and we have a long way to go, but a foundation of cross-cultural ancestor remembrance cultivated by Freecano culture feels like the right place to start.

14

A SUSTAINABLE GOOD PLACE

In Africa there is a concept known as "ubuntu"—the profound sense that we are human only through the humanity of others; if we are to accomplish anything in this life it will in equal measure be due to the work and achievements of others.

NELSON MANDELA

There are three steps for defeating ethnocide, and all of them require consistent effort. The first step is to recognize and raise awareness of ethnocide and create reactionary structures for combatting it, such as laws and policies. It would be inconceivable, in a society that combats ethnocide, to pardon former Confederates after their war against American democracy. A lack of punishment for Donald Trump's blatant attempt to steal the 2020 presidential election and instigate a failed coup d'état at our Capitol would likewise be inconceivable. Instead of a societal norm that excuses ethnocide, America would have a language, philosophy, and laws and policies to respond to these crimes. Secondly, in order to combat ethnocide, we must forge ethnogenesis and cultural naissance. Encouraging communities of color to proactively gather, tell their stories, heal from the generational trauma of ethnocide, and celebrate their culture begins the process of creating culture. We must defeat the destruction of culture by creating culture. Finally, we must cultivate a philosophy for focusing our thoughts toward creating good—not simply countering bad. If we aspire to create a proactive culture, but are primarily engaging in ethnogenesis as a reaction to ethnocide, our vision will be muddied. There must be a word and a practice to anchor our proactive thoughts and actions. At The Sustainable Culture Lab, this word is Eŭtopia.

Eŭtopia means "sustainable, nurturing good place" and it derives from the Greek *eu-*, meaning "good," and *topia*, meaning "place." We have added the caron diacritic to indicate the pronunciation "ev-topia," as a way to distinguish the idea from *utopia* and its corrupted meaning in the vernacular. Importantly, Eŭtopia is a proper noun, and capitalized as such. It is imperative that Eŭtopia exist as a real place that we actively sustain, rather than an impossible ideal. Utopia, despite meaning "nonexistent good place," primarily exists as an aspiration, and we must be able to do more than merely hope for Eŭtopia. We must be able to create it.

When I first began thinking about Eŭtopia, the core question centered on the meaning of "good," and how one's concept of "good" can shift depending on one's essence. The concepts of good that derive from an essence-focused perspective are not inherently bad, but they do open the door to a subjective interpretation of good that may not have any attachment to facts. A goodness guided by essence might include actions that make one feel "good," but are not beneficial to anyone. The good of Eŭtopia needed to be an objective goodness attached to existence.

A simple example: a good friend is not "good" because they are good at something in particular. They do not have to be attractive, rich, or even have many shared interests. A good friend is a person that you can rely on, someone you can trust. This friend is good because they help sustain and nurture you. Good friendships help people live longer. A bad friend does not sustain or nurture you, yet we are often attracted to the bad friends because they possess attributes that are considered "good," like wealth, popularity, or attractiveness. Having wealth, beauty, and power can be good, but being a good person and a good friend outweighs these essence-focused concepts of good. A dystopia is bad because it is unsustainable and does not nurture human life, and an ethnocidal society is anything but sustainable and nurturing.

On the Japanese island of Okinawa, children are set up in a friend group, called a *moai*, that lasts a lifetime. One's *moai* becomes one's longest relationship, and this collection of friends support each other from childhood until death. The residents of Okinawa have one of the longest and healthiest life spans on earth. Knowing that you will always have a group of friends whom you can depend on makes people less stressed, more active, and helps cultivate a meaningful life because you know that you are never alone.

Eŭtopia is a cultural practice with an attachment to place, and one might cultivate Eŭtopia anywhere. On an individual scale, if you aspire to get in shape and lead a healthier life, you can view your body as an Eŭtopian place and the practices you engage in to nurture and sustain your body as Eŭtopian practices. If you are in a relationship and you live with your partner, annoying household chores might be recast as actions for cultivating an Eŭtopian home. Both of you should want to engage in practices that sustain and nurture your relationship, and your home is an important part of that relationship. There is a power to articulating our actions as an expression of Eŭtopia. It becomes much easier to distinguish between existence- and essence-based concepts of good. Instead of attempting to articulate the supremacy of one's essence or idea and persuading another person to submit or agree, the conversation shifts to one about each person's individual and collective existence while also taking into consideration each person's essence. Making your partner a nice breakfast in the morning can be an Eŭtopian practice, and remembering their dietary preferences can make this practice more successful and sustainable. One's essence can change, but our commitment to sustaining and nurturing existence should not.

Articulating Eŭtopia focuses our thoughts and actions toward doing good and not just countering bad. By actively engaging in Eŭtopian practices, we are reminded that Eŭtopia is not perfect. Eŭtopia acknowledges and embraces imperfections while providing the framework for improvement. We all forget to do the dishes and neglect to clean our homes, but if we remember that this labor works toward creating an Eŭtopian space, it may be easier to commit yourself to engaging in the work in the future, and to finding purpose and meaning from your endeavors. All of us can cultivate our own Eŭtopian practices, and the beauty of language and philosophy are that they are inherently communal.

Language exists from the need to communicate with others. A language for one person would not require words or symbols. Every second of every day, we communicate with our bodies without the need for words or symbols. I do not need to think of the words "Move my hand up" for my hand to move, but I do need words to get someone else's hand to move up. We need the language of Eŭtopia not solely for ourselves, but to express ourselves in the hope of being in *communeship* with another person. The sustainable, nurturing good place that we cultivate must have a name so that we can share it with others. The nature of language and philosophy is inherently communal. But America's ethnocidal society—which celebrates individualism and thrives off a corrupted language—prefers to repackage philosophical ideas and practices as "self-help." Our individualism makes life less meaningful.

Philosophy and language are interwoven. Philosophy provides the meaning and wisdom that supports and expands our words. Eŭtopia is just a word, but the meaning behind the word speaks to the philosophy. Understanding the distinction between existence- and essence-based notions of good provides Eŭtopia's meaning, and through that meaning it becomes possible to create meaningful Eŭtopian practices. And as with language, a philosophy that exists only within ourselves is not a philosophy.

The magical thing about Eŭtopia is that once you shift your focus, it becomes much easier to notice the Eŭtopian practices that we neglect and misinterpret. For example, not too long ago the Danish practice of *hygge* became a popular design fad in the United States. Americans became mildly obsessed with this hard-to-translate Danish word that loosely means "coziness." Americans wanted to design their homes with the coziness of *hygge*, but unsurprisingly our desire to consume and commodify the culture of another people meant that we misunderstood the underlying philosophy, language, and culture. The cold climate influenced greatly by the North Sea can make the weather in Denmark fairly inhospitable, so the Danish created a culture of warm and cozy homes to cultivate a cheery and warm disposition. Also, the coziness of *hygge* expands beyond the individual. A family can also practice *hygge*, and part of the appeal of a cozy home is that it is welcoming, warm, and nurturing to your guests. But perhaps more importantly, *hygge* is also the practice of infusing your energy and soul into your home. A valued morning routine that can empower you after you leave your house is also *hygge*. Carving out the time in the morning for a nice breakfast within your cozy home is an integral part of *hygge*.

This facet of Danish culture is not a commodity that can be bought and consumed. It is a philosophical practice condensed into a single word.

To the untrained eye and mind, *hygge* appears effortless, an easily consumable product that can perfectly fill America's cultural void. Ethnocide inclines people to attempt to find meaning by turning meaningful actions and philosophies into meaningless products for consumption. By shifting our perspective toward Eŭtopia, it is easier to recognize *hygge* and many other cultural practices from around the world as Eŭtopian practices. This shifting of perspective inclines us to cultivate and appreciate these practices instead of consuming and appropriating. We do not need to mass-produce a *hygge* aesthetic to understand the sustainable, nurturing importance of taking the time to create a home and daily routines that provide you and others with meaning, warmth, and strength.

Throughout this book, the ideas that I have used to help explain and combat ethnocide have been Eurocentric, but this has nothing to do with a supremacy of European ideas. Instead, I employed a Eurocentric focus because the linguistic, philosophical, and cultural familiarity made it easier to articulate the flaws of ethnocide and potential solutions. In America, we live in a society shaped by European ideas and language. This is what we understand, regardless of whether we like it or not, so I believed that the most effective way for people to understand potential solutions to these European-created problems was to explore if Europe already had the language and philosophy to help solve these problems. However, as we shift our focus toward Eŭtopia, it is very important to shift our perspective beyond European and European-derived ideas, yet we must ensure that we do not commodify these non-European ideas.

When I think about Eŭtopia, I think about the practice of *moai*, but I also know that it may be impossible to replicate Okinawa's *moai* in America. Americans may not be able to match our children with a community of other children who nurture and sustain each other for the rest of their lives, but we can understand the philosophy and meaning of *moai* to help us become better friends and people. I enjoy the Japanese practices of *wabi-sabi* and *kintsugi*, which remind us of the imperfection of existence. In *wabi-sabi*, craftsmen intentionally leave in or create imperfections so that we are reminded of the imperfections of existence. *Kintsugi* derives from *wabi-sabi*, and is the practice of repairing broken objects using a gold adhesive to mend cracks. The beauty of the objects is enhanced by the visible, vivid imperfections. When looking at a *kintsugi* pot or running your finger across a dimple in your favorite coffee mug, you experience a subtle reminder of imperfection and existence. Of course, interpretations of these philosophies often oversimplify their meaning by describing them as teaching the "beauty of imperfection." More importantly, they are meant to bring us closer to existence and nature by reminding us of the imperfection of all living things, and to encourage us to make something beautiful and meaningful from imperfection. We must have an active, not passive, relationship to beauty and meaning.

In the language of Camus, *wabi-sabi* and *kintsugi* are rebellions against the meaninglessness of existence, yet his language was forged in the chaos of twentieth-century Europe. *Wabi-sabi* and *kintsugi* have been practiced since the fourteenth and fifteenth centuries in Japan, and derive from Zen Buddhism, which officially arrived in Japan around the twelfth century, but whose ideas derive from the sixth century B.C.E. when Buddhism was created. Eŭtopia can manifest as a coffee mug or plate that you use every day, but the meaning and philosophy that inspired its creation may have begun thousands of years ago. Unfortunately, as *wabi-sabi* and *kintsugi* have become more popular in America, our ethnocidal society attempts to create culture-less replicas with a *wabi-sabi* or *kintsugi* façade whose meaning and philosophy have been stripped away.

The newness of the United States and our ethnocidal foundation make it harder for Americans to recognize and cultivate Eŭtopia. We do not have a history of creating good—despite what we tell ourselves. We can look at an Eŭtopian practice and misunderstand its meaning, and often we only feel comfortable embracing the practice once its meaning has been stripped away. Yet even when we do understand the importance of these practices, we lack the language and culture to articulate and manifest our appreciation. Eŭtopia helps provide the capacity to express our respect and appreciation for the sustainable, nurturing cultures of other societies that we should aspire to emulate.

—

Another obstacle for conveying and sustaining the meaning of words is the necessity of an abundance of words to articulate the meaning of one word. Sartre's *Being and Nothingness* is nearly eight hundred pages, and it was only the beginning of the discussion on Existentialism. I have no idea why Europe latched onto the philosophy of Descartes, but I'm confident that the ability to summarize his ideas with only five words played a significant role in shaping European minds. You do not need to be a scholar or even literate to understand "I think therefore I am." Unbeknownst to the practitioners of this idea, their essence-driven philosophy would have disastrous consequences for the world. As we shift our focus toward existence, we also need a phrase to anchor our thoughts and provide meaning to our words and actions.

Ubuntu is a southern African philosophy that can be summarized as "I am because we are," and in five words it is clear that Ubuntu is the philosophical antithesis of "I think therefore I am." Ubuntu suggests our being is inextricably connected to the being of others, and Descartes suggests our being is connected to the thoughts that populate our minds. The former encourages us to be a part of existence and commune with others, while the latter inclines us to be apart from existence and to live within our imagined essence. The togetherness of Ubuntu encourages us to think beyond our shared humanity, and to embrace the connection we share with our environment. The food we eat, the water we drink, the air we breathe, and the climate and topography of where we live all help shape us. "I am because we are" encourages an empathy that extends beyond our humanity and into the environment and inanimate objects, such as a *wabi-sabi* bowl from fourteenth-century Japan, or the capacity to feel-into a work of art from nineteenth-century Germany. The philosophy of Ubuntu must influence our thoughts and actions as we forge Eŭtopia, and Ubuntu already has a successful track record of combatting ethnocide.

Nelson Mandela practiced Ubuntu as he challenged apartheid in South Africa, and the collectiveness of Ubuntu empowered him to work with white Afrikaner South Africans while still ensuring the dignity of Indigenous African people. He did not aim to find common ground with the ethnocider. Instead, he demonstrated the benefit of Ubuntu to shatter their ethnocidal philosophy. Apartheid and ethnocide create a social construct of "us vs. them," but not a "we." Under systemic, normalized division, "we" normally speaks to various tribes and factions, but there is no collective "we" to speak of. Ubuntu encouraged Mandela to forge a collective "we" in South Africa, and this collective had to include all South Africans regardless of race. Mandela countered the normalized "us vs. them" of apartheid not by inverting the power dynamics of ethnocide, but by altering the philosophy of the country and creating a new cultural "we." Ubuntu challenged ethnocide by articulating a theory of ethnogenesis that could create an Eŭtopian place. The unity and cultural healing that Mandela forged among South Africans by bringing them together in support of the national rugby team during the 1995 Rugby World Cup in South Africa was a manifestation of Ubuntu, and is still regarded as a cultural turning point that showed the potential of a new, unified South Africa.

Archbishop Desmond Tutu is also a practitioner of Ubuntu, and he used its philosophy of togetherness during South Africa's landmark Truth and

Reconciliation Commission. His goal was to confront the unpleasant truth of the past while creating a framework for collective healing. The goal of confronting the past was not to inflict retributive justice on the wrongdoers, but to attempt a process of restorative justice that could restore the humanity of all South Africans while creating the safeguards to prevent a relapse into a regressive culture dependent on destruction. South Africa's *crimen injuria* law—which makes it illegal to call an Indigenous South African *kaffir*—legally protects the dignity of African people while combatting a potential cultural regression to ethnocide. The philosophy of Ubuntu allows its practitioners to demonstrate a humanity that those accustomed to ethnocide struggled to imagine, and this is how we can transcend ethnocide. This is the cultural obligation of all victims of ethnocide: both ethnocider and ethnocidee.

Mahatma Gandhi's Satyagraha can be expressed with the easy maxim "holding on to truth." Satyagraha influenced Dr. King's philosophy of nonviolence, and a more complete definition of the word demonstrates that Satyagraha does not just defend the truth, but protects the soul, culture, or *Geist* of a people. "Satyagraha is literally holding on to Truth and it means, therefore, Truth-force. Truth is soul or spirit. It is, therefore, known as soul-force." The ethnocidee fights to preserve their soul within an ethnocidal world, and it's not surprising that a prodigious Black minister whose profession was to enliven the soul of his congregation would understand the connection between soul and truth as a way to strengthen his community and combat oppression. A dystopian ethnocidal society exists to destroy the souls of the ethnocidee and ethnocider, and in so doing ethnocide also depends on destroying the truth. The soullessness of Donald Trump and his supporters exists to wage a perpetual, Ur-Fascist war against the truth.

Ubuntu and Satyagraha both speak to universal truths, and the leaders of their movements in the twentieth century have inspired Americans who champion equality. In America's ethnocidal society, the truth has always been a distant second to white ethnocidal dominance, and holding on to truth has always been an act of rebellion. Today, ancestor remembrance traditions can be one facet of this peaceful rebellion just as sitting at segregated lunch counters and demanding a return of your voting rights were in the 1960s. By holding on to the truth, we demand that the oppressors confront their dangerous untruths, but unlike in Gandhi's India, the end goal cannot be convincing the ethnocider to leave the country. Our oppressors, unlike British colonizers, have severed their national ties to Europe, with nowhere they can retreat to. Articulating the horrors of ethnocide will not be enough, so we must forge a new culture built around a philosophy committed to making a sustainable, nurturing culture in America that transcends racial division. A cross-cultural ancestor remembrance tradition both holds on to truth and is one step toward forging the new equitable culture that American society needs.

Ubuntu's maxim "I am because we are" has already helped forge a new culture in South Africa, and Satyagraha's "holding on to truth" has helped liberate India from the British. As America works to emancipate ourselves from ethnocide, we must always hold on to truth and work to create a cultural "we." Americans celebrate our constitution because of the words "We the people," but we casually dismiss the fact that the "we" is not a collective "we." This truth is uncomfortable, and far too many of us embrace the lie because it can be manipulated to suit our emotional or essence-based needs. America can only truly have "We the people" when we acknowledge that thus far America has never strived to create a collective cultural "we."

—

A sustainable good place requires effort. It is not an impossible and perfect ideal that sustains itself without communal effort. It may be a nice idea to believe that one can exist as a passive participant in a heaven on earth, but this concept has no connection to existence. We must all cultivate our gardens. Eŭtopia is a place that can fall apart when we choose to cease nurturing it. Negligence, whether by yourself or others, can shatter an Eŭtopian practice. Eŭtopia is the constant process of sustaining existence and creating meaning from our actions. It will always be easier to undermine Eŭtopia than create it, because destruction is easier than creation. However, because of its simplicity, people inevitably attempt to find meaning and purpose from destruction. Ethnocide is one such attempt.

Cultivating an Eŭtopian space does not preclude cultural regression, but it does mean that we must have the tools to confront this problem and find our way back to Eŭtopia's cultivation. America's ethnocidal society celebrates destruction, and America suppresses the truth by existing in bad faith. We have lived in this destructive *mauvaise foi* for so long that we struggle to imagine language, philosophies, and practices that could liberate us from our ethnocidal norm. Because ethnocide is all we have ever known, America is fearful of life without ethnocide. Far too often we attempt to comfort ourselves by corrupting the truth and convincing ourselves that the harm of ethnocide is beneficial or does not exist.

To create a sustainable, nurturing, good place, you need to be able to identify and articulate the aspects of existence that harm us, and we will always need to pursue this work. In early 2020, few people anticipated that the COVID-19 outbreak would become a deadly pandemic that radically reshaped the world, but there have been obvious distinctions between people's existence- and essence-based responses. In the United States, far too many Americans perpetuated our society's essence-based worldview. They proclaimed nonsensical, contradictory theories regarding COVID-19, drawing conclusions that encouraged them to act as if the deadly pathogen did not exist. These Americans proclaimed that COVID-19 was a hoax, that wearing masks did not help stop the spread of the disease, and that

China intentionally made the disease in a laboratory. Their illogic encouraged them to behave as if we were still in a pre-COVID-19 world. Then President Trump championed these delusional ideas; his negligence and essence-based ideology both exacerbated the problem and galvanized his supporters who yearned for someone to embrace their essence. Trump's campaign rallies, and even the ceremony at the White House to announce the nomination of Amy Coney Barrett to the Supreme Court, were superspreader events. Trump's supporters actively prioritized their essence ahead of their existence during a deadly pandemic. One half of America confronted an existential crisis, and the other an essentialist crisis.

By prioritizing essence ahead of existence, these Americans became incapable of addressing the pressing concerns of existence, and they made existence harder to sustain. Throughout 2020 Trump and his supporters even expressed the belief that wearing a mask, staying inside, and adjusting their life due to COVID-19 constituted a theft of their freedom, but their concept of freedom was grounded in their essence, and not their existence or the existence of hundreds of millions of other Americans. They wanted the freedom to be destructive and dangerous without any repercussions. They wanted the essence of the master-slave dialectic. They did not want to be free to live alongside their fellow human, but sought instead an imagined freedom where they dominate and are untouched by existence. As Americans were dying at unprecedented rates, and hospitals struggled to cope with the surge in infections, Trump and his sycophants followed the lead of Marie Antoinette and France's ancien régime and said, "Let them take hydroxychloroquine" as the administration failed to provide the American public with adequate safety guidelines or economic relief. When President Barack Obama left the White House in 2017, his administration had even left the incoming Trump administration a playbook for how to address a deadly pandemic. As an extension of America's Lost Cause, Trump dismissed the legitimacy of Black existence, ideas, and intellect, and ignored Obama's advice.

In 2020, America's biggest threats were COVID-19 and ethnocide. It only took a matter of months to identify and name COVID-19, but it has taken centuries to do the same with ethnocide. When I first started talking to people about ethnocide, many asked me if naming the destruction of culture while keeping the people was actually necessary. They questioned the impact that one word could have, but comparing ethnocide to COVID-19 linguistically made it easy for people to understand the life-altering impact of one word. I would ask people to imagine what their life would look like if COVID-19 existed but the world had never identified or named this global killer. All we knew was that people were suddenly falling ill and dying as they went about their normal lives. The disease attacked all people regardless of age, race, or income. No place was safe from this mysterious phantom that could strike you down anywhere and at any time, and no one would have a clue about how to protect themselves. The absence of a language for what ails you not only results in catastrophe, but condemns humanity to live in a state of powerlessness where the only expectation is that the chaos will continue and the only hope is divine intervention. America has attempted to combat ethnocide, but without naming the crime. This is why we hope for a savior to rescue us from our crime without a name, yet also anticipate they will come up short, be killed by a *letzter Mensch*, and society will tragically remain the same. We expect to not transcend our problems, yet want to call these anticipated failures "progress."

The creation of new words can be an empowering endeavor because when we can name and define the world around us, we become equipped with the tools to proactively interact with the world. We are not consumed with angst and anxiety due to the fear of the unknown, but instead use our freedom and language to turn the previously unknown into the known.

Unsurprisingly, Germany—with their glorious compound words—has confronted the COVID-19 pandemic by creating over a thousand new words for describing and coping with this new reality. When Germans go outside, they make sure to wear their *Alltagsmaske* (everyday mask) and maintain a *Mindestabstandsregelung* (minimum distance regulation). As they follow the necessary safety protocols, they exist in an *Anderthalbmetergesellschaft* (one-and-a-half-meter society) that includes a *Fussgruss* (foot greeting) to ensure that they can still forge physical connections in our socially distanced world. The process of cultivating life-affirming language is more than just defining the problem that imperils your society, such as COVID-19 or ethnocide. In addition to defining the problem, we must also cultivate and create the plethora of words to describe our reality within this all-consuming plague. We need these derivative words to make us less fearful of the present and to help us proactively combat, confront, and solve the previously unnamed problem. We cannot engage in *aufheben* without new language.

Eŭtopia is not a place or a way of life that has the answers to all of our questions. Instead, it will help us ask the right questions so that we can find the answers that we need. Still, there will never be a time where we will have all of the answers and no need for questions. When COVID-19 hit America, an Eŭtopian perspective might have prevented us from asking how to blame China or why Democrats supposedly wanted to take away Americans' freedoms. Instead, we would have asked questions about the nature of the illness so that we could name it, begun the process of developing treatments and vaccines, and then asked Americans about the sacrifices we can collectively make to help ensure that we can remain healthy and safe during a time of crisis. An Eŭtopian question asks not what your fellow man can do for you, but what you can do for your fellow man. These are questions and answers based on existence and not essence, and they already have a track record of empowering Americans to work to become their best selves.

After we name and diagnose the problem, we can then ask questions about how we can create an equitable culture that brings us together. The new culture we create will require a name, and we will need to create practices to sustain and nurture us. In the post-COVID-19 era, our new cultural practices might include regularly wearing face masks, getting COVID-19 vaccines, not shaking hands, and working from home more often. To combat ethnocide, we must first name the destructive cultural plague that has consumed American society and then take measures to prevent it from spreading. We must create a new culture that precedes our racial divisions and focuses on creating a collective culture built upon truth. I have no idea if Freecano will be embraced, but I do know that I arrived at this answer by asking the right type of questions. By synthesizing the many cultures of America into something new and constructive, we can engage in *aufheben* and lift ourselves up from the destructive status quo of ethnocide. As we work to transcend ethnocide, we must create the language, philosophy, and practices to maintain our non-ethnocidal way of life in a sustainable good place. Ethnocide is unsustainable due to its essence-based philosophy, parasitic relationship with humanity and the earth, dependence on lies, and ideological disconnect from existence and sustaining life.

As we cultivate Eŭtopia, it is inevitable that some entity will challenge the importance of doing good, and sustaining life, because it will always be much easier to do bad, and destroy life. The wisdom of Eŭtopia should always provide a response that justifies the necessity of sustaining and nurturing existence. Eŭtopia helps us ask the right questions, so that we can find the answers to help support a sustainable, nurturing existence.

Oh my body, make of me a man who always questions!
FRANTZ FANON, *Black Skin, White Masks*

AFTERWORD

American *Geist* and Soulless Language

What is your aim in philosophy? To show the fly the way
out of the fly-bottle.

LUDWIG WITTGENSTEIN,
Philosophical Investigations

On May 25, 2020, then-Minneapolis police officer Derek Chauvin murdered George Floyd by kneeling on his neck for nine minutes and twenty-
nine seconds. Chauvin forced the air out of Floyd's lungs, and everyone
who watched the video filmed by Darnella Frazier—who was only seventeen at the time—saw a man's soul being forced out of his body as he
begged for life. The chant of "I can't breathe"—which had become a pillar
of Black Lives Matter marches and protests after Eric Garner was stran-
gled to death by New York City police officer Daniel Pantaleo on July 17,

2014—took on a new resonance: despite the seismic efforts and illusion of progress, we heard the same cries for help and witnessed the same soulless outcome.

When I watched the video of Floyd's murder, I saw ethnocide, *Geistmord*, and the banality of American evil. America and the world watched a white male police officer nonchalantly squeeze out the life and soul of a Black man. The crime Floyd had committed to justify his arrest and brutal killing on a street in Minneapolis, Minnesota, according to Chauvin and the three other assisting police officers, was that he allegedly attempted to purchase goods at a local convenience store using a counterfeit twenty-dollar bill; an alleged fraud of twenty dollars gave Chauvin and his fellow officers all the justification they needed to murder Floyd in broad daylight. In 2014, Garner was murdered because law enforcement suspected him of selling cigarettes without a tax stamp, and this alleged crime probably amounted to less than twenty dollars. Floyd's murder was evil incarnate—not merely the evil embodied by the police officers who committed and oversaw Floyd's murder, but that of an entire society and culture built upon taking life and destroying souls. America has condoned this evil for centuries.

When Chauvin murdered Floyd, I thought about the photos of lynchings that white Americans fondly gazed into and shared with their friends and family, those postcards and souvenirs that later became the subject of Ken Gonzales-Day's *Erased Lynching* series. Those white Americans felt empowered by their soulless existence, and depictions of *Geistmord* and ethnocide brought them joy. When they engaged in terror, captured depictions of terror with their cameras, and shared them with their community, they perceived their atrocity as a normal and necessary action to sustain their way of life. As Chauvin slowly killed Floyd without a hint of remorse, anxiety, or concern—despite being filmed committing this act of terror—it became abundantly clear that he perceived his actions to be normal and an extension of the power bestowed upon American law enforcement. Chauvin kept the peace and sustained law and order in the manner of the American slave patrols who existed to capture runaway slaves. Denying Black Americans freedom sustained ethnocide, and American law enforcement was largely created to sustain America's dystopian status quo. Following Garner's murder, no charges were brought against Pantaleo, and he continued to work as a police officer until he was fired in 2019, more than five years after he murdered Garner. On June 25, 2021, Chauvin was sentenced to twenty-two and a half years in prison.

After Floyd's murder, I wrote about ethnocide in the mainstream media for the first time, with articles appearing in *The Daily Beast* and the *BBC*. The linguistic and cultural connection to Nazism no longer seemed like a step too far for mainstream media. I was glad that my language had been deemed relevant, acceptable, and necessary for articulating the inherent terror of American life, but I was saddened by the amount of Black death required for American society to legitimize the language a Black person uses to articulate the systemic terror that has always shaped our society and terrorized Black people. I cried when my words made it into print; I could not celebrate. My minor success had already come at too great a cost.

—

Following Floyd's murder, Black Lives Matter protests engulfed the nation and spread around the world. The impending presidential election energized the American people. We knew that President Trump would not listen to our cries, but we hoped that then-presidential candidate Joe Biden would. But worldwide protests did not prevent American law enforcement from killing Black Americans, and soon the protests that emerged following Floyd's murder also carried the names of the other Black Americans who had been killed or seriously injured in the ensuing months. On August 23, 2020, Jacob Blake was shot in the back four times—paralyzing him from the waist down—by Kenosha, Wisconsin, police officers, and soon thereafter protesting consumed the city. Two days later, seventeen-year-old Kyle Rittenhouse arrived at a protest in Kenosha brandishing an AR-15-style rifle.

Rittenhouse articulated that he desired to confront protestors in order to defend and save property, and he was willing to use lethal force to do so. Rittenhouse's terroristic logic is more of the Anglican credo embodied by John Smith and articulated by John Locke that prioritizes property and wealth ahead of human life and considers property to be an essential component to freedom. Rittenhouse expresses a greater capacity to sympathize with a building or a business than other human beings because he, and many other Americans, believe that a building and a business are an extension of their whiteness. The existence of non-white people fighting for freedom presents an essentialist threat to ethnocidal Americans that they often suppress with lethal force.

Black Americans and their allies destroying property and no longer behaving as the property of white Americans equates to the destruction of what ethnocidal Americans call freedom, and Rittenhouse was willing to engage in terror in order to preserve ethnocidal freedom. Rittenhouse killed two people, Joseph Rosenbaum and Anthony Huber, and injured Gaige Grosskreutz—none of whom are Black—as he clashed with protestors. Their allyship and desire to forge community with non-white people made them a threat to ethnocide, so they too became the recipients of ethnocidal terror. After the murders, Rittenhouse fled Wisconsin and returned to his home state of Illinois, and on August 26, he turned himself in to the authorities.

Prior to his attack in Kenosha, Rittenhouse also articulated his support of Blue Lives Matter, and in the months following his arrest, ethnocidal Americans including law enforcement officials have articulated support for him and even donated money to his legal defense. Rittenhouse was able to post a $2 million bond, and was released from custody in November 2020. This phrase, "Blue Lives Matter," demonstrates how meaningless, soulless language can create soulless people who use terror to sustain a soulless way of life.

Following the emergence of the Black Lives Matter movement after the 2012 murder of Trayvon Martin, American conservatives and the Republican Party actively pursued creating their own slogan that would delegitimize "Black Lives Matter." "Blue Lives Matter" became arguably the most popular, with "All Lives Matter" a close second, and this phrase has allowed Americans to claim that they support law enforcement without explicitly denouncing the Black Lives Matter movement or using racist language. Blue Lives Matter is a phrase created to mask racism under a veil of supporting law enforcement, yet as the Capitol attack of January 6, 2021, shows, a respect for law enforcement is quickly dismissed if it stands in the way of ethnocidal terror. The phrase does not have any true meaning apart from delegitimizing the language and existence of Black Americans. Blue Lives Matter is ethnocide and *Geistmord* condensed into three words. It is a meaningless phrase fueled by white essence, whose sole purpose is to turn the meaningful culture, language, and existence of people of color into meaningless gibberish, so that ethnocide can remain the dominant force in America. It is a dominance forged by reducing existence into a meaningless void.

This is the language America often opts to speak when confronted with the existence of those without a white essence, and this destructive discourse can corrupt and imperil the most noble of institutions and principles. America's soulless language has already corrupted the First and

Second Amendments to the U.S. Constitution, and this corruption has made our society ill-equipped to prevent the hate-filled discourse and violence that has become our dystopian norm. Instead of the United States' founding document professing freedom and security, it now professes hate and terror due to ethnocidal corruption.

—

It is fair to say that America's Founding Fathers who enshrined the rights of free speech and to bear arms into our Constitution never intended to include or extend those rights to people of color. Indigenous and Black people did not have protected speech, and they were not encouraged to take up arms to combat the spread of the white ethnocidal and genocidal tyranny that destroyed their communities. From America's inception, ethnocide has created a diseased language with the explicit purpose of forcing non-white people to live in a perpetual state of dis-ease. However, faith in democracy resides in the belief that it can remedy its afflictions. Therefore, as toxic, dangerous speech and deadly gun violence continue to consume the nation, we must examine why American democracy has thus far been unable to cure our disease. In hindsight, there are many examples of when America could have actively remedied our affliction, but for the sake of brevity, I will focus on two Supreme Court cases.

In the summer of 1964, Ku Klux Klan member Clarence Brandenburg invited a local television news reporter to attend and document a KKK rally in Ohio. At this rally, in addition to spewing the racist language that had long been the American norm, Brandenburg spoke of the need to seek revenge following the passage of the landmark Civil Rights Act of 1964. "We're not a revengent organization," said Brandenburg. "But if our president, our Congress, our Supreme Court continues to suppress the white,

Caucasian race, it's possible that there might have to be some revengence taken." (In this statement, Brandenburg coined the words *revengent* and *revengence* not to fill a profound linguistic void in American society, but to account for his ignorance of the words *vengeful* and *vengeance*. Brandenburg struggles to even articulate his intent, but there is no ambiguity about what he meant to say.)

At the time, Brandenburg's language violated Ohio's criminal syndicalism statute that prohibited both the rally and his speech. Ohio's law prohibited both the advocating of crime, violence, or unlawful methods of terrorism and voluntarily assembling with a society or group to teach or advocate for the prohibited speech. Brandenburg was charged, convicted, and sentenced to one year in prison, but he challenged the decision, claiming that it violated his First Amendment rights. The Supreme Court's decision in this case has shaped American free speech ever since.

In 1969, in *Brandenburg v. Ohio*, in a per curiam decision, the Supreme Court sided with Brandenburg, stating that abstract speech could not be prosecuted, and instead created a new standard for policing speech called "imminent lawless action." Essentially, since they could not connect Brandenburg's speech to a specific or imminent lawless action, his speech was abstract. Brandenburg did not immediately leave the rally and seek revenge; therefore, in the eyes of the court, his language was abstract and needed to be protected. At the time, the court's decision was not controversial. Brandenburg was represented by the ACLU, and Americans across the racial divide viewed this decision as a preservation of freedom of speech in America. In hindsight, this decision is absurd and dangerous, because the decision is based upon ignoring or removing from the equation the historical and existing threat of America's white ethnocidal terrorism. The ramifications of defining the expression of white ethnocidal terrorism as abstract speech have shaped our society for the worse, and in 2021, Donald Trump has used this standard as his defense against being prosecuted for inciting the January 6 riot on the Capitol. He wants the law to define his words as abstract and meaningless so that he suffers no consequence for his deadly actions. Trump speaks the language of Brandenburg.

Brandenburg was a member of a known and established American terrorist group. His words came with a history of terror, and he uttered his words during a time of volatile racial tensions in America. From 1964, when Brandenburg uttered his dangerous language, to 1969, when the Supreme Court defended his right to propagate white ethnocidal terrorism, countless people of color were terrorized by the KKK, and so were the white Americans who supported the Civil Rights Movement. Martin Luther King Jr. was assassinated in Memphis, Tennessee, on April 4, 1968, by a white supremacist, so the normalization of America's dangerous and diseased speech had already killed and terrorized many of the Americans who fought to save the soul of the nation.

Brandenburg's language was not abstract. The only way one could perceive his language as such would be to view him as a singular individual and not as an extension of a toxic culture. Brandenburg was not some random individual who expressed hate-filled language on a random day in 1964. He was a member of a terrorist organization that held a rally to profess the need to seek revenge against the federal government for extending rights and freedoms to people of color. This terrorist group had existed for a century at the time of Brandenburg's dangerous words, and there has never been any ambiguity about their beliefs and the terror they are willing to inflict to sustain them. Throughout the 1960s, this organization and its sympathizers acted upon their dangerous speech and terrorized the nation. There is nothing abstract about Brandenburg's speech. In fact, the underlying philosophy of his speech is that he believes that denying him the capacity to articulate the necessity of terrorism equates to a denial of his First Amendment rights.

Without terror, Brandenburg and his ilk do not believe they can be free. Without terror they have been silenced. For them, TERROR IS FREEDOM, and the most powerful court in America agreed with them. In the end, Brandenburg did not need to seek "revengence" against the Supreme Court.

When I talk to people about my frustration with *Brandenburg*, I often bring up the concept of dangerous speech, which is a simple yet controversial idea in America. By implementing laws to regulate dangerous speech, societies that are attempting to recover from a domestic atrocity or society-altering act of domestic terrorism work to limit the speech that precipitated the dystopian event in hopes of preventing a similar catastrophe in the future. Germany and France, for example, have laws that prohibit anti-Semitic speech. South Africa's *crimen injuria* law is also a regulation of dangerous speech. These societies are aware of their history, and as they work toward becoming a sustainable, nurturing, and dignified culture, they seek to regulate destructive, dangerous language with a history of emboldening their worst and most-base selves. You can neither work-off-the-past nor have a memory culture when you live in an ahistorical society committed to destroying culture.

More often than not, Americans find the notion of dangerous speech incredibly troubling, because they perceive the regulation of speech as precipitating a descent into the total absence of free speech. If a person in Germany is reprimanded for anti-Semitic speech, some Americans interpret this scenario as an example of the dangers of policing speech. Frequently, they will even cite Orwell and express a fear of a dystopian Big Brother who polices everything they say and do, yet they rarely grasp that the freedom they are protecting is actually the manifestation of Orwell's doublethink. For the last fifty years, a core principle of America's freedom of speech has been allowing all Americans—but in reality, mainly white Americans—the right to profess the necessity of terrorism in the name of freedom. These two contradictory ideas are now interwoven and perceived as one and the same. America interprets a solution to our problems, such as regulating dangerous speech, as the precursor to a dystopian way of life. We have this inverted, diseased perspective because we do not want to confront the reality of the bad place within which we already live.

Brandenburg exists because America prefers to imagine that white ethnocidal terror does not exist. If the KKK, America's present racial tensions, and the history of our society are removed from the equation, then Brandenburg is just a random individual who said something unpleasant but ultimately harmless in 1964. From this perspective, it would be absurd and dangerous to imprison Brandenburg, but the dangers and absurdity of this perspective should be just as clear. America's misinterpretation of freedom speaks to a corrupted and diseased language, and from our unhealthy, soulless discourse springs a language that professes the necessity of hate and terror to sustain what a segment of our population considers freedom. America's ethnocidal language—built upon the erasure of the awareness of ethnocide—also influences the Second Amendment.

In *Nunn v. State of Georgia*, Hawkins H. Nunn sued the state of Georgia, claiming that its 1837 ban on the sale of certain weapons, including various knives and pistols, was a violation of the Second Amendment, and in 1846, the Georgia Supreme Court sided with Nunn. In the court's decision, it ruled that Georgia could not ban the sale of weapons, but it could regulate whether people could conceal carry weapons. Following this ruling, open carry became the norm in Georgia, and this decision still influences American gun laws today. In the U.S. Supreme Court's landmark 2008 decision *District of Columbia v. Heller*, which overturned the nation's capital's ban on handguns, Justice Antonin Scalia referenced *Nunn v. State of Georgia* in the majority opinion stating that the case protected the "natural right of self-defense" in the Second Amendment. The *Heller* decision opened the floodgates on the deregulation of weapons in the name of self-defense and has helped create the increasingly violent and dangerous society we live within. In 2021, Greg Abbott, the Republican governor of Texas who is staunchly pro-gun, made it legal for Texas residents to carry a gun without a license or training. Similar bills are being proposed in other states.

As with *Brandenburg*, the decisions in *Heller* and *Nunn* only make sense if you remove white terrorism and ethnocide from the equation. In 1846, Georgia was still a slaveholding state, and nearly half of the population was enslaved. Georgia's ethnocidal way of life could not exist without weapons, because white Georgians needed them to oppress the state's large population of enslaved people. Additionally, the rights articulated in the Second Amendment did not de facto extend to people of color. The cultural requirement for white Americans to carry weapons also increased the likelihood that white Georgians would turn their weapons on other white Georgians. Instituting a ban on certain weapons would seem like a logical solution for Georgia's white-on-white crime, but this solution would never work, because the state's need to perpetually oppress Black Americans meant that you could not have a society without guns. Instead, the illegality of certain guns in Georgia increased the likelihood that white Georgians would illegally obtain a gun and conceal it when they carried it. When guns cannot be removed from a society, laws to regulate guns create a black market for weapons and a more dangerous society. In the 1840s, the prevalence of Georgians concealing illegal guns made it almost impossible for Georgians like Nunn to protect themselves from other white Georgians. In today's language, the good guy with the gun was getting shot by the bad guy with a gun, yet since both the good guy and the bad guy in this society perpetuate terror against non-white Americans, the true reality is that both are bad, and their society is starved of goodness.

When your society's default is the perpetual terrorization of Black

Americans, instructing white Americans to open carry their weapons equates to protecting the freedom and safety of white Americans. Terror again equals freedom in this society, but now we are talking about the actions and not just the words that precede the actions. Within this dystopian world, overturning Georgia's weapons ban while also banning conceal carry was Georgia's solution, and in the present, America still applies this illogic to shape our gun laws. By ignoring how ethnocide has diseased our laws and language, America perpetuates terror in the name of freedom, and still we wonder why we feel less safe and less at ease.

When a white teenager brings an AR-15-style rifle with the goal of inflicting terror to defend freedom, he does so because America's language and laws have encouraged him to see the world in this way. When a white American perceives racial equality, civil rights, and voting rights as threats to their existence that must be suppressed with violence and terror, they are merely continuing America's corrupted ethnocidal norm. When law enforcement perceives Black existence as inherently criminal and a threat to white existence, they do so because our society has encouraged them to think this way and given them the authority to use lethal force to exterminate the threat of Black existence. When Americans spew hate-filled, racist, anti-Semitic rhetoric, we believe that the dangers of these words exist in the abstract. We believe that the language has only moral or ethical ramifications, but hardly any real-world impact. These words and those who utter them supposedly pose no imminent lawless threat; therefore, they are essentially meaningless. When America's hate-filled language is considered meaningless, America concludes both that it must be protected and that it would be absurd to punish someone for meaningless words. Instead, America punishes people for their meaningless words only after they have committed a crime inspired by the words, and thus their previously meaningless language becomes meaningful hate speech.

There is a dangerous absurdity to America's soulless language, and one can see the soullessness of America's way of life only through seeing and respecting the souls of those who have been victims of American ethnocide and genocide. In 2020, George Floyd showed the world that the soul of America far too often is shaped by soulless people and the destruction of souls.

—

In America, discussions pertaining to soul are primarily reserved for theologians, and not philosophers. One's soul is an ecclesiastical concern in America. It is rarely discussed in relation to the present, and Americans do not equate one's soul with one's mind or intelligence. America's cultural reliance on religion and not philosophy to shape our soul ironically inclines Americans to lead a soulless life in anticipation of a soulful death.

Intriguingly, as *Einfühlung*, or empathy, grew within philosophy, so did the study and examination of our living soul and people who struggle to empathize. Soon thereafter, the words *psychopathy* and *psychosis* emerged. *Psycho-* derives from Greek, meaning "soul, mind, spirit," and *-pathy* is also a Greek derivative, meaning "suffering or disease." With *empathy*, *-pathy* means "feeling," because it is shared with another, but with *psychopathy*, it means "suffering or disease" due to a lack of connection. *Psychopathy* means "soul suffering," and *psychosis* means "abnormal soul," and these words came into existence as Europe worked to define, examine, and rectify the horrors of being unable to empathize. This is an understanding of soul grounded in reality, and as Americans demonize others by calling them "psychos," we remain tragically unaware that soul has just become a pejorative. America's culture of individualism and division makes our souls suffer, and inclines us to be fearful of the diverse, inclusive, empathetic world we need to embrace.

America cultivates a culture of fear masked by the *mauvaise foi* of American Exceptionalism, and due to this, America wages culture wars both big and small, international and domestic to sustain our ethnocidal way of life.

I prefer using *Geist* instead of *soul*, because the philosophical examination of *Geist* makes it easier to lead a soulful life. Saying *Geist* reminds me that my individual and shared collective soul is firmly grounded in the present while also being a continuation of the past. *Geist* also reminds me that one's mind and intelligence are more than quantifiable attributes that can be measured on an exam. One's *Geist* includes the hard-to-explain, unique attributes that are so influential in shaping our personality and life. The unmeasurable and hard-to-explain attributes of a person and of a people have long been the purview of the philosopher, so to further examine the soul of America, we should quickly discuss two plays by Jean-Paul Sartre.

The Respectful Prostitute (*La Putain respectueuse*) was first performed at the Théâtre Antoine in Paris in 1946. The play is set in the American South, and its accurate depiction of American life under Jim Crow inclined Americans to describe the play as anti-American. The plot of the play is a familiar American narrative on par with the expectation of police brutality and gun violence today. A Black man is accused of raping a white woman, and American society must inflict its injustice in the mask of justice. Lizzie, the prostitute, is the white woman, and the play is devoid of a hero.

At the beginning of the play, the Black man accused of raping Lizzie finds her in her hotel room and begs her to tell the truth. Lizzie promises the man, who is never given a name and is listed as The Negro, that she will tell the police and the judge that he did not rape her. Lizzie is from New York City, and does not believe in the South's iteration of justice. Later in the play, Lizzie has a client named Fred. Fred is the son of a powerful senator, and Fred's cousin Thomas is accused of killing a Black man. The false narrative being spread around town is that The Negro and his Black friend attempted to rape Lizzie on a train, and that Thomas intervened to save Lizzie. During the struggle, Thomas killed the Black man, and now the town is hunting The Negro so that they can lynch him. The true story is that Thomas was drunk and approached Lizzie on the train. After she rejected his advances, he started to sexually assault her. The Negro and his friend were sitting across from Lizzie on the train, and a scuffle broke out between them and Thomas. Thomas pulled out his gun and killed the Black man.

After enlisting Lizzie's services, Fred tries to convince Lizzie to change her story and say that the Black men raped her. Lizzie refuses and declares that she intends to tell the truth. Fred responds, "There is no truth; there's only whites and blacks, that's all. Seventeen thousand white men, twenty thousand niggers. This isn't New York; we can't fool around down here." The large number of Black Americans in the South and white America's commitment to perpetual oppression means that there is no room for truth in this society. It is us vs. them, and white America's zero-sum essence means that they can only survive via nonstop oppression.

Eventually, Fred, with the assistance of his father, The Senator, convinces Lizzie to change her story. As they persuade Lizzie, they remind her that Thomas comes from a "good family" and profess the absurdity of sending a white man to prison for killing a Black person. They proclaim that Black people are the devil, and that Lizzie is also the devil if she sides with Black people. They also work to describe Thomas's life as meaningful, and impress the heartache his mother will feel if her son is sent to prison. The Negro's life, however, is expressed as meaningless and disposable, and no one will miss him if he is gone. In the end, Lizzie agrees to change her story, but soon thereafter she regrets her decision.

In the next act, the town is consumed with angry white men going from door to door looking for The Negro. A lynch mob has formed, and The Negro seeks refuge in Lizzie's hotel room. She says that he can stay there because it is the last place that the mob would look. When the mob arrives at her door, she tells them that he is not there, but wishes them "good luck."

Eventually, Fred returns to Lizzie's room, and Lizzie hides The Negro in the bathroom. Fred tells her that the mob found another Black man and lynched him instead. Fred knew that it was the wrong man, but he did not care because this Black man's death made it easier for him to claim that his lie was the truth. A Black man's death sustained a white society's lies. This is American *mauvaise foi*.

Fred did not return to Lizzie's room to relay the news. He returned because the sight of a Black man hanging from a tree—Fred was part of the lynch mob—made him realize that he wanted to marry Lizzie. "You are the Devil. You've bewitched me," said Fred. "I was with them, I had my revolver in my hand, and the nigger was swinging from a branch. I looked at him, and I thought: 'I want her.'"

Fred eventually discovers The Negro hiding in Lizzie's room. The Negro escapes from the hotel room and Fred chases after him, shooting his gun. When Fred returns to Lizzie's hotel room, he claims that he missed and did not shoot The Negro. Fred continues to court Lizzie and the play ends with them embracing and Fred happily saying that "everything is back to normal again."

Apart from being an accurate depiction of American life, *The Respectful Prostitute* reminded me of another play by Sartre that explicitly talks about soul. In *No Exit* (*Huis Clos*), three souls are condemned to hell for eternity, and they are charged with torturing one another. Their only tools for implementing terror are their personalities, and the three of them are confined to a room. Being their awful selves is the extent of their collective torture, and there appears to be no exit from their suffering. Yet during the play the door to their room opens and they have the opportunity to leave, but they decide to stay because they believe the hell they know is better than the unknown.

These three awful people might have been sent to hell, but when given the opportunity to leave, they decide to say. As the three confront their chosen hell, Garcin—the male character—exclaims, "There's no need for red-hot pokers. Hell is—other people!"

No Exit is known for this statement by Garcin, and I kept on thinking about this hellacious statement as Fred proclaimed that Black people and anyone who protects them are the devil. In Fred's real-world environment hell is other people, yet he erroneously believes he is not a part of this hell on earth despite it being the creation of his ethnocidal culture. Fred proclaims that Black people are the devil as he lynches an innocent Black person. The sight of America's strange fruit hanging from the poplar tree as a Black body swings in the southern breeze suddenly makes Fred realize that he loves Lizzie and wants to embrace this white demon. He has no desire to escape this hell, and instead aspires to revel within it. He admits that within this world there is no truth, and he embraces the void. Existence is just a constant battle with the other that they demonize. There are no heroes in this world. Instead, brutes such as Thomas are depicted as heroes, as the truth that exists within the ethnocidee is exterminated. Thomas represents the Lost Cause of ethnocide.

During Derek Chauvin's murder trial, the defense attempted to propagate a false narrative that drug abuse was responsible to George Floyd's death, and not the fact that Chauvin kneeled on his neck for nine minutes and twenty-nine seconds. They wanted the truth to die with Floyd. They essentially argued that Floyd killed himself as Chauvin engaged in routine police duty. Chauvin wanted the authority to kill without being held responsible for murder. This was the master-slave dialectic in the courtroom, and despite the vulgarity of Chauvin's defense, the American public had little confidence that he would be found guilty. In America's white vs. Black ethnocidal culture, it is rare for a police officer to be found guilty of killing a Black American regardless of the veracity of the evidence. America knows that the survival of truth is a rarity in our society. Chauvin being found guilty has given America hope that we may be able to escape our ethnocidal hell and save our collective soul.

—

The acceptance of lies, the perpetual demonization of the other, and a diseased language serve as a foundation for an American hellscape that proclaims itself to be a paradise and a pillar of truth, justice, and equality, but in order to save our collective soul we must be able to recognize our society for what it is, find a way to escape from our delusions, and have the wisdom and courage to reconstruct our world. The sheer size of the United States means that reconstructing our society into one that empowers our souls will require monumental effort that can seem nearly impossible because we must remake a nation that is almost the size of a continent.

For change to come from within and from the ground up, protests and activism need to consume cities and upend a society's way of life for an unavoidable and sustained period of time. Change from the top down will require wealthy and powerful Americans to emancipate themselves from the unsustainable, exploitative, and ethnocidal structures that have brought them relative success, and embrace the fact that cultivating inclusive and nurturing structures will be both a smarter investment for themselves and for society as a whole. Sustained activism and political engagement from the bottom and top can then lead to policies and laws that can remake society for the better, but the larger the nation the larger and more sustained the activism must be in order to move the needle. In Europe, with countries that are smaller than American states, it is much easier for protests to consume a nation, and as a result politicians feel more pressure to listen to the people. It is easier for the people's voices to be heard. In America, a massive protest in Washington, D.C., or New York City will have no impact on the lives of Americans in the South or on the West Coast, and it can easily be forgotten and ignored by many Americans as they remain preoccupied with the daily struggles of making ends meet. The threshold for activism is much harder to reach in America, and as a result, Americans can become more prone to apathy and resignation to an inescapable existence within an unsustainable, divided, and violent society. People end up focusing on surviving in America instead of transcending, and when *Aufhebung* seems like an impossibility, *mauvaise foi* can comfort you from the world you fear confronting. American society employs a nihilistic iteration of capitalism that alienates all of us from existence, but thankfully the ethnocidee and our cultural yearning for freedom still insist on rebelling against American ethnocide and engaging in the thus-far Sisyphean struggle to save the soul of America.

Following George Floyd's murder, protests spread not only across America, but around the world. Protests have occurred in over two thousand cities and sixty countries, and Derek Chauvin was convicted of his murder. These protests and the growing influence of Black voters helped the Democratic Party win control of the White House and Senate and maintain control of the House of Representatives, yet Republican obstructionism still prevents the progress that our society needs. This is the gargantuan scale of the change that must occur to reconstruct America, but the outcome must be greater than the conviction of one ethnocidal police officer and one successful election cycle.

The collective yearning for change that compelled Americans to vote, and people from around the world to take to the streets in the midst of the deadly threat of COVID-19, has definitely commenced the reconstructing of our society, yet it can still feel like not much has changed. The expansive scale of our nation means that most people need to see sweeping changes to believe that change has occurred. The requisite change must become a sustained reverberation that washes across the nation, stretching from the Atlantic and Pacific Oceans. This geographical impediment combined with the obstacles that ethnocidal Americans create—such as voting restrictions that may linguistically appear race neutral, but disproportionately harm people of color—mean that people can become discouraged because they cannot see the incremental changes taking place that can precede and create greater change.

Additionally, the nature of America's required changes mean that we must confront the unsavory truths that for far too long America has concealed by distorting and corrupting reality. Brandenburg's language can no longer be abstract, open carry does not make society safer, and neither Thomas from *The Respectful Prostitute* nor Rittenhouse is a brave American from a good family. They are a continuation of America's diseased, ethnocidal culture that exists to both conceal and perpetuate terrorism. As the capacity of ethnocidal Americans to conceal the truth weakens, America must now witness the domestic ethnocidal terrorism that has always existed in our country, but that we have been taught was nonexistent.

As more and more videos emerge of police officers and everyday Americans feeling justified in terrorizing the other that they have defined as a demon, our society gazes into the soul-sucking, hellacious cultural void created by ethnocide. Today's images and videos of domestic American terrorism can feel debilitating and heartbreaking, and thus dynamic progress can feel like a regression. Americans might yearn for a time when they were encouraged to believe that such terror did not exist. Compared to a century ago, fewer Americans feel joy when they see an image of a Black American being terrorized, but far too many prefer to imagine that the problem never existed. When I see news reports about another person of color being unjustly killed in America, I think about my uncle Vernon's classmate who was killed by a white man in Alabama because he urinated behind a gas station. I think about my aunts and uncles who told me how fortunate I was to live in this iteration of America. The murders of Breonna Taylor, Philando Castile, Ahmaud Arbery, Tamir Rice, Ronald Greene, Walter Scott, Elijah McClain, and so many others make the news today, yet in years gone by America would have acted as if their murders had never happened and their lives had always been meaningless. In the past, the truth about America's terrorism also died when people of color were murdered, but that is not always the case today.

In response to George Floyd's murder, the support for the Black Lives Matter movement increased across America and across our racial divide, but in the subsequent year, support for the movement has followed a predictable path. Support among white Americans, and especially conservative Americans, has decreased. However, despite the predictable regression toward violence and soulless words such as "Blue Lives Matter," an inspiring coalition of people of color and our white allies has emerged, and we cannot underestimate the profound impact of this movement to save the soul of America.

Over the past year, as I have worked on this book, many people have asked about George Floyd and Black Lives Matter, and if this era is merely more of the same or something truly different that could transcend ethnocide and reconstruct America. In many ways, this era is not too dissimilar from those of the past, but what makes this era different from the 1960s and the 1860s are the interracial friendships that have formed in our society. In the 1960s, the white Americans who fought for civil rights did not do so because of a long friendship with a Black America that preceded their activism. When they joined the movement, it was because of a moral objection to segregation and Jim Crow. Once they uprooted their lives and became trusted members of the movement, friendships could form. This dynamic is not too dissimilar from the 1860s, when carpetbaggers relocated to the South and worked to create relationships with emancipated Black Americans. In neither scenario did the friendships precede the movement, but that is not the case today.

In today's America, it is much easier for children of all races, ethnicities, and religions to form friendships at an early age, so when people of color are subjected to abuse, it is easier for all Americans to imagine this terror befalling a childhood friend, a coworker, or a neighbor. The white Americans who continue to support BLM, civil rights, voting rights, and racial equality are not merely acting on behalf of a moral calling. Instead, they are fighting to preserve the shared connections they have had with people of color for most of their lives. The terror inflicted upon people of color has long been beyond their comprehension, so in this regard they need to cultivate empathy, yet what brings many of them into the movement is a oneness or sympathy with those Americans whom ethnociders had previously labelled as demons.

For example, I have childhood friends who did not understand the dynamics of being a Black man in America, but they still regarded me as a friend. When they see videos of Black people being terrorized, they can imagine something that they had considered inconceivable happening to their friend. This convergence of empathy and sympathy can transcend ethnocide, and we cannot underestimate the potential for this subtle yet seismic shift to transform and reconstruct America. A white man becoming president of the United States largely due to his friendship with a Black man also speaks to the transformational impact of these friendships.

The diversity of this coalition helps ensure that the fight for equality extends to all of the communities of color who have been victims of ethnocide. Black Americans may have been the primary targets of an ethnocidal agenda and the creators of the Black Lives Matter movement, but it is obvious that ethnocide works to destroy the culture of all people of color in the Americas as ethnociders destructively work to sustain their culture-less existence. Therefore, the philosophy of Black Lives Matter can improve the lives and preserve the culture and soul of Indigenous people, Asian Americans, Latino Americans, Muslim Americans, Palestinians, and oppressed people around the world. There is the potential to transcend our dystopian norm and cultivate a new shared culture. In the American Cycle, this is the reconstruction that occurs after abolition. My non-Black friends asking me if they could also become a part of Freecano culture speaks to this desire to create a new culture. These are profoundly meaningful changes that are often overlooked but can make all the difference in the world.

—

The NBC sitcom *The Good Place* starts with the premise of *No Exit* in that the main characters are condemned to torture each other for eternity, but the show deviates from the play in that the characters are originally unaware that they are in hell and that they are heroic enough to step into the unknown in order to escape. In America, we are encouraged to consume meaningless entertainment so that it can distract us from the unpleasant world that we live within, and due to this expectation, the meaningful ideas and philosophies expressed in some American entertainment are often dismissed and perceived as merely meaningless spectacle. *The Good Place* is four seasons of philosophical comedy that derives from a profound question: "How do you escape a hell of your own creation that you erroneously thought was a heaven?" This is a question that all Americans must ask.

To answer this question, the characters in the show turned to philosophy and cultivated friendships because both of these actions strengthened their souls, helped them become better people, and empowered them to make a better world. Philosophy and friendships helped give them the courage to step through the door and overcome their fears. The cultivation of sustainable, nurturing, empathetic friendships with each other also gave them the strength to persevere on their arduous journey, and philosophy gave them the wisdom to make smart decisions along the way. *The Good Place* is a modern-day version of Dante Aligheri's Divine Comedy where the protagonist escapes hell, travels through purgatory, and finally makes it to paradise. (*Dead Souls* was Gogol's rendition of Dante's *Inferno*, but tragically he died before he could write how Chichikov escaped hell, traversed purgatory, and made it to paradise.)

As America works to save the soul of the nation, we must remember that when you resign yourself to a life within a perpetual hellscape, you have decided that hell is and will always be both yourself and other people. Lies and *mauvaise foi* serve as a fragile shield for the dystopian world you have created. However, if you are brave, heroic, and empathetic enough to step into the unknown and forge a better world, you will find that your salvation will come from your good-faith connections to other people. This is how you save your soul. The diverse friendships that are remaking American society have given us a fighting chance to save the soul of America, and live in a society that promotes freedom, justice, and equality for all. We may finally be able to emancipate ourselves from and transcend the demonizing ethnocidal mantra of hell being other people and embrace an immutable and soulful fact that ethnocidal America has long existed to destroy: Freedom is other people.

ACKNOWLEDGMENTS

A book about language, philosophy, and American society requires a lot of communal support.

The work that occurs before you find the right word or phrase can be a messy and uncomfortable endeavor. Conversations where you misspeak and say something uncomfortable as you challenge a troubling American norm are an unavoidable part of the process. Yet for the process to continue, the person you are speaking with must have faith in your desire and capacity to find the right words. Otherwise they would leave the conversation, ending the process and impeding progress. You must forge good-faith relationships within a society shaped by bad faith, and this can be incredibly difficult.

My process both during and before writing this book has mirrored this dilemma, so I need to thank each and every person who listened to me, gave me advice, and encouraged me to keep on speaking before I even knew what to say. The list of people I need to thank and acknowledge is incredibly long, so I apologize for being unable to list everyone.

This book would not be possible without Andrea. She has always encouraged me and supported my work, and without her love none of this would be possible. I need to thank my good friend Brian for enthusiastically reading all of my draft chapters and giving me feedback as I worked through the numerous iterations of this book and kept on working despite countless rejections from publishers. I must thank everyone who supported my vision of a cross-cultural ancestor-remembrance celebration. I need to thank all of my friends at Eaton for taking the time to engage in conversation with me, cultivating a welcoming atmosphere, and encouraging me to create The Sustainable Culture Lab. Also, I must thank my team at SCL who have remained committed to giving my work life and helping it grow so that we can reconstruct America into a more nurturing and sustainable society.

Lastly, I could have never written this book without the support of my family. From my parents to my sister, my aunts and uncles, cousins, grandparents, and ancestors, all of them have played a role in this process. I have never felt unloved, and with that foundation you can achieve anything.

BIBLIOGRAPHY

Alford, Terry. *Prince Among Slaves: The True Story of an African Prince Sold into Slavery in the American South.* Oxford: Oxford University Press, 2007.

Arendt, Hannah. *Eichmann in Jerusalem: A Report on the Banality of Evil.* London: Penguin, 2006.

Bakewell, Sarah. *At the Existentialist Café: Freedom, Being, and Apricot Cocktails.* New York: Other Press, 2017.

Beckett, Samuel. *Waiting for Godot.* New York: Grove Press, 1982.

Byrd, William. *The Secret Diary of William Byrd of Westover, 1709–1712.* Richmond, VA: Dietz Press, 1941.

Camus, Albert. *Caligula and 3 Other Plays.* New York: Vintage Books, 1958.

———. *The Plague.* New York: Modern Library, 1948.

———. *The Stranger.* New York: Vintage Books, 1988.

Case, Anne, and Angus Deaton. *Deaths of Despair and the Future of Capitalism.* Princeton, NJ: Princeton University Press, 2020.

Clavero, Bartolomé. *Genocide or Ethnocide, 1933–2007: How to Make, Unmake, and Remake Law with Words*. Milan: Giuffrè Editore, 2008.

De Botton, Alain. *The Consolations of Philosophy*. New York: Vintage, 2000.

Debord, Guy. *The Society of the Spectacle*. New York: Zone Books, 1995.

Descartes, René. *Discourse on Method and Meditations on First Philosophy, 4th Edition*. Indianapolis, IN: Hackett, 1999.

Du Bois, W. E. B. *Black Reconstruction in America, 1860–1880*. New York: Free Press, 1998.

———. *The Souls of Black Folk*. New York: Barnes & Noble Classics, 2003.

———. *W. E. B. Du Bois's Data Portraits: Visualizing Black America; The Color Line at the Turn of the Twentieth Century*. Edited by Whitney Battle-Baptiste and Britt Rusert. New York: Princeton Architectural Press, 2018.

Eco, Umberto. "Ur-Fascism: Freedom and liberation are an unending task." *The New York Review of Books*, June 22, 1995.

Fanon, Frantz. *Black Skin, White Masks*. New York: Grove Press, 2008.

Ferry, Luc. *A Brief History of Thought: A Philosophical Guide to Living*. New York: HarperCollins, 2011.

Foner, Eric. *Reconstruction: America's Unfinished Revolution, 1863–1877*. New York: Perennial Classics, 2002.

Frankl, Viktor E. *Man's Search for Meaning*. Boston: Beacon Press, 2006.

Freire, Paulo. *Pedagogy of the Oppressed*. New York: Bloomsbury Academic, 2015.

Fromm, Erich. *Erich Fromm and Karl Marx: Marx's Concept of Man*. London: Bloomsbury Academic, 2013.

Gandhi, Mahatma, *Gandhi on Non-Violence*. Edited by Thomas Merton. New York: New Directions, 1965.

———. *The Selected Works of Mahatma Gandhi, Volume Five: The Voice of*

Truth. Edited by Shriman Narayan. Gujarat, India: Navajivan Publishing House, 1969.

Gogol, Nikolay. *Dead Souls*. London: Penguin Classics, 2004.

Gopnik, Adam, ed. *Americans in Paris: A Literary Anthology*. New York: Library of America, 2004.

Haley, Alex. *The Autobiography of Malcolm X: As Told to Alex Haley*. New York: One World, 1992.

Harris, Ruth. *Dreyfus: Politics, Emotion, and the Scandal of the Century*. New York: Picador, 2010.

Hegel, Georg. *Phenomenology of Spirit*. Oxford: Oxford University Press, 1977.

Jaulin, Robert. *La paix blanche: introduction à l'ethnocide*. Paris: Éditions du Seuil, 1970.

Jeffries, Stuart. *Grand Hotel Abyss: The Lives of the Frankfurt School*. London: Verso, 2016.

Kass, Arielle. "Calls grow for Gwinnett elections board chair to resign." *The Atlanta Journal-Constitution*. January 19, 2021.

Kendi, Ibram X. *Stamped from the Beginning: The Definitive History of Racist Ideas in America*. New York: Nation Books, 2016.

Kierkegaard, Søren. *The Concept of Anxiety: A Simple Psychologically Oriented Deliberation in View of the Dogmatic Problem of Hereditary Sin*. New York: Liveright, 2015.

Larkin, Emma. *Finding George Orwell in Burma*. London: Penguin, 2011.

Lemkin, Raphael. *Axis Rule in Occupied Europe: Laws of Occupation – Analysis of Government – Proposals for Redress*. Washington, D.C.: Carnegie Endowment for International Peace, 1944.

———. *Totally Unofficial: The Autobiography of Raphael Lemkin*. Edited by Donna-Lee Frieze. New Haven, CT: Yale University Press, 2013.

Locke, John. *Second Treatise of Government*. Indianapolis, IN: Hackett, 1980.

Marx, Karl. *Selected Writings*. Indianapolis, IN: Hackett, 1994.

Marx, Karl, and Friedrich Engels. *Basic Writings on Politics & Philosophy*. New York: Anchor Books, 1959.

Metzl, Jonathan M. *Dying of Whiteness: How the Politics of Racial Resentment is Killing America's Heartland*. New York: Basic Books, 2019.

More, Thomas. *Utopia*. London: Penguin, 2003.

Morris, Roy, Jr. *Fraud of the Century: Rutherford B. Hayes, Samuel Tilden, and the Stolen Election of 1876*. New York: Simon & Schuster, 2003.

Nabokov, Vladimir. *Nikolai Gogol*. New York: New Directions, 1961.

Neiman, Susan. *Learning from the Germans: Race and the Memory of Evil*. New York: Farrar, Straus and Giroux, 2019.

Nietzsche, Friedrich. *Thus Spoke Zarathustra*. London: Penguin Classics, 2003.

Orwell, George. *Animal Farm*. Orlando, FL: Harcourt, Brace, 2003.

———. *Down and Out in Paris and London*. New York: Harvest Books, 1961.

———. *Homage to Catalonia*. New York: Harcourt, Brace, 1980.

———. *1984*. New York: Signet Classics, 1977.

Paz, Octavio. *The Labyrinth of Solitude and Other Writings*. New York: Grove Press, 1985.

Perarnau, Martí. *Pep Confidential: The Inside Story of Pep Guardiola's First Season at Bayern Munich*. Edinburgh: Arena Sport, 2014.

Power, Samantha. *A Problem from Hell: America and the Age of Genocide*. New York: Perennial, 2002.

Sartre, Jean-Paul. *Being and Nothingness*. New York: Washington Square Press, 1992.

———. *Existentialism Is a Humanism*. New Haven: Yale University Press, 2007.

———. *No Exit and Three Other Plays*. New York: Vintage International, 1989.

Smith, Adam. *The Theory of Moral Sentiments*. New York: Penguin Classics, 2010.

———. *The Wealth of Nations*. New York: Bantam Dell, 2003.

Staples, Brent. "The Haunting of Tulsa, Okla." *The New York Times*. December 26, 2020.

Winner, David. *Brilliant Orange: The Neurotic Genius of Dutch Soccer*. New York: Overlook Press, 2008.

Wright, Richard. *Black Boy*. New York: Harper Perennial, 1993.

Voltaire. *Candide, or Optimism*. New York: Barnes & Noble Classics, 2003.

BARRETT HOLMES PITNER is a columnist, journalist, and philosopher whose work has been published in *The Daily Beast*, BBC, *The Guardian*, and elsewhere. He is the founder of The Sustainable Culture Lab, a think tank with the goals of influencing policy by working with legislators and decision makers, and impacting culture at a grassroots level through events, work, and cultural offerings. He lives in Washington, D.C. Find out more at barrettholmespitner.com.